Canadiens, Canadians and Québécois

CANADA
Issues & Options

A series designed to stimulate intelligent inquiry into crucial Canadian concerns

Canadiens, Canadians and Quebecois

BRUCE W. HODGINS

Professor, Department of History, Trent University

RICHARD P. BOWLES

Associate Professor, Faculty of Education, University of Toronto

JAMES L. HANLEY

General Manager, Educational Media Division, Ontario Educational Communications Authority

GEORGE A. RAWLYK

Professor, Department of History, Queen's University

P
PRENTICE-HALL ♦ OF CANADA, LTD
Scarborough h *Ontario*

PRENTICE-HALL, INC., ENGLEWOOD CLIFFS, NEW JERSEY
PRENTICE-HALL INTERNATIONAL, INC., LONDON
PRENTICE-HALL OF AUSTRALIA, PTY., LTD., SYDNEY
PRENTICE-HALL OF INDIA, PVT., LTD., NEW DELHI
PRENTICE-HALL OF JAPAN, INC., TOKYO

Library of Congress Catalog No. 74-6749

ISBN 013 112888-4

3 4 5   78 77 76 75

PRINTED IN CANADA

Contents

Preface

The *Canada: Issues and Options* series focusses on a number of vital continuing Canadian concerns. Each volume probes the nature of a complex issue in both its contemporary and historical contexts. The issues were chosen because of their relevance to the life of the Canadian teenager as well as the general Canadian public.

Every volume in the series provides a wide variety of primary and secondary source materials. These sources are interdisciplinary as well as analytical and descriptive. They embody many divergent points of view in order to provoke critical in-depth consideration of the issue. They are arranged in a manner designed to personally involve and confront the reader with the clash of opinions and options inherent in the various issues. The historical sources have been carefully selected to provide a better understanding of the roots of the issue under consideration. It is hoped that this method will establish in the reader's mind a meaningful relationship between the past and the present.

The organization is flexible. If a chronological study of the development of the issue is desired, this can be accomplished by treating the historical sources first and later examining the contemporary manifestations of the issue. By reversing this procedure, the reader can first deal with the contemporary section. This approach will provide the reader with a brief overview of the issue, a case study designed to put it into personal and immediate terms, and a more detailed examination of the issue in its contemporary setting, prior to examining its historical roots.

Questions designed to stimulate further research are also included. These questions do not limit examination or prescribe answers, but raise more questions and suggest aspects of the issue which might be further investigated.

Throughout these volumes, a conscientious effort has been made to avoid endorsing any one viewpoint. No conclusions are drawn. Rather, the reader is presented with information which has been arranged to encourage the drawing of his own tentative conclusions about the issue. The formation of these conclusions involve the use of the skills of inquiry and the examination and clarification of personal values.

Acknowledgments

The authors are deeply indebted to Peter and Sandra Gillis for their considerable help in assembling basic material for this volume. Further research was carried out by William and Diana Summers.

Particular thanks are due Wendy Cuthbertson for her help, advice and hard work in the final preparation of this material. Without her assistance this volume might never have been published. Thanks are also due to Paul Hunt and Norma Andrew of Prentice-Hall of Canada, Limited, for their help and hard work.

The authors thank the many writers and publishers who have granted them permission to use various materials. Source references are provided with the documents.

Every reasonable effort has been made to find copyright holders of material used in this book. Please notify the publishers in case of omission so that appropriate credit can be given in subsequent printings.

Introduction

Ever since the British conquest of French North America in 1759–60, relations between French and English Canadians have been a recurring issue in Canadian life. These relations have played a significant role in many of the events in this country's past and will in its future.

The problems and tensions which in recent years have called the very structure of Confederation into question have no simple answers. This volume will not provide any. Rather, it raises such additional questions as:

— What are the actual issues and tensions? What do French, English and other Canadian groups think and feel about these issues?

— What are some of the political, social and cultural dimensions of these issues?

— Can Quebec remain within Confederation and still satisfy the aspirations of the Québécois?

— How has our past contributed to the present and what does the future hold?

The authors hope the wide variety of opinions and sources provided in this book will stimulate you to clarify your own attitudes as you probe these questions and many others. In this manner it is possible for you to develop a better understanding of present problems and contribute to their resolution in the future.

The Issue:
Some Opinions

What follows is a collage of documents reflecting some of the varied opinions about French-English relations in Canada. What are the issues? How do you feel about them? Why do you feel the way you do?

1. CANADA'S GREATEST CRISIS

In this excerpt from the Preliminary Report of the Royal Commission on Bilingualism and Biculturalism *(Ottawa, 1965), the commissioners stated without reservation that the issue of French-English relations in Canada constituted the greatest crisis in this country's history. (Reprinted by permission of Information Canada.)*

The Commissioners have been driven to the conclusion that Canada, without being fully conscious of the fact, is passing through the greatest crisis in its history.

The source of the crisis lies in the Province of Quebec; that fact could be established without an extensive inquiry. . . . But, although a provincial crisis at the outset, it has become a Canadian crisis, because of the size and strategic importance of Quebec, and because it has inevitably set off a series of chain reactions elsewhere.

What does the crisis spring from? Our inquiry is not far enough advanced to enable us to establish exactly its underlying causes and its extent. All we can do is describe it as we see it now: it would appear from what is happening that the state of affairs established in 1867, and never since seriously challenged, is now for the first time being rejected by the French Canadians of Quebec.

Who is right and who is wrong? We do not even ask ourselves that question; we simply record the existence of a crisis which we believe to be very serious. If it should persist and gather momentum, it could destroy Canada. On the other hand, if it is overcome, it will have contributed to the rebirth of a richer and more dynamic Canada. But this will be possible only if we face the reality of the crisis and grapple with it in time.

(Reprinted with permission *Toronto Star.*)

"How do you spell Ann Landers?"

2. A PROBLEM OF FEDERALISM

In his article "The Five Faces of Federalism" (in P. A. Crépeau and C. B. Macpherson, eds., The Future of Canadian Federalism *[© University of Toronto Press 1965]), Professor J. R. Mallory outlines the strains that a rising Quebec nationalism was placing on Canadian federalism.*

The French-Canadian community has developed a new set of expectations from government, and looks to the power of the state to satisfy their new wants and to bring the economic development which will enlarge opportunities for all. For them, these things must be done by their own French-Canadian state of Quebec, and not by Ottawa. . . .

It is these new forces which have created the latest crisis in Canadian federalism. The growing centralization of the past fifty years created no great problems in Quebec as long as the province was seeking to contract out of the twentieth century. But with the French-Canadian community determined to use to the full the resources of the provincial government to achieve a national revival, a whole range of problems has emerged in Canadian federalism which will require substantial readjustments in the system. The mechanics of this readjustment will not be easy, and the issues at stake are very large indeed.

3. A PROBLEM OF LANGUAGE

In 1967 Pierre Elliott Trudeau, then justice minister, suggested a method for ending French-Canadian dissatisfaction. A report of Trudeau's remarks by Brian Upton was published in the Montreal Star, *September 6, 1967. (Reprinted by permission of* The Montreal Star.*)*

Roughly 95 per cent of French Canadian gripes would be wiped out if language and education rights were spread across the country in an entrenched bill of rights, Justice Minister Pierre Elliott Trudeau said yesterday.

Mr. Trudeau said Ottawa was "putting its cards on the table" at the proposed 1968 federal-provincial conference and rejected as "unworkable" Quebec proposals of special status, a two-nation state for Canada, or associate status.

4. A PROBLEM OF WEALTH

Journalist Anthony Westell reported the remarks of R. W. Bonner, chairman of Macmillan-Bloedel, in an article in The Globe and Mail, *Toronto, on 28 November, 1967. (Reprinted by permission of* The Globe and Mail, Toronto.*)*

Canada's real problem is that some regions are rich while others are relatively poor, wealthy British Columbia told the Confederation of Tomorrow Conference yesterday.

Attorney-General R. W. Bonner brushed over questions of the French language and culture to argue that the basic strain in Confederation is that living standards in the Atlantic provinces and, to a lesser extent, Quebec, are not catching up with standards in other parts of the country.

5. AN OBSOLETE CULTURE

P. L. Saunders, a history teacher at the Lindsay Collegiate and Vocational Institute in Lindsay, Ontario, argued that the expanding nationalism in Quebec represented the last gasps of an obsolete culture. This report of Mr. Saunders' remarks was published by the Lindsay Post Mercury on January 20, 1968. (Reprinted by permission of P. L. Saunders.)

"No culture is more certain of death than one refusing to adapt and modify, and no isolated enclave can survive in the twentieth century Western World" said LCVI history teacher P. L. Saunders in addressing the Lindsay Kiwanis Club, Thursday.

The subject of his address was "Separatism, the myth that French-Canadian culture can be maintained."

6. THE CONQUERED PEOPLE

This selection is an excerpt from the article "Why I Support a Policy of English Unilingualism," by Mark Alchuk for Excalibur, the York University student newspaper. The article was published February 11, 1971. (Reprinted by permission of Excalibur.)

Unfortunately terrorism may succeed in creating a feeling of indifference among English Canadians who are tired of hearing about Quebec and its separatists. Such an attitude is as deadly to Canadian survival as the FLQ terrorism. English-speaking Canadians have a numerical, historical, economic, constitutional and legal right to the predominance of the English language over the French. The French Canadians are the conquered people; it is time they accept the English fact!

7. LIBERTY FOR QUEBEC

This declaration by René Lévesque appeared in Option for Quebec (1968), the book in which Lévesque argued in favour of Quebec's separating from the rest of Canada. (Reprinted by permission of The Canadian Publishers, McClelland and Stewart Limited, Toronto.)

For our own good, we must dare to seize for ourselves complete liberty in Quebec, the right to all the essential components of independence, i.e., the complete mastery of every last area of basic collective decision-making.

This means that Quebec must become sovereign as soon as possible.

Thus we finally would have within our grasp the security of our collective "being" which is so vital to us, a security which otherwise must remain uncertain and incomplete.

Then it will be up to us, and us alone, to establish calmly, without recrimination or discrimination, the priority for which we are now struggling feverishly but blindly: that of our language and our culture.

8.   THE MYTH OF POLITICAL INDEPENDENCE

Pierre Vallières, a colleague of Pierre Elliott Trudeau during the 1950s, became the leading thinker of the revolutionary-terrorist group, the FLQ. After the October Crisis of 1970, fomented by the FLQ, Vallières became converted to the democratic separation of the Parti Québécois, led by René Lévesque. This excerpt is taken from Vallières' White Niggers of America (1971), written during the author's FLQ days. (Reprinted by permission of The Canadian Publishers, McClelland and Stewart Limited, Toronto.)

Political independence is only a myth (a luxury we can do without, bled white as we are!), except on condition that it is preceded by the expropriation of foreign capital (American and other) and the nationalization of natural resources, banks, and other enterprises that presently belong to foreign capital; the modification in depth of the monetary, financial, commercial, and customs relations that enslave us to the United States; and a social transformation that can lead to the disappearance of the parasitic classes (the English-speaking and French-speaking petty bourgeoisies of Quebec) which are tied to imperialism and profit from the sale of Quebec to foreigners. This condition is therefore tantamount to the necessity for a total revolution.

9.   IT'S TOO LATE

Toronto journalist Graham Fraser reached what he called a "bitter conclusion" concerning Canada's future in his essay, "A Sense of Being," written for Notes from a Native Land, *edited by Andy Wainwright (Ottawa: Oberon Press, 1969). (This excerpt is reprinted by permission of Oberon Press.)*

A large part of my personal agonizing about Canadian national identity has been concerned with Quebec. I learned French—principally out of some sort of sense of national duty and some kind of belief in a bilingual Canada. But in fact, being a bilingual Canadian is rather pointless and a bit of a pain in the neck. After innumerable student conferences, debates, interviews, earnest conversations in French with federal politicians from Quebec, and three summers working in French in student groups whose underlying aim was to prove that bilingualism is a good thing, I've decided the hell with it. I can decide to live in Quebec, in French, or in Toronto, say, in English.

10. CAN ENGLISH CANADA SURVIVE?

Professor William Neville, a political scientist teaching at Trent University, wrote an article for the November 1971 Canadian Forum *entitled "After Victoria: The Choice for English Canada," from which this excerpt is taken. (Reprinted by permission of* Canadian Forum.*)*

It is time that we began to recognize that English Canadians too have aspirations and preferences, that we have problems to solve, that we have things to accomplish; it is time, too, that we thought about the problems—and the advantages—that Quebec's departure will confer in reaching our goals.

National unity and unity of purpose are noble objectives, but they no longer exist in Canada outside the rhetoric of the politicians. If we do not face that fact squarely, then we shall be totally unprepared for the bombshell that almost certainly lies ahead.

11. QUEBEC SETS EXAMPLE

Fraser Duff of Markham, Ontario, wrote the following letter to the editor which was published in the Toronto Star, *January 14, 1972. (Reprinted by permission of Fraser Duff.)*

In the light of changing attitudes in Quebec I can't help but feel enormous admiration and respect for the people of that province. The people of French Canada have reached the point where they are saying "enough."

The French culture on this continent may be, and probably is, doomed to absorption into the English culture around it. But the Québécois will not let their culture and their nation go down with a whimper and a sigh. They will go out, if need be, with flags flying and with guns blazing.

If English Canadians continue their suicidal race toward greater dependence on the United States, Quebec not only has the right, it is its duty, to secede. Why should we in English Canada insist that Quebec care .about the country when English Canadians don't?

What do you think?

1. (a) Of the eleven statements you have just read, which, if any, come closest to stating your views?
   (b) Which statement seems to you to be most logical and reasonable?
   (c) Was your choice the same in (a) and (b)?
2. What issues in French-English relations did you find in the above documents? What issues do you think have been omitted? In your opinion what is the most important problem today in French-English relations in Canada? Why?
3. Summarize the points of view contained in any three of the foregoing documents. Compare them. What might the author in each case suggest for the resolution of the issue?

2

Encounter

Yesterday the Children Were Dancing, a play written by Gratien Gélinas, a leading French-Canadian actor and playwright, was first performed in English by the Charlottetown Festival in Prince Edward Island on July 5, 1967.

The following excerpt has been taken from the last two scenes of the play. In the preceding action, Pierre Gravel, a lawyer, has been offered the federal justice portfolio but is unexpectedly faced with the opposing views of André, his son and the leader of a terrorist plot to dynamite public monuments symbolic of "British imperialism." André is determined not only to proceed with the bombings but also to give himself up to the police afterwards, thus assuring the ruin of his father's political career. The older Gravel is himself a French-Canadian nationalist (who is planning to deliver a strongly-worded speech supporting French-Canadian expansion, to the Canadian Club in Toronto the next day), but André's activities both dismay and outrage him. Gélinas portrays the bitter conflict resulting between two strong men whose great affection for one another only aggravates the feelings created by their political differences.

Gratien Gélinas is a moderate French-Canadian nationalist who was closely associated in the public mind with the Quiet Revolution of the early 1960s. This play was written several years ago—a fact which should be borne in mind while reading it.

How well has the play stood up to the passage of time? Are positions like André's likely to occur now or in the future? Do you think that the same degree of feeling exists today? How might you alter these scenes to make them more relevant to the present situation, if at all?

ANDRÉ: The issue dividing the two of us, Mother, has to do with the future, not the past. It has to do with building what's going to be our world: don't you understand! The world where Nicole and I and the rest of our generation will have to live, long after his generation—which is determined to run everything, to decide everything without us—has gone with the wind. If we differ, too bad! I won't bow down before him. I haven't the right!

GRAVEL: What nonsense!

ANDRÉ, *to his mother*:   When the workers rebelled a hundred years ago against being exploited like slaves, the capitalist plutocrats reacted just like him—oh yes! They cried, "Nonsense!" When fifty years ago the women decided to be something more than diaper-changing machines, the males huffed in indignation—oh yes! It happened all the same. [*To his father*] So brace yourself: the next offensive will be launched by the young.

GRAVEL: Against the old, I take it?

ANDRÉ: Yes! It's all over, that revolting little game where the beds of war and politics are never made by the young suckers who sleep in them.

GRAVEL: It'd be worth seeing, this Quebec kindergarten of yours, built to order by babies still in diapers!

ANDRÉ, *to* NICOLE, *perhaps*:   Not so long ago it was the parents who chose, according to their own greed and vanity, the dumb heiress their weak-kneed son would marry. . . . By now, we've made some progress: in private affairs a young person is allowed to plan his life without too much interference. But in public affairs, my boy, you get a hiding if you refuse to shack up for the rest of your days with the fat mare with eyes crossed coast to coast who was picked for you without your say-so by Daddy Pearson! The bride we spend our political future with, thank you, we'll choose ourselves—and it'll be in keeping with our age, not yours, you can be damn sure!

GRAVEL: You're making great sense, all right! "Watch, beloved countrymen, the boxing match is on: a battle royal, to the finish, between the fathers and sons of French Canada! Experience, Logic and Reason versus Recklessness, Conceit and Ignorance—in their natural state: that is, unpolluted by parents. To be won once and for all, the Garden of Eden in your backyard, bananas off the trees in January and old-age pensions when you get out of college!" [*To* LOUISE] To hear eyewash like that from your own son, when you've surmounted handicaps that he and the other young sheikhs of his age'll never know! I jumped into life right in the middle of the Depression. Instead of hanging around with my pockets full of my father's money, waiting for the right moment to slap him down, I had to work nights washing dishes at the Northeastern Lunch to pay my school fees. Just avoiding starvation was considered a lucky break. If a man can be judged by the trials he's taken in stride, then you're no match for us, my smug young friends, when it comes to the survival of the fittest!

ANDRÉ: Sure, you're respectable. You were born in winter, deep in the national woods—the deepest. The simple fact you've come out alive is a triumph in itself.

GRAVEL: Start putting your ten fingers to work for you, and let your idle brain get busy, before you cry "Crap!" and flush us down the drain! Then you might have a right to claim our generation is blocking the glorious destiny of a mixed-up bunch of spoiled brats!

ANDRÉ: Unhappily for you and for us, the challenge you had to face makes it impossible for you—no matter how willing—to understand the challenge we have to face.

GRAVEL: That's right! Spring has sprung: the air is warm, life is easy. Fade away, old men, we don't need your mitts and snowshoes any more!

ANDRÉ: It's not your fault, but you grew up in a colonial world, where submission to the English and licking their boots were taught you as national virtues. Your most inspiring motto? "Endure to endure!" You sat blissfully on your rear ends at the side of the road, watching the English parade by, minting money and swelling with power, and you smiled approval like dear little friars under a vow of eternal poverty. And now you'd like to apply your system to our national heritage?

GRAVEL: Yes, but today all that's being changed!

ANDRÉ: You've always been ordered around, so now you're obsessed with the notion you could never stand on your own two feet. If Ottawa lets go your hand, bingo!—you're convinced you'll forever fall down and go boom. Know what you've got? The complex of the dog on the leash, who'll never go farther than his lousy doghouse, even if the leash is removed and he's whipped. How can you lead us to freedom? It's got you as scared as the plague and VD combined.

GRAVEL: Bull!

ANDRÉ: You complain that today's youth is quitting on you? Then where do we find the blind faith that could draw us after in your inspiring footsteps? Among your compromisers? your maybe-things-are-all-for-the-best gents? your healers of a dying Confederation? your political boxers with their hands tied by party strings?

GRAVEL: Stop piling it up: I get the drift. According to you, Ottawa must be the Sodom and Gomorrah of Canadian politics: not a single honest man—all traitors, thieves and imbeciles! Trash for the fires of the Separatist heaven! Who do you think you're fooling with these fables?

LOUISE: André, you exaggerate, with all the passion and intolerance of your age. The right, the truth, are never wholly on one side. Life is going to teach you some hard lessons if you won't admit that.

ANDRÉ: I've never doubted it.

LOUISE: Whatever you may think, there are men there of integrity and ability, as dedicated as you are to our people.

GRAVEL: Granted, French Canada has a whole litany of grievances. I've admitted that in my speech for tomorrow, as bluntly and bitterly as you might. But good God, if we want to defend our rights let's stop barricading ourselves in the cellars of the Chateau de Ramezay and draw swords where the battle rages.

ANDRÉ: No government in Ottawa can grant Quebec half its demands without automatically demolishing itself.

GRAVEL: What do you know about it?

ANDRÉ: Your own party is up to its neck in the dilemma: either bow to Belle Quebec and lose the nine Ugly Sisters on the deal, or get tough with her to please the rest of the country, and so lose power, Quebec, and all. If you won't accept evidence as clear as that, then you're the visionary, the spinner of dreams.

GRAVEL: Your delicate sophistries might have carried weight three years ago, or even last year. But while you were plotting your little revolution, I'll have you know, the problem was daily being resolved upward without the inestimable advantage of your brilliant co-operation.

ANDRÉ: Oh yes: the way cancer gets cured by morphine.

GRAVEL, *to* LOUISE: And now his dud fireworks are ready for lighting, he'll try on any caper, any paradox, to justify what he's doing.

LOUISE: André, no matter what you've said—and I've learned a good deal from it—I still think your father's right when he says that by different means he'd achieve there the same ends you're after here.

ANDRÉ: No, Mother: it would be a waste of an honest man's good life, trying to work out a compromise with English Canada. He'd let loose with an occasional outburst in French, just to scare them, followed by a curtsy in English to show them there are no hard feelings. And he'd burst with pride, every third session or so, at getting through some itty-bit reform that'd keep Quebec from screaming too loud but wouldn't upset the Liberals in Ontario, in Newfoundland, in Alberta . . . and other beauty spots in the land of our fathers.

GRAVEL: You don't know what you're saying!

ANDRÉ: Itty-bit reforms you'd get, naturally—along with a slap on the back and broad smiles by the dozen! "Sure, Peter, but what does Quebec really want, after all? Be a good boy and state it over again, will you? No, we don't get you. Why don't you try spelling it backwards for a change? But don't worry, Peter: believe it or not, we have big plans for you. The time is coming damn fast when we'll be ready to kick you right in the ass! Another thirty years or so. What with immigration and the Pill, authoritative sociologists tell us that by the end of the century the damn Pea-Soupers won't represent more than seventeen per cent of the population. And then, chums, you can yell your heads off: we won't care a hoot. In back of the backwoods, that's where you'll find the French identity, and it can stay there till Doomsday!"

GRAVEL, *to* LOUISE, *exasperated*:   How can you answer rubbish like that? You have a go at him: I'm fed to the teeth.

LOUISE: André, the odds are not fair. You dreaded this confrontation, so you've been steeling yourself for it for a long time. But it's hit us like a thunderclap and we're stunned. So it's easy for you to outmanœuvre us. I can't find anything to say to you, either. But I know that all the words I wish I could think of now to hold you back, words I can't find in my poor empty head, will come back to plague me weeks and months later . . . when it's too late, when I spend my nights picturing you on your cot: you, a wild bird, caged, stifled, paralyzed behind bars! [*After a sob which* NICOLE *cannot quite restrain*] Oh yes, Nicole my dear, we're bewitched by the pride men have, but it's hard to live with. [*To the other two*] My darlings, I don't know any more which of you is the least unreasonable. Only one thing I'm sure of: the winner of this trial, whoever he is, will come out of it as pitiful as the loser.

ANDRÉ: Perhaps more.

LOUISE: André, you're the only one who could still call a halt. . . .

ANDRÉ, *achingly*:   I can't.

LOUISE: You are headed straight for calamity with your fists clenched. Are you sure you've considered how ugly it can be?

ANDRÉ: Where I'm headed I've tried to figure out at least a dozen times. But I know the real thing will be worse than the worst I've imagined.

GRAVEL: Yes, my boy! You're above fear! You don't care about the hard knocks, you don't give a damn about your father or anyone . . . but in all charity I warn you: you're going to find playing at revolution an expensive hobby. Expect the sacred flame to get a shower bath.

ANDRÉ: I'm under no illusions, believe me.

GRAVEL: You'd better not be. Remember one thing above all: you're going to throw yourselves into the arms of the police—one a night for fifteen days—hoping to gain public sympathy by ridiculing the forces of law and order. But just wait: you've no idea yet what a humiliated cop is like. He won't forgive you for making a fool of him. After two or three days, when they've got the picture, they'll use any means at their disposal to make someone squeal and bring the farce to an end.

ANDRÉ: I've foreseen that too.

GRAVEL: You're the leader, and the only one, according to you, who knows the whole gang; so be prepared, poor devil, to scream out before you pass out.

LOUISE, *in revulsion*:   Pierre . . . no . . .

NICOLE *goes upstage for a moment to hide her emotion.*

GRAVEL, *as grieved in his own way as the two women*: What! You think I enjoy talking like that to my own son? Good God, this is no time for sugar-coating the pill! [*He withdraws, panting.*]

ANDRÉ: Don't try to frighten me, Dad. For days I've been scared out of my wits. [*Troubled*] It's not that I don't give a damn about the hard knocks, about prison and all the woes in store for me. I'm afraid all right. Or that I don't care about the loss of your friendship, or the harm I'm doing you, or the suffering I cause Mother, or Nicole's heartache. Away from all of you, I'll be so miserably unhappy I'll be tempted often to curse the demon that drove me there.

LOUISE: So much suffering . . . for such a dubious purpose, such a debatable one . . . it makes no sense, my child, it makes no sense.

ANDRÉ: If I were a soldier, if they put a gun in my hands, and made me risk my skin in some absurd war started, as always, by comfortable old men, anxious to vindicate their mistakes and hold onto their loot, even if you were sad to see me go, would you try to hold me back?

GRAVEL: And your own little war, which no one else is forcing you to start: you're certain-sure it's super-legitimate and sacrosanct? In your heart of hearts, all's bright and light?

ANDRÉ: No. I'm not absolutely certain I'm not making a mistake.

GRAVEL: You're in doubt about it? You admit it?

ANDRÉ: Yes.

GRAVEL, *to* LOUISE: But his mind's irrevocably made up, all the same, to carry us all down together into his abyss!

LOUISE, *to* ANDRÉ: If you're not completely convinced, how can you take on such a frightening responsibility?

ANDRÉ: Need a priest prove to himself he's absolutely right to believe in God before he commits his life to Him? He may reason it out for years, but there'll come a time when he's got to rely on faith, and faith can't ever exclude doubt.

GRAVEL: Mister Toad ducks again! "It's a matter of faith . . . in the spirit of the saints, I argue no more." You're evading the issue! You've run out of your festering arguments, your back is against the wall, so you scurry like a rat into a hole.

ANDRÉ: No, I'm not evading anything. The biggest risk I'm taking hasn't got through to you yet—and you a lawyer! If fascination with your own wound'd let you be more objective, you'd have realized by now that the sentence I'll get will cut me off for life from the practice of law. Code of the Bar, Chapter Two, Article Forty-eight. [GRAVEL *reacts as if struck.*] The independence of Quebec will give me the only chance I'll ever get to return some day to my chosen profession. So you see, I'm not trying to cheat: I'm jumping without a net. If I miss the trapeze I've had it.

GRAVEL: Louise, it's utter madness!

ANDRÉ: Nicole, nothing, absolutely nothing, forces you to take the jump with me. On the contrary, everything points the other way if you decide I'm not the one you thought you loved. Better to cry for a while than make us both miserable by not facing up to it honestly and courageously.

GRAVEL, *to* ANDRÉ: That's an easy way to play the martyr, taking for granted that next month a revolution will be announced with a trumpet blast . . .

ANDRÉ: No . . .

GRAVEL: . . . and a delirious crowd'll sweep in, break your chains and switch your crime sheet to a national hero's diploma! But you're writing yourself a Batman serial, boy!

ANDRÉ: No, I know the battle will be long.

GRAVEL: You won't live to see the end of it. . . .

ANDRÉ: Long . . . and bitter enough for a man to cry quits.

GRAVEL: . . . Ever! The public will never go along!

ANDRÉ: But some day it'll have to come to an end . . .

GRAVEL: Who cares about independence when he's happy the way he is?

ANDRÉ: . . . even if you wait till the year two thousand.

GRAVEL: To them a new road or a raise in salary will always speak louder than principles.

ANDRÉ, *mainly for himself*:   Whatever you want, let them prove you have no right to it . . .

GRAVEL: It's stupid, but that's the way it is!

ANDRÉ: . . . but if you have a right to it, don't let them tell you you can never have it.

GRAVEL: You're not going to change any of that!

ANDRÉ: Justice always wins in the end.

GRAVEL, *seeking a way to keep him*:   There are things which are possible and things which are not!

ANDRÉ: It's a question of patience, that's all. . . .

GRAVEL: Say what you like and do as you please, you can't live without compromise.

ANDRÉ: . . . All the more reason not to give up.

GRAVEL, *pleading*:   Don't waste your life crying out in the desert!

ANDRÉ, *stubbornly*:   Give up, and you'll never find peace . . .

GRAVEL: You're nothing but a bunch of visionaries!

ANDRÉ: . . . you'll kick yourself as long as you live.

GRAVEL: Even those who're with you now will drop you, one by one . . .

ANDRÉ: Even if you were alone . . .

GRAVEL: . . . and tell you it's better to live in the real world after all!

ANDRÉ: Even if you were all alone, it wouldn't change a thing. . . .

NICOLE *comes and sits by him and takes his arm.*

GRAVEL, *sensing that* ANDRÉ *has eluded him*:   You talked about Sweden a moment ago: the United States would never let us set up a socialist state right next door to them.

ANDRÉ: . . . That's why there's no point discussing it any further.

GRAVEL: With ten provinces we've all the trouble in the world seeing they don't take over in every way conceivable.

ANDRÉ, *fed up*:   There's no point!

GRAVEL: How do you expect Quebec to go it alone, lost in an ocean of two hundred million speaking English?

NICOLE, *champing at the bit*:   He has no choice, can't you see? Sure it'd be easier for him to give in and live happily ever after, but he can't. It's not his fault: he can't do it! Everyone can't be born meek and mild and careful!

GRAVEL, *to* NICOLE: Listen—

NICOLE, *pouring out her heart*:   If he's daring and a little crazy, good for him. It's a change! Since 1759, haven't we had it up to here with cowards, weaklings and sissies?

GRAVEL, *wanting to recapture control of the discussion*:   Nicole, this is something for us to—

NICOLE, *a small fury*:   Listen yourself! You've been jawing away long enough: now it's my turn. And if you don't want to hear what I have to say, cover your ears! It won't make any difference, 'cause you don't understand anything anyway. It's not surprising you two don't get along: you don't speak the same language! What he calls independence, an open window on the world, freedom to support Quebec's interests over Ontario's, you and the other alumni of the Faculty of British Sciences call narrow separatism, going back into a shell, collective suicide, a Chinese Wall around Quebec and a medieval ghetto!

GRAVEL: Catch his hay fever if you want: you'll soon get over it—you'll see!

NICOLE: Have you any idea what a colonial you are, even in your own home? [*Practically under his nose*] An hour ago, on the phone, you were talking to your big boss, the Prime Minister of what you quiveringly call my beloved country. Had you felt the temptation, perfectly legitimate for a free man, to make him answer you in your mother tongue, can you imagine how bewildered the poor dear great man would've been? And yet three out of ten of "his people" speak French. And Confederation is hardly a surprise—it's been around for a century! What's more, a Nobel Prize winner isn't usually a dunce. So? He can't speak our language, or he won't speak it? Either way, you can kiss every finger of both his hands if you want to, but personally I say, "Nuts! Crap!" [To LOUISE]. . . . When his trials are over he'll have triumphs instead. I'll put it in writing! The instant, ready-mix victory you were after is chicken feed compared with the one he'll win in the long run! . . . [*She falls back beside* ANDRÉ, *short of breath*] Whew! I'm beat! [*To* ANDRÉ] Now, love, it breaks my heart to have to tell you, but when I looked at the clock five minutes ago it was ten to nine.

ANDRÉ, *waking up*:   Yes: that's right. I must go. [*He gets up painfully.*]

GRAVEL, *going to him*:   No, André . . . don't go.

ANDRÉ: Please . . . let me by.

GRAVEL, *begging*:   Today, you're the stronger: don't take advantage of it. I'll be grateful as long as I live.

ANDRÉ: It's too late. . . .

The clock begins to sound nine.

GRAVEL: If I've wronged you in any way, I humbly ask your forgiveness.

ANDRÉ: It's too late. I've got to go.

GRAVEL, *panic-stricken*:   I'm not asking for myself. Give this up and I'll never touch politics again, not with a ten-foot pole, I swear.

ANDRÉ: It's out of my hands now. . . .

GRAVEL: Don't go! You said, didn't you, that someone else could take your place?

ANDRÉ: It wouldn't make any difference.

GRAVEL: You'll explain to them what happened: they'll understand.

ANDRÉ: If I let my replacement do it, it wouldn't make any difference: don't you see?

GRAVEL, *gripping* ANDRÉ *by the lapels*:   André, André! You can't do this to me! [*He slaps him.*] My favourite son, my pal . . .

ANDRÉ, *putting up no defence and almost crying himself*:   It wouldn't prevent the scandal. . . .

GRAVEL, *continuing to strike him*:   My pal . . . the apple of my eye!

ANDRÉ: Don't you get it? My replacement is—[*Another slap cuts off the sentence.*]

LOUISE, *a cry*:   It's Larry!

ANDRÉ: Yes, it's him.

GRAVEL, *letting him go, stunned*:   What?

ANDRÉ: It's Larry! Yes, I tell you it's Larry!

SCENE EIGHT

O'BRIEN *enters from the outside.*

O'BRIEN, *without troubling to doff his coat*:   In the cab, I just heard that the monument to Edward VII, in Wolseley Park, went down three minutes ago.

LOUISE, *to* O'BRIEN: Larry . . . where is he?

O'BRIEN: He left me at the Windsor. I thought he'd be here.

LOUISE, *faced with the evidence*:   Oh my God, it's him!

O'BRIEN: Who? [*Coming to* ANDRÉ] Your replacement?

The telephone rings.

O'BRIEN, *answering, since he is closest to the phone*:   Yes? . . . Where are you, Larry? . . . Just a minute. [*To* ANDRÉ] He wants to speak to you.

LOUISE, *to* O'BRIEN: Where is he?

O'BRIEN: At my place.

ANDRÉ, *on the phone*:   Why so early? It wasn't time yet . . .

O'BRIEN, *after consulting his watch, he taps* ANDRÉ *on the shoulder*: It's now nine-thirty. [*Ill at ease*] Before I left, a while ago, I put back the clock.

ANDRÉ, *on the phone*:   Okay, Larry: I didn't know . . . Nobody saw you? . . . Don't move from there, you hear? [*Despite his exhaustion, he is once more the leader.*] As agreed, I go to the police. . . . Don't argue: that's an order. . . . [*Gently, before hanging up*] Larry . . . thanks, kid.

LOUISE: André . . . why did you choose . . . him?

ANDRÉ: He had to do his share. I thought I'd found a good way of keeping him at arm's length. [*To* O'BRIEN] Thanks to you, I failed.

O'BRIEN: May I go with you?

ANDRÉ: No, look after Larry, right away. Keep him from doing anything foolish. That's all I ask.

O'BRIEN *goes out.*

ANDRÉ: I'll get my things ready.

He goes up to his room. NICOLE, *after a moment's hesitation, goes after him and takes him by the arm.*

GRAVEL, *crushed, after a silence*:   Louise . . .

LOUISE, *through her own sorrow*:   Yes, dear?

GRAVEL: Louise . . . what's happening to us?

LOUISE: Yesterday, they were children dancing in the house. . . . Today they've become men . . . ready to fight in the street.

GRAVEL: Against us?

LOUISE: Against their fate.

GRAVEL: They had everything to make them happy.

LOUISE: Others, perhaps . . . not them.

GRAVEL, *lost*:   What's to be done now?

LOUISE: Refuse what isn't yours to accept, any more. But give that talk of yours tomorrow.

GRAVEL: I wouldn't have the strength.

LOUISE: You've got to find it. To make their way, your sons have pushed you into the ditch. But you can't stay there. Their right to assert themselves as men doesn't rob you of the right to continue on your way. If your convictions haven't changed . . .

GRAVEL: Their solution isn't the right one, that I know!

LOUISE: Then you don't have a choice either. Your duty is clear. Don't be afraid: those who hear you tomorrow will not despise you. Courage always commands respect. [GRAVEL *gets up with an effort*.] You can tell them truths which more than ever they'll have an obligation to understand.

The doorbell rings, and the SECRETARY *appears discreetly in the hallway.*

SECRETARY, *greeting* LOUISE: Evening, Mrs. Gravel. [*To* GRAVEL, *putting her evening's work down*] Well, it's all copied.

GRAVEL: Thank you.

SECRETARY: Except the ending. If you've got it, I could take it down now.

GRAVEL: Would you?

SECRETARY: I'd be delighted to. [*She has already removed her coat and sits, ready to take dictation*.] By the way, your reservation has been confirmed for the ten-thirty plane.

GRAVEL, *dictating*:   Gentlemen . . . by now, you all know that my own house is divided over the problem that—together—we have faced today.

ANDRÉ, *a small suitcase in his hand, comes down the stairs after* NICOLE. *During the following speech he goes to his mother and embraces her.*

GRAVEL, *still dictating*:   I know that you share my distress. . . .

LOUISE, *holding* ANDRÉ *by the hand as he starts to go*:   Pierre . . . I think your son would like to shake hands with you.

ANDRÉ *lowers his head. After a short moment of hesitation, he goes slowly to his father. In silence, scarcely looking at one another, they shake hands. Then* ANDRÉ *goes upstage, where he stands a moment, lost.*

GRAVEL, *picking up his dictation*:   I know that you share my distress, and that of my wife. . . .

NICOLE, *after waiting in the hallway, she has come to get the bag which* ANDRÉ *left on a chair when he came to embrace his mother*:   Let's go. [*She takes* ANDRÉ *by the arm.*]

During the following speech, LOUISE, *sitting near her husband, watches the young couple disappear out the door.*

GRAVEL, *dictating*:   . . . For my divided house will not go down without shaking yours to its very foundations.

The curtain falls.

What do you think?

1. (a) Who has been proved to be more correct in assessing the problems of and solutions for French-English relations in Canada, André or his father? Why?
   (b) Whom do you identify and sympathize with more, André or his father? Why?
   (c) Was your choice the same in (a) and (b)? If not, why not?
2. How has reading this selection affected the perception you had of French-English relations at the end of Part 1? Why?
3. Do you feel that the play is accurate or inaccurate in its portrayal of the relationship between French Canadians and English Canadians and relationships among French Canadians? Why?

3

The Contemporary Scene

In its Preliminary Report, the Royal Commission on Bilingualism and Biculturalism reported that the crisis in French-English relations in Canada stemmed from the fact "that the state of affairs established in 1867, and never since seriously challenged, is now for the first time being rejected by the French Canadians of Canada."

What "state of affairs" is French Canada rejecting? What are the grievances that underlie this rejection? What changes are French Canadians demanding? How are these demands being received in English Canada?

In this section dealing with the contemporary aspects of the French-English issue, you are encouraged to probe into the sources, extent, and effects of the crisis that has raised these questions, by first looking at the Quebec scene from a cultural, economic and political perspective and by then examining the reaction to Quebec in other parts of Canada.

Inside Quebec

Not all French Canadians, of course, live in Quebec. But the French-English issue in Canada as we know it finds its source for the most part in the province of Quebec. Quebec has been undergoing for some time, and still is undergoing, profound changes in its social structures and social thinking. Inevitably the pressure for change expresses itself politically, and thus what is at first a provincial phenomenon becomes a national concern, as Quebec demands a re-assessment of Confederation and a redefinition of her role in it to reflect the vast transformation in her own society.

What has been the nature of this transformation? How does it express itself in the spheres of culture, economic life and politics? What demands do these changes make on the rest of Canada and why?

Cultural Tensions

What is the significance of the term "Québécois"? What does the fact that French-speaking Quebeckers prefer to call themselves Qué-bécois rather than French Canadians tell you about the Quebec culture and the Québécois's attachment to their province? Why do the Québécois feel a strong sense of uniqueness, of identity, of cul-tural homogeneity—rare things in Canada? What apprehensions do the Québécois have about the future of their culture and how do they want to protect it?

The following section includes readings about the nature and vitality of the Québécois culture, including an examination of the crucial language issue.

How important is the preservation of the Québécois culture to you? Why?

1. WE ARE QUÉBÉCOIS

In his book, Option for Quebec *(1968), René Lévesque, leader of the democratic separatist Parti Québécois, describes what it is like to feel oneself a Québécois. M. Lévesque also points out some of the problems faced by the Québécois in preserving their cultural identity. What are some of these problems? (Reprinted by permission of The Canadian Publishers, McClelland and Stewart Limited, Toronto.)*

What that means first and foremost—and if need be, all that it means—is that we are attached to this one corner of the earth where we can be completely ourselves: this Quebec, the only place where we have the unmistakable feeling that "here we can be really at home."

Being ourselves is essentially a matter of keeping and developing a personality that has survived for three and a half centuries.

At the core of this personality is the fact that we speak French. Everything else depends on this one essential element and follows from it or leads us infallibly back to it.

*   *   *   *   *

Until recently in this difficult process of survival we enjoyed the protection of a certain degree of isolation. We lived a relatively sheltered life in a rural society in which a great measure of unanimity reigned, and in which poverty set its limits on change and aspiration alike.

We are children of that society, in which the *habitant,* our father or grandfather, was still the key citizen. We also are heirs to that fantastic adventure—that early America that was almost entirely French. We are, even more intimately, heirs to the group obstinacy which has kept alive that portion of French America we call *Québec.*

All these things lie at the core of this personality of ours. Anyone who does not feel it, at least occasionally, is not—is no longer—one of us.

*   *   *   *   *

On the other hand, one would have to be blind not to see that the conditions under which this personality must assert itself have changed in our lifetime, at an extremely rapid and still accelerating rate.

Our traditional society, which gave our parents the security of an environment so ingrown as to be reassuring and in which many of us grew up in a way that we thought could, with care, be preserved indefinitely; that quaint old society has gone.

Today, most of us are city dwellers, wage-earners, tenants. The standards of parish, village, and farm have been splintered. The automobile and the airplane take us "outside" in a way we never could have imagined thirty years ago, or even less. Radio and films, and now television, have opened for us a window onto everything that goes on throughout the world: the events—and the ideas too—of all humanity invade our homes day after day.

The age of automatic unanimity thus has come to an end. The old protective barriers are less and less able to mark safe pathways for our lives. The patience and resignation that were preached to us in the old days with such efficiency now produce no other reactions than scepticism, or indifference, or even rebellion. . . .

The dangers are striking enough.

In a world where, in so many fields, the only stable law seems to have become that of perpetual change, where our old certainties are crumbling one after the other, we find ourselves swept along helplessly by irresistible currents. We are not at all sure that we can stay afloat, for the swift confusing pace of events forces us to realize as never before our own weaknesses, our backwardness, our terrible collective vulnerability.

*   *   *   *   *

The only way to overcome the danger is to face up to this trying and thoughtless age and make it accept us as we are, succeeding somehow in making a proper and appropriate place in it for ourselves, in our own language, so that we can feel we are equals and not inferiors. This means that in our homeland we must be able to earn our living and pursue our careers in French. It also means that we must build a society which, while it preserves an image that is our own, will be as progressive, as efficient, and as "civilized" as any in the world. (In fact, there are other small peoples who are showing us the way, demonstrating that maximum size is in no way synonymous with maximum progress among human societies.)

To speak plainly, we must give ourselves sufficient reason to be not only sure of ourselves but also, perhaps, a little proud.

What do you think?

1. (a) What does it mean to be a Québécois, according to M. Lévesque? How would a French Canadian living outside Quebec react to Lévesque's remarks?
   (b) Describe how you think a Québécois might feel about being a Canadian.
2. What cultural challenge is Quebec now facing, in M. Lévesque's view? What do you think brought this about?
3. Does René Lévesque feel that a culture based on tradition can be compatible with "progress" and "modernity"? Do you agree with him? Why or why not?

2.   CULTURAL VITALITY IN QUEBEC

Professor Ben-Z. Shek of the University of Toronto presented this background paper, "The Search for Identity and the Development of Quebec Culture," to the Committee for an Independent Canada in the fall of 1972. How does a sense of identity contribute to a people's cultural vitality? (Reprinted by permission of the Committee for an Independent Canada. Excerpt from Mon Pays *by Gilles Vigneault, reprinted by permission of Les Editions Du Vent Qui Vire et Les Nouvelles Editions De L'Arc, Montreal.)*

De mon grand pays solitaire
Je crie avant que de me taire

A tous les hommes de la terre
Ma maison c'est votre maison
Entre mes quatre murs de glace
Je mets mon temps et mon espace
A préparer le feu la place
Pour les humains de l'horizon
Et les humains sont de ma race . . .

The above words are from *Mon pays,* written and composed by Quebec's most famous *chansonnier,* Gilles Vigneault. This song is practically a hymn today in Quebec, because its sensitive creator has been able in it to touch certain chords common to thousands of his compatriots. In spite of what we have been told by those in high places that French-Canadian nationalism is to all intents and purposes a reactionary, xenophobic phenomenon, Vigneault's song is proof of the contrary. The word "race," so much a part of the inward-looking, mythical vocabulary of traditional right-wing Quebec nationalism, has here been turned into its opposite, and is now applied to all of humanity, equally welcome to sit before the singer-poet's cosy fireplace. The neo-nationalism so evident today in Quebec's burgeoning culture is largely a positive, confident and realistic acceptance of the Québécois by themselves. Its approach is open to the world, and not chauvinistic, and stresses, as poet Fernand Ouellette said recently during a visit to Israel with other Quebec cultural leaders, that one contributes to universal cultural values by developing one's own people's artistic and psychological talents.

*　　*　　*　　*　　*

In my view, it is no accident that within the last ten years or so, as national consciousness has grown in Quebec, so too has the number of *chansonniers,* that rather unique breed of poet-composer-performer. Alongside Gilles Vigneault there are Georges Dor, Robert Charlebois, Jean-Pierre Ferland, Claude Léveillé and the *chansonnier-interprète* Pauline Julien, to name only a few. Their songs have become beloved household objects to people in every corner of Quebec, because they have found the right turn of phrase, the right register to express people's hopes and fears, joys and sorrows, and to name the places, rivers, towns, hills and valleys, that are familiar and dear to them.

*　　*　　*　　*　　*

The novelists of Quebec, particularly its younger ones, those between twenty-five and forty, have, too, reflected the collective search for identity in their successful works. As they became more "Québécois" in their writing, they also made a greater impact on France, where they have won prizes and created great interest. Among such writers are **Jacques Godbout, Hubert Aquin, Marie-Claire Blais, Claude Jasmin, Réjean Ducharme**. The "universalists" of the generation (and some of the entourage) of Prime Minister Trudeau, like Robert Elie, André Giroux and even a latter-day convert such as Roger Lemelin, have ceased to write novels altogether. Even controversial works such as Jacques Renaud's *Le Cassé,* written in the truncated, highly anglicized, deformed *joual* of the uneducated Montreal poor, have won wide acclaim because of their authenticity and powerful, emotional rendering of the most deprived social strata.

It was in the field of poetry that there first emerged a movement united around the theme of *le pays*. It was the poets grouped around the Montreal publishing house, L'Hexagone, headed by Gaston Miron, who during the 1950's began to give expression to the phenomenon of a French-language culture in a North American context. Fernand Ouellette, Jean-Guy Pilon, Paul-Marie Lapointe, Gatien Lapointe and others identified the emotional geographical framework in which they lived and strove for creative expression, often linking the loved one with the country to be possessed. In the 1960's many younger poets emerged, and today not a week goes by without the publication of two or more collections of verse. The oral tradition is very much in evidence as poets read before large audiences. A case in point was the *Nuit de la poésie,* held in March, 1970, when more than 4,000 Montrealers stayed up a whole night to hear some 35 poets recite their work at the Gésu Hall. . . .

*   *   *   *   *

Many English-speaking Canadians are aware of the vitality of Quebec film-making because of the exposure given such recent films as Jutra's *Mon oncle Antoine* and Perrault's *L'Acadie, l'Acadie*. In 1971, forty-three feature-length films were produced in Canada, and of these, twenty-nine were made in Quebec, almost all by French-speaking directors. Quebec film directors have been very prominent among the winners of 1200 prizes awarded Canadian films during the past several years at such international festivals as Poitiers, Dinard and Chicago. Clearly the effervescence seen in French-language film production in Quebec is linked with the stronger sense of identity which has grown among the Québécois these past ten years. This is seen both in the subject matter of many of the films as well as the controversies that develop around them within the National Film Board.

In this rapid bird's-eye view of Quebec's recent cultural awakening and its relationship to the quest for identity and positive self-assertion, I have tried to show that healthy nationalism and its cultural expression can greatly enrich the life of a people while at the same time contributing to mankind's varied storehouse of artistic treasures. Is there a lesson to be learned here for English Canada?

What do you think?

1. *(a) Why is Quebec culture gaining such enormous vitality?*
   (b) "Is there a lesson to be learned here for English Canada?" Is there? If so, what do you think the lesson is?
2. *How do you think the Québécois regard English-Canadian cultural life? How would this feeling influence their attitude towards English-French relations in Canada? Why?*

3. A LAST DITCH STAND

George Grant, who teaches religion at McMaster University in Hamilton, has written extensively and sensitively about the effects of technological homogenization on national cultures. In his influential book Lament for a Nation *(Toronto: McClelland and Stewart, 1965), Grant wrote pessimistically about the future of Canadianism. Below are his remarks on the prospects for French-Canadian culture. (Reprinted by permission of The Canadian Publishers, McClelland and Stewart Limited, Toronto.)*

Nevertheless, indigenous cultures are dying everywhere in the modern world. French-Canadian nationalism is a last-ditch stand. The French on this continent will at least disappear from history with more than the smirks and whimpers of their English-speaking compatriots—with their flags flying and, indeed, with some guns blazing. The reality of their culture, and their desire not to be swamped, cannot save them from the inexorable facts in the continental case. Solutions vary to the problem of how an autonomous culture can be maintained in Quebec. But all the answers face the same dilemma: Those who want to maintain separateness also want the advantages of the age of progress. These two ends are not compatible, for the pursuit of one negates the pursuit of the other. Nationalism can only be asserted successfully by an identification with technological advance; but technological advance entails the disappearance of those indigenous differences that give substance to nationalism.

What do you think?

1. *"Those who want to maintain separateness also want the advantages of the age of progress." What does the author mean by this statement? Do you feel this is generally true of Quebeckers? Explain why you feel the way you do.*
2. *Compare George Grant's views with those of René Lévesque (Pt. 3—The Contemporary Scene, Reading 1). How do they differ? Whom do you agree with and why?*
3. *Do Grant's remarks shed any light on the problem of English Canada's search for a national identity? If so, why?*

4.   A BULWARK AGAINST THE UNITED STATES

The remarks of Quebec Premier Robert Bourassa concerning the role of Quebec in preserving Canada from U.S. cultural absorption were reported in the Toronto Star, *April 29, 1971. (Reprinted with permission* Toronto Star.*)*

Canada could sink under a flood of Americanism "without a Quebec which is strong, dynamic and culturally sure of itself," Quebec Premier Robert Bourassa warned last night.

He said Canadians should not see Quebec as a problem, but as an essential element for the reinforcement of a truly Canadian identity before the growing U.S. influence in Canada.

The premier was guest speaker at the annual dinner of the Canadian Press, the co-operative newsgathering agency serving 104 Canadian newspapers as well as radio and television stations.

"More and more, English-speaking Canada seeks to protect itself against American encroachment," he said. "In this quest for true Canadian identity Quebec is a precious ally, an exceptional asset."

He warned that if Quebec people see their language and culture endangered they may turn to separatism and the remaining provinces probably "would slowly slip into the American wake."

"What all Canadians must admit is that any downgrading of French culture in Quebec, and in the country, can only mean downgrading the claim to an authentic Canadian personality in favor of an even greater integration into American culture," he asserted to loud applause.

What do you think?

1. *Compare the views of Premier Bourassa with those of*
   (a) René Lévesque (Pt. 3—The Contemporary Scene, Reading 1).
   (b) George Grant (Pt. 3—The Contemporary Scene, Reading 3).
   Who do you think is right and why?
2. *Compare the situation of Quebec vis-à-vis Canada with Canada's situation vis-à-vis the United States. What differences are there? What similarities? On the whole, is the comparison a fair one? Why or why not?*

5.   THE IMPORTANCE OF LANGUAGE

The preceding documents in this section have dealt with French-Canadian culture in very general terms. These next few documents have been selected to provide you with an opportunity to examine one facet of that culture—language.

This article, "Cultures in Conflict: the Imperative of Language," is by Raymond Gagné and was published in Canadian Dimension Magazine *in the August-September 1969 issue. In this piece, Gagné examines the role that language plays in the vitality of a national culture. (Reprinted by permission of* Canadian Dimension Magazine.*)*

Most French Canadians are aliens on the greater part of Canadian soil, even in their own fortress of Quebec. Any significant study of the crisis in French Canada today must deal with the causes of this alienation and its effect on all aspects of French-Canadian existence. This sort of study must necessarily employ such words as culture, language, and personality, broad concepts which themselves are in need of clear definition. Modern anthropologists apply the term culture, not to the individual as such, but to the entire set of forces visibly and *imperceptibly* at work in the shaping of an entire society, all that goes into the information and formation of the individual. In this sense everyone born and brought up in the confines of a given society inherits a culture, a language and a *collective personality* that is freely and unconsciously transmitted from one generation to another. The formal educational system we sometimes regard as the chief repository and transmitter of culture and language is but one of the many sub-structures of the total set that constitutes culture. Family life, television, radio and the cinema are other obvious examples in our culture. If schools were a *sine qua non* of culture and language, the Eskimos along with the great majority of the world's population would be meaningless non-entities, since they have no formal school system. In its broadest anthropological sense, culture is the school par excellence of every human being, whatever culture he belongs to, and with no tuition fees to boot.

  * * * * *

It is generally accepted that language is the most important vehicle of culture. There are other modes of cultural expression, notably art and music, but even these, at least in certain cultures, have been described and transmitted in part through the medium of words. . . . The very structure or grammatical categories of language imposes on its speaker a particular view of the universe, and conditions his *emotive* responses to this distinct view of reality. Language is not merely an instrument to communicate ideas and feelings, but is itself the molder of thought and emotion. It is a tool that limits the speaker's perception of objective reality.

  * * * * *

United Nations translators have observed that different languages seem to imply different attitudes—the English pattern is said to be pragmatic and inductive, whereas the French pattern is generalizing and deductive. Anyone who has kept up with the great Canadian constitutional debate in recent years may have recognized that the French Canadians want to revamp the sum and substance of the B.N.A. Act and inject it with broad declarations of principles and rights, whereas the English Canadians would be content to touch up certain details here and there. The custom of legal precedent is deeply rooted in British history but not so in French history. This might explain in part why the revolution of 1789 took place in France and not in England. It must never be forgotten that the manifestation of contemporary culture has deep historical roots, just as the language we use today echoes deep into the halls of time. All this, then, to show that we are all more or less unconsciously prisoners of our own linguistic and cultural patterns, which give us a particular view of the world and a particular way of reacting to it emotionally and rationally.

*   *   *   *   *

When a given language, in this case, French, is constantly under pressure to express the structures of a foreign culture, in this case, English, as well as the remnants of its own culture, it ill serves both groups and is, in fact, rejected by both.

This is exactly what is happening in Quebec and Canada at large today. French Canadians themselves look down on their own language because they realize it is neither fish, flesh nor fowl. They know it is *hybrid* and mongrelized, the product of a hybrid culture.

Always keeping in mind the inseparability of culture, personality and language, we can state that the average French Canadian scorns himself because he has contempt for the hybrid language he is forced to speak and the hybrid culture that necessarily shapes him. His self-contempt is increased by the fact that he is not only rejected by English Canadians, but also by all the various ethnic brands of new Canadians who naturally prefer to assimilate into the powerful and prestigious English minority group of Quebec.

*   *   *   *   *

This is the very heart of the French-Canadian crisis. The French Canadian today is saying: "I do not like what I am and where I am going; now that I am beginning to understand the forces that made me so, I want to change the structures in order to become what I want to be." The sixty-four dollar question is, of course, is it too late? René Lévesque's new **Parti Québécois** does not think so, although it certainly emphasizes the extreme urgency of the situation. It is now or never, they say. It is a huge gamble, they recognize, but, they hasten to add, who has ever rejected a great risk when his very life is at stake? The independence movement in Quebec springs from one prime malaise, and it is not essentially economic, as most people believe. The independence movement in Quebec is aimed, first and foremost, at saving the French culture, language and personality on the North American continent. In essence, it is a linguistic-cultural revolution. It is based on the desire to transform the sociodynamics of Quebec into essentially French channels of expression and creation.

What do you think?

1. (a) *Explain the role that language plays in the cultural differences between peoples.*
   (b) *Do you feel that language is the most important form of cultural expression? Why?*
2. *Discuss the following:*
   (a) *Speaking French does not ensure "Frenchness."*
   (b) *Without its language, a culture became a set of mere artifacts.*
3. *According to Gagné, what does the French Canadian think of his language? Why does he feel the way he does? How are these feelings likely to influence his attitude towards English Canadians and their attitudes towards him?*

6.   LES ENGLISH SONT COMING

The cartoon below appeared in a French-language magazine, but the actual source is unknown.

What do you think?

1. Examine the above cartoon. What do you think the cartoonist is trying to say?

7.   SEARCH FOR A LANGUAGE POLICY

Montreal journalist James Ferrabee wrote the following article on Quebec language policy for the Montreal Gazette, *January 11, 1972. The article was entitled "In Linguistic Policy-Shaping, the Focus is on Montreal," and focusses on the debate of language education policy in Quebec. (Reprinted by permission of the* Montreal Gazette.)

Yet while this delicate diplomatic work [the B and B Commission's efforts to protect French minorities outside Quebec and to render the federal civil service bilingual] was being done from 1963 to 1967, and several generations of attitudes were crumbling in English Canada, the perspective on the problem was shifting radically in Quebec.

The main cause of the shift was a declining birth rate which slid from a high of close to 30 per 1,000 inhabitants in the late 1950s—several points above the national average, and nearly four points above Ontario's —to 17 per 1,000 population by 1967, lower than the national average, including Ontario. It was the first time in more than 200 years that Quebec's birth rate was equal to or below the national average.

The birth rate had been the one constant factor through good times and bad, through waves of immigration from Europe and the United States, and waves of emigration out of Quebec. It maintained the French fact in Quebec, which assured "survival." But the drop in the Quebec birth rate meant that survival of the French fact in Canada as an issue was overtaken by survival of the French fact in Quebec itself. As a consequence, to many intellectuals in Quebec, the B and B Commission became out-dated, even irrelevant.

One event in 1968 was to illuminate the new shift in thinking even more clearly. It was the crisis in the Montreal suburb of St. Leonard which pitched parents mainly of Italian origin against a group of French-speaking Canadians controlling the local school board over the issue of the board attempting to phase out English-language education in the schools. This was the first time the right of parents to choose the language of instruction of their children had been challenged in the province. The move was not aimed at English-language schools for English-language children as much as at the half million or more new Canadians who had come to the province in the preceding 20 years. The children of the relatively new arrivals, the French-speaking members of the board said, were assimilating with the

1,000,000 English-speaking minority, and not with the 5,000,000 French-speaking majority and here was the main threat to the future of the French fact, they said. The [Italian] parents replied that they were not choosing sides, only assuring that their children would be able to speak both French and English. English was the language which assured mobility.

* * * * *

[*Many prominent Québécois, faced with evidence from studies showing that between Quebec's declining birth rate and immigrant families' learning English rather than French, and feeling that the French language was endangered in Quebec, advocated provincial laws which would require non-Anglophone immigrant and non-immigrant parents to send their children to French schools.*]

The powerful argument which [these] Francophone Quebecers use is that the rights of the "collectivity"—the French community which is 80 per cent of Quebec—must take precedence over individual rights.

It is difficult, if not impossible, to legislate "collective" rights in this context without taking away someone's individual rights.

What do you think?

1. *Do you feel that Quebec nationalists are exaggerating the danger to their language and culture? Why?*
2. *In the language issue, as exemplified by the St. Leonard crisis, explain how "collective" rights and "individual" rights collide.*
3. *Would you support legislation which sought to actively protect the rights of a certain group or would you oppose such legislation on the grounds that since it treats the group separately, it is discriminatory? Why?*

8. CULTURAL CRISES COMPARED

On March 10, 1973, the influential Montreal newspaper Le Devoir *published a series of five articles on the subject of English Canada's search for a cultural identity. This selection is a précis of one of those articles. The original was written by Guy Rocher, a University of Montreal sociologist. (Reprinted by permission of* Le Devoir.*)*

In an article entitled "Is English Canada Experiencing a Cultural Crisis?" Guy Rocher sets out to study the similarities and differences between English- and French-Canadian cultures. He assumes, from the beginning, that there is such a thing as an English-Canadian culture, despite the fact that French Canadians have always monopolized the subject of culture.

Among the similarities, Guy Rocher notes: the interrogation on the existence of a specific culture, distinguished from the American or "Commonwealth" culture in English Canada. English Canada has tried to base its cultural originality on multiculturalism (as opposed to the "melting pot" theory in the U.S.). These are the similar and yet opposite positions of both Canadas. French Canada has sought its originality in ethnic and linguistic homogeneity; English Canada in heterogeneity.

Most enlightening, though, are probably the differences between the two groups. The cultural and identity crisis in English Canada has not become as visible as it is in Quebec. It has not been expressed in social and political movements and parties, nor has it led to popular demonstrations. In English Canada, it is more of an elitist movement which has not been voiced outside the intellectual community.

This seclusion, added to the lack of communication (which Rocher calls the "high wall of silence and ignorance") between the two communities, has kept English Canada's interrogation very isolated.

Another difference is that English Canada has identified the invasion of American culture as a dangerous threat to its own (this reaction is especially violent in English-Canadian universities, where it sometimes becomes mere xenophobia or anti-Americanism), whereas Quebec is still busy struggling to free itself from the rest of Canada.

The third difference between the two communities is that Quebec has never suffered a real brain-drain (Quebec intellectuals are deeply attached to their country and rarely do they leave for France or the U.S.), whereas there has been strong emigration of the English-Canadian intelligentsia towards the U.S., Britain and other parts of the Commonwealth (this phenomenon is not unlike American emigration towards Europe in the early 20th century). English-Canadian artists, writers, researchers thought they could not be recognized on the international scene if they remained in Canada.

"What can this brief comparison teach us?" Guy Rocher wonders in his conclusion. We French Canadians are not the only ones wondering what we are and what we would hope to be on the North American continent. It might therefore be interesting to pay heed to what people in the same position have to say, and to see how they handle the situation. They might teach us how to react to the invading American civilization, which is still too unconsciously felt in Quebec.

It would be naive to believe that French and English Canadians can work together in solving their particular identity crisis since the problems take different forms.

Comparing the two, though, might be enlightening and enable us to measure the difficulties and the chances of overcoming them.

What is meant by?

"monopolized"
"homogeneity"
"heterogeneity"
"xenophobia"
"intelligentsia"

What do you think?

1. Why does Rocher feel that the cultural and identity crisis is more visible in Quebec than in English Canada? How would this difference affect attitudes of the two language groups towards one another?
2. Do you think that the Québécois should be more wary of the American influence than M. Rocher seems to think they are? Why or why not?
3. Do you agree that the identity crisis in English and French Canada "takes different forms"? Defend your answer. Do you agree with M. Rocher that the two language groups cannot work together to solve their identity problems? Why?

Economic Problems

Are there economic roots to many of the grievances expressed by the Québécois? Do the Québécois experience discrimination in economic areas—on-the-job treatment, earning power, or opportunities for advancement? Do the Québécois feel that the Quebec economy does not "belong" to them at the present time? Are Québécois feelings of economic discrimination or of alienation from economic decision-making justified?

The following readings examine the reasons for some of the complaints made by the Québécois about their economy. What is the significance of the Québécois economic ambitions for French-English relations?

9. THE BOTTOM OF OUR DIFFICULTIES

Claude Ryan, editor-in-chief of the famous Montreal French-language daily, Le Devoir, *is one of the most respected voices in French*

Canada. In an editorial appearing in Le Devoir, *July 11, 1972, Ryan analysed the relationships between economic and social problems and those concerning culture and language. (Reprinted by permission of* Le Devoir.)

If the questions of culture and language are to be approached in an atmosphere of complete calm and impartiality, people must all be able to feel themselves economic and social equals; they must have the impression that everybody has an equal opportunity in life.

Now under existing economic conditions, anglophones start off with undisputed advantages. Until economic power is distributed on a more uniform basis—and this means a good deal more than government programs for the redistribution of income—we shall be begging the question.

Actually, the sharing of power also goes farther than what is called the working-language question. It covers all structures issuing economic decisions. Whatever the cost may be, francophones must make their way into these structures. There is no doubt that they control the promotion, duration, and vitality of their language.

What do you think?

1. *Why do you think Ryan feels that only when people have economic and social equality can they discuss culture and language calmly and impartially?*
2. *According to Ryan, what will guarantee French Canadians social and economic equality? What problems do you think French Canadians face in trying to achieve this goal?*

10.   THE ROOT OF THE CRISIS?

This selection, which briefly outlines some of the economic problems of Quebeckers, has been taken from a student handbill published during the October Crisis of 1970.

The crisis [October 1970] in Quebec is the outcome of a long history of staggering unemployment, starvation wages, and foreign ownership and exploitation. These are the bread-and-butter roots of the crisis which the government and the press have left unmentioned. These are the issues that have moved the Québécois to form a popular movement for independence.

TODAY, ONE OUT OF ELEVEN PEOPLE IN QUEBEC IS OUT OF A JOB.

Quebec has the highest unemployment figure in all Canada—8.9 per cent. Quebec has held the championship in unemployment for a long time. From 1958 to 1968 the average has been 7.3 per cent compared with 3.9 per cent in Ontario. For the last fifteen years, the number of unemployed workers in Quebec has ranged from 20 to 40 per cent more than Canada as a whole.

ENGLISH CANADIANS AND AMERICANS CONTROL MOST OF QUEBEC'S ECONOMY.

Although English-speaking Canadians make up less than 13 per cent of the population, they control, together with Americans, all the important sectors of the economy—banking and finance, manufacturing, and the resource industries. About fifty large industrial corporations control 75 per cent of industrial and mining production in Quebec. Only three of these are controlled by local Québécois capital. French-Canadian companies were responsible for only 5 per cent of the $3.4 billion worth of exporting from Quebec in 1961. English-Canadian companies accounted for 44 per cent and foreign companies for 52 per cent.

IT PAYS NOT TO SPEAK FRENCH IN QUEBEC.

Among male non-agricultural workers in Quebec, the average income for those who speak only English is $5,502. They are 11.1 per cent of the population. For workers who speak both languages, the average income is less—$4,772. They are 52.2 per cent of the population. For workers who speak only French, the average income is $3,099. They are 36.5 per cent of the population.

The average income of English-speaking workers is 41 per cent higher than that of French-speaking workers. No government program of bilingualism and biculturalism can disguise this blatant fact.

What do you think?

1. *In this reading, it was claimed that the popular movement for independence in Quebec has as its source certain economic conditions.*
   (a) What are these conditions?
   (b) Are the conditions referred to in this reading the same conditions referred to by Claude Ryan in the preceding one?

2. *Why do you think some French Canadians feel that only inde-*
pendence will correct these economic conditions? Do you agree
with them? Why or why not?

3. *To what extent are you willing to trust the statistics above in form-*
ing your opinion of the economic life of the Québécois? Explain
your answer.

11. MAÎTRE CHEZ NOUS

Toronto Telegram *staff reporter Claude Renault examined the reasons*
for the income disparity between French Canadians and English
Canadians in an article published in the Telegram, *June 17, 1969.*
(Reprinted by permission of the Toronto Sun Syndicate.)

"Tu n'es pas maître dans ta maison quand nous y sommes."

These words, the words of the chorus of an old French Canadian
song, say in translation that "you are not the master in your own home
when we are there." To some extent this seems to be the message which
non-French Canadian finance and enterprise are driving home in Quebec
and, not surprisingly, French Canadians seem to be rejecting both the
medium and the message. The *Telegram* survey has shown that French
Canadians in Quebec do not feel they are the masters in their own home,
and economic statistics show that this feeling is quite correct.

Yesterday's *Canada 70 Report* illustrated clearly just how far the
French Canadian in Quebec is from being master in his house, just how
alienated from his own environment he is in reality.

The question is why.

Before going into the explanation, however, it might be necessary,
as a reminder, to stress the fact that more than 80 per cent of Quebec's
population is French Canadian and that, of this proportion, almost half
speak French only.

With this fact in mind, let's move on to some others which I recently uncovered. The following brief resume of facts is taken straight
from a Bilingualism and Biculturalism research study which, until today,
was still secret and unpublished anywhere.

Value-added manufacturing enterprise in the province of Quebec
is only 10 per cent under financial control of French Canadians. In mineral-
rich Quebec only 2 per cent of value-added mining operations is under
financial control of French Canadians. Only one-third of the value-added
commercial services (retailing, wholesaling, insurance, etc.) in Quebec is
financially controlled by French Canadians.

These facts, the documents say, go a long way toward explaining why, in his own province, the French Canadian is in an underprivileged position. The person who gave these statistics to the *Telegram* added as a summation that "therefore big enterprise is evidently still under the control of Anglophones in Quebec and this explains why certain types of top positions have been reserved for other Anglophones."

Is this really an explanation of anything? In conducting its interviews in Quebec, the *Telegram* team has uncovered clear indications that many average French Canadians think this is the answer.

Pierre Desmeules, an oil refinery worker in east-end Montreal, says that "there is a ceiling in all large companies for French Canadians. This is not something you need to know, you sense it as soon as you begin to work." A personnel officer for a large English-Canadian firm in Montreal, French Canadian but studying for his Bachelor of Commerce degree during the evening at the English-language McGill University had this to report about his hiring instructions:

"I am to hire a French Canadian who is bilingual and an English Canadian who is unilingual equally. However, I am told to reject the French Canadian if, when speaking English, his accent is too strong, even if his grammar is all right."

The *Telegram's* control group studies show that, almost universally, French-Canadian Quebeckers believe that large companies have a ceiling beyond which French Canadians may not trespass. This, however, is merely a belief; it is not a fact. So, to test this belief against facts, the *Telegram* talked to a number of economists. Most of the French-speaking economists interviewed readily admitted they favored the pro-independence Parti Québécois. Their opinions, perhaps unreasonably, automatically became suspect. For this reason, we sought an economist who would be entirely unbiased on the issue and came up with Professor Benjamin Higgins, now teaching at the Université de Montreal.

He has worked for the B and B Commission on matters related to economics and language and recently headed the federal commission which favored Ste. Scholastique (much against the Quebec government's will) as the site for Montreal's future jumbo jet airport and also has prepared a report for the Quebec government on regional economic disparities. In other words, he is as close as you can get to objectivity.

His considered opinion was that "English-speaking management of big business in Quebec prefers to have English-speaking top management, scientific personnel and top level technical personnel, and this results, between the French and the English, in some difference in occupational status for a given level of education." Professor Higgins, probably privy to a good deal of still classified information, was being discreet; nevertheless, by his statement, he roughly confirmed both the B and B survey results and the opinion of the "average" French Canadian.

*   *   *   *   *

Professor Higgins went on to say that if you eliminate the educational difference, the occupational difference and the difference of age and sex, "you have explained 95 percent of the difference in income between the French and Anglophone Canadian."

"Therefore," he added, "the problem is not really that the French Canadian Doctor of Science or Engineering gets paid less than the Anglophone in the same job. The problem is that the Doctor of Science who speaks French is not in the job. The owner or his supervisor wants not only someone who is English speaking but someone with the same background and type of technical training as his own. In other words, the difference in the level of education explains about half the difference in income. The other factor is that for a given education status there is some difference in the occupational status, because of the degree to which Quebec enterprise is under the control of English Canadians."

Why was the gap between French and English growing, despite increasingly better French-Canadian education in Quebec?

"The difference in occupational status is increasing because higher levels of education bring less increase in income to the French Canadian than to the English Canadian and, again, you come back to the issue of financial control. The point is that the difference in occupational status is increasing rather than improving. My own hunch is that this is because the French Canadian does not have equal access to certain kinds of high-income occupations, because of the continuing predominance of Anglophone ownership in the province of Quebec."

What do you think?

1. *The author of this selection uses the word "alienated" to describe how the Quebecker feels about his environment. Do you agree with this point of view? If so, how and why do economic conditions in Quebec create this feeling of alienation?*

2. *Do you feel that there is a connection between economic alienation, as described in this selection, and cultural alienation, as described by Raymond Gagné (Pt. 3—The Contemporary Scene, Reading 5)? If so, explain the connection.*

12.   A LACK OF DYNAMISM

M. Gérard Filion, president of the Canadian Manufacturers' Association from 1971 to 1972 and former publisher of Le Devoir, spoke to the Richelieu Club in Montreal on the subject of Quebec's economic problems. Excerpts from M. Filion's speech were published in the

Globe and Mail, *Toronto, April 28, 1969. (Reprinted by permission of M. Gérard Filion.)*

The people of Quebec have not displayed much dynamism in industrial development. Quebec was industrialized from the outside; Quebec built its industry with capital that came from abroad and was administered by teams recruited abroad following a spirit and methods imported from abroad. . . . The French-Canadian Quebecker has taken refuge in agriculture, in lumbering and in sawmills, the building of doors and window frames, in furniture and shoemaking, with a little textile around the edges. While the neighboring province was industrializing, we were preaching a return to the earth. While the great industrial complexes were being formed, we were praising the merits of small business.

I have already stated in a bittersweet tone that Quebec has been afflicted for 100 years with governments of lawyers who understand nothing of business. It would have been more precise to say "governments of professionals," for the education system we have given ourselves and for which we were alone responsible, inevitably led to a scorn for economic things and an exaltation of so-called cultural values. It was not the Americans, it was not the English Canadians, it was not even the English-speaking Quebeckers who inflicted on us for 100 years the education system we had. It is the French-Canadian society which gave itself this system, with the consequences we observe today.

   *   *   *   *   *

The social climate of Quebec is hardly favorable to economic progress. By a bad social climate, I don't necessarily mean separatism, student rebellion and bombs. I wish rather to denounce the open contempt which the public displays for business and for people concerned with it. In this regard we are dragging a long intellectual heredity, a prejudice rooted in an unreal morality and reinforced by a situation as a minority people. One always scorns the wealth one does not have, but one cherishes the wealth one possesses. Those who have nothing are full of obsequiousness, those who have something display the arrogance of "beggars on horseback." The production of goods and services is not more contemptible when achieved by an industrial manager, a shopkeeper or a financier than it is when done by a farmer or an artisan.

   *   *   *   *   *

A country is not rich because of the abundance of natural wealth. There are poor countries which are full of resources, and rich countries which have none. It is grey matter which makes all the difference. Let us use more of it in Quebec and we will catch up to the others.

What is meant by?

"obsequiousness"
"artisan"

What do you think?

1. (a) According to Gérard Filion, how was the Quebec economy developed? What was the significance of the nature of this development for French Canadians in the Quebec economy?
   (b) Why do you think French Canada developed an educational system and a social climate that "led to a scorn for economic things and an exaltation of cultural values"?
2. George Grant (Pt. 3—The Contemporary Scene, Reading 3) claims that it is in the rejection of economic progress on the part of French Canadians that French Canada has been able to preserve its culture. Do you think it is possible for French Canadians to become more dynamic, as M. Filion recommends in the preceding article, in the economic area without imperiling their culture? Why?

13.   FRENCH-CANADIAN BLACKMAIL

Mark Alchuk was a first-year student at York University when he wrote an article for the student newspaper entitled "Why I Support a Policy of English Unilingualism." This excerpt is from Mr. Alchuk's article, published in the Excalibur, *February 11, 1971. (Reprinted by permission of* Excalibur.*)*

Separatism is explained away today by drawing attention to the high unemployment in Quebec. We are constantly bombarded with such facts as English Quebeckers are better paid than French Quebeckers; French Quebeckers have higher unemployment and are second class citizens. We are never told why French Canadians are unemployed and receive low wages—they just do somehow.

The guilt for all this however is placed squarely on English Canada. English Canadians are being told that they alone are responsible for whatever is wrong in Quebec. English Canada is to blame for unemployment, English Canada is to blame for low wages, English Canada is suppressing the Québécois. Using such absurd reasoning, I wonder if Quebec is responsible for unemployment in Ontario. I wonder if Quebec is responsible for the injustice committed against the real founding races of Canada, the

Indians and Eskimos? I wonder if Quebec wants to take any blame itself for what is wrong in the province; it seems very unlikely!

The economic backwardness of the French Canadian has always been blamed on the energetic, competitive English entrepreneur. Most of French Canada's problems can be explained by the fact that it is a small cultural island in an English-speaking business world with which it cannot compete; its backwardness stems from unreformed institutions, decades of governmental corruption, Catholicism, and antiquated laws.

All these relevant considerations have been brushed aside and the French Canadian, maintaining he is guiltless of Quebec's economic backwardness, continues to believe in some English-Canadian conspiracy against him. This twisted logic used to blackmail English Canada into accepting the bilingual policy has become intolerable.

What do you think?

1. *Compare Mr. Alchuk's views with those of Gérard Filion in the reading preceding this one. Where do they agree? Where do they disagree? Explain why.*

14. A TOTAL REVOLUTION

Pierre Vallières, a one-time associate of Prime Minister Trudeau's during the 1950s, became the leading thinker for the FLQ. After the October Crisis of 1970 Vallières renounced his connection with the FLQ, throwing his support to the democratic separatist party, the Parti Québécois. This selection has been taken from Vallières' book, White Niggers of America: (McClelland and Stewart, 1971), written during his FLQ days. (Reprinted by permission of The Canadian Publishers, McClelland and Stewart Limited, Toronto.)

But when it comes to the Québécois "Terrorists," the nature of their actions, so to speak, is regarded as radically different by the indigenous petite bourgeoisie, which feels its own privileges threatened by the "terrorism" of the Front de libération du Quebec (FLQ). That is why the petite bourgeoisie of Quebec, notwithstanding the political struggle it is waging against Canadian colonialism, insists on considering the partisans of the FLQ as "criminals" or, at best, as irresponsible and dangerous "anarchists."

Of course, it would be very different if the FLQ were the armed avant-garde of the nationalist petite bourgeoisie and were content to demand legal, formal, purely political sovereignty for Quebec. But the FLQ is, on the contrary, the armed avant-garde of the exploited classes of Quebec: the workers, the farmers, the petty white-collar workers, the students, the unemployed, and those on welfare—that is, at least 90 percent of the population. The FLQ is struggling not only for the political independence of Quebec, but also and inseparably for the revolution, a total revolution which will give all power to the workers and students in a free, self-administering, and fraternal society. Only a total revolution will make it possible for the Québécois, in collaboration with the other peoples of the earth, to build a Quebec that is truly free, truly sovereign.

The nationalist petite bourgeoisie is incapable of leading this revolution, or even desiring it, because it is completely dependent on American imperialism, in whose hands—in the framework of the Canadian Confederation, or in the future framework of a "sovereign" republic—it is only an obedient puppet. A parasitic class par excellence, the French-speaking petite bourgeoisie of Quebec can demand and obtain only the appearance of power. The true masters are on Wall Street and in Washington, for only total revolution will be able to destroy the economic, political, and cultural bases of the domination of Quebec by the U.S.A. The nationalist petite bourgeoisie, caught between American imperialism, which tomorrow may use it as a screen—in place of the English Canadians—and the exploited classes whose interests are radically and definitively opposed to its own, can survive as a semi-ruling class only on the condition that it becomes the sole manager of imperialist interests in Quebec. For the Québécois, petite bourgeoisie separatism is the only means that will enable it to play the same role in Quebec that the Anglo-Saxon petite bourgeoisie plays in Canada as a whole, the parasitic role of prison guard and policeman of American interests. That is why the petite bourgeoisie of Quebec is separatist.

The exploited classes of Quebec are also separatist, but for quite different reasons. For them, separatism, along with the destruction of the capitalist structures, is the means of wresting Quebec from the clutches of American imperialism. It is a struggle for both the national liberation of Quebec and the total social liberation of the Québécois.

The petite bourgeoisie may achieve its ends by means of elections, an invention of the capitalists designed to give the masses the illusion of a certain degree of democracy. But as in many other so-called decolonized countries, it may also have to resort to violence to overcome the stubborn resistance of the "Rhodesians" of Quebec, the Anglo-Saxon minority which has hitherto been all-powerful.

The exploited classes, on the other hand, have no choice. The only way in which they can oppose the organized violence of imperialism and its local representatives (English-speaking or French-speaking) is by the revolutionary violence initiated by the FLQ in 1963.

What is meant by?

"indigenous petite bourgeoisie"
"partisan"
"anarchist"
"avant-garde"
"parasitic"
"Rhodesians"

What do you think?

1. *How do you think André, the young protagonist in* Yesterday the Children Were Dancing *(Part 2), would have reacted to this passage by Pierre Vallières? How would André's father have reacted? Why?*
2. *Why is the FLQ separatist as well as revolutionary?*
3. *Are there groups in English Canada who feel about "American imperialism" the way Vallières does? If so, compare them with the FLQ, explaining any similarities and differences. How do you think the FLQ would feel about such groups and why?*

15.   THE PUSH FOR AUTONOMY

McGill University economist Kari Levitt, in her influential book about American investment in Canada, Silent Surrender *(1970), discusses the relationship between Quebec's economic woes and that province's desire for greater independence. (Reprinted by permission of The Macmillan Company of Canada Limited.)*

The relationship between English Canada and Quebec is a special one. Quebec is both a province within Confederation and the *patrie* of the French-Canadian nation. The demand for more autonomy by the province of Quebec thus has a dual character. In part, it resembles demands for increased provincial powers expressed by all the larger provinces; in part, it is the political form in which the desire for self-determination of French Canada expresses itself.

Clearly, there can be no national equality for French Canada without power over economic decisions. In the area of public policy, we thus have the demand for a larger share of revenue, and for a voice in tariff, monetary and immigration policy. For French Canada, more economic power for the government of Quebec is crucial, because the provincial public sector is the only effective lever by which French Canadians can influence decisions affecting their lives. While the English-Canadian elite is rapidly relinquishing economic control to the American corporations, the French-Canadian elite urgently desires entry into private corporate power. Such entry is highly restricted at present, and the situation has been fully documented by John Porter in his book *The Vertical Mosaic*. Yet national equality requires that economic decisions affecting Quebec must be made by French Canadians, not by English-Canadian or American corporations. Nothing less can assure the continued existence of a French-speaking community on the North American continent.

The experience of linguistic domination also explains the lack of discrimination in French-Canadian resentment between English-Canadian and American domination. It is interesting that public opinion polls constantly show less concern about American domination in Quebec than anywhere else in Canada, and no less a politician than René Lévesque does not appear to fear the consequences of "liberating" Quebec from the domination by the English-Canadian financial elite with the help of more powerful American capital. What difference, after all, to the French-Canadian worker in Arvida, whether orders are received in English from a foreman employed by a Canadian company like Alcan, or an American company, like Union Carbide?

The French-Canadian middle class is comprised of self-employed professionals, small businessmen and bureaucratically employed technocrats. No private French-Canadian entrepreneurial group can effectively challenge the powers of the anglophone corporations. The logic leads from nationalism to state entrepreneurship. This was the policy which guided the more radical elements of the Lesage administration during the so-called Quiet Revolution. It was symbolized by the creation of Hydro-Quebec as the first step to a more extensive expansion of the public sector into the resource industries of the province.

What is meant by?

"patrie"
"technocrat"
"entrepreneurial"
"state entrepreneurship"

What do you think?

1. "Clearly, there can be no national equality for French Canada without power over economic decisions." Why does Ms. Levitt feel this way? Do you agree? Why or why not?

2. (a) Why does the author feel that "no private French-Canadian entrepreneurial group can effectively challenge the powers of the anglophone corporations"?

(b) *How do some Quebeckers intend to resolve this problem? Why?*

(c) *How does this solution affect federal-provincial relations? Why?*

Politics in the Seventies

How are the cultural and economic tensions in the province of Quebec being expressed in the political arena? How do the political parties of Quebec reflect the sometimes opposing attitudes of various Quebec social groups towards these tensions and their solution? Why do extra-parliamentary forms of dissent exist in Quebec? How does the political situation in the province affect Quebec's relationship with English Canada and with the federal government?

These are some of the questions which you are encouraged to examine in the following section. This section includes a survey of Quebec's political parties and their performance in the 1973 provincial election, brief looks at the 1970 provincial election, the 1970 October Crisis, and the labour unrest of spring 1972.

How would you account for the extraordinary range and vitality of political expression in Quebec? How do these characteristics of Quebec politics affect French-English relations today? What do they imply for the future?

16. THE PARTI QUÉBÉCOIS

How do the platforms of Quebec's four major political parties reflect the differing attitudes of various Quebec social groups to the economic and cultural tensions in their province? The next few readings attempt to provide you with some idea of what each of Quebec's major political parties represents socially, economically and politically.

The Parti Québécois (PQ) promises that should it form the government of Quebec it will immediately initiate negotiations with the government of Canada to create a politically separate Quebec, bound to Canada only by certain economic treaties. The following description of the Parti Québécois was written by journalist Nick Auf der Maur for the Montreal-based magazine, the Last Post, *in January 1973. Mr. Auf der Maur's article was called "The Making of the President." What is the significance of this title? (Reprinted by permission of the* Last Post.*)*

Mme G. is an industrious, hard-working, dedicated Québécois. She's vice-president of the Parti Québécois riding association in Montreal–St. Jacques and lives in a basement flat on Carré St. Louis, a mildly fashionable square in the basically working-class district.

The photos and flags that adorn her flat bespeak her political inclinations. First off, the flags. She has both the blue and white Quebec Fleur-de-Lys, given to the province by Maurice Duplessis, and the red, white and green colours of the 1837 Patriote rebels.

The prominent photos are of John F. Kennedy, Fidel Castro, Charles de Gaulle and René Lévesque—the Kennedy image, a youthful reformer, a Catholic martyr; Castro, the little guy standing up to the big guy, doing something for his people; de Gaulle, who oversaw the liberation of his own nation and gave official sanction to the liberation of another; Lévesque, who encompasses all these virtues. If there is such a thing, Mme G. is a typical Péquiste militant.

*   *   *   *   *

Recently in Washington, a high-powered team of Canadian negotiators showed up at an international economic conference. As they walked into the conference room, they recognized a man who had been a familiar figure at Ottawa-Quebec negotiations. "What are you doing here?" they inquired. "I'm here as a consultant to look after the interests of Switzerland and a few other countries," Jacques Parizeau replied smiling.

Jacques Parizeau may not be typical, but he's a good example of the PQ leadership,—competent, thorough, strong—and supremely confident.

Along with Mme G. and Parizeau, the Parti Québécois is made up of about 70,000 paid-up members and a million and more sympathizers in the province. They hope to bring about the independence of Quebec by 1974 at the earliest, or the election after next at the least. Already, after just four years of existence, the PQ lays claim to speaking for 24 per cent of the electorate. It has every possibility of increasing that figure, if not in one fell swoop, at least slowly but surely. Almost everything since 1970, from the October federal elections which underscored Quebec's isolation from the rest of Canada to Premier Robert Bourassa's bumbling inability to produce the 100,000 jobs and economic security he promised in his election campaign, seems to be helping the PQ down what it sees as the inexorable road to independence.

René Lévesque himself is optimistic, although not recklessly over-confident.

"We expect to increase our vote substantially in 1974," (the expected date of the next provincial elections), he said over lunch in late November [1972]. "We'll form the official opposition, which is what we really are right now." He mentioned that there's a chance the PQ might "accidentally" win power in the next election, but the main PQ objective was to secure a majority in the following election.

[*In a passage omitted here, Mr. Auf der Maur goes on to analyse the origins of the Parti Québécois, describing Lévesque's role in the 1960–66 Liberal government, his conversion to separatism, and his subsequent withdrawal from the Liberal party in 1967. In 1968 the Parti Québécois was formed with Lévesque as leader.*]

A year and a half later [1970], the PQ ran its very successful election campaign. The party projected an image of being young, dynamic and, most crucially, positive. Instead of the somewhat negative "Ottawa non" slogans of past independentist groups, the bright young men of the PQ centred their campaign on the positive theme of "Let's build Quebec together." The main slogan was simply "OUI," Yes. The thousands of red and blue OUI buttons and stickers became the most visible symbol of the whole campaign. . . .

*   *   *   *   *

. . . a short time before the April 29 elections, polls showed the PQ and Liberals running almost neck and neck, 26 per cent to 29 per cent, with a very large bloc of undecideds.

Then, just a few days before the election there occurred an incident which still rankles very deeply in the PQ. It later came to be called the "Brinks coup." The Royal Trust Company arranged for several Brinks trucks loaded down with securities to be shipped secretly out of Montreal to Ontario. Photographers and TV crews were thoughtfully tipped off.

It was an example of the "economic terrorism" that so embitters Lévesque.

*   *   *   *   *

Nevertheless, the PQ picked up almost a quarter of the vote in 1970—more like a third of the French vote, since the 20 per cent of Quebecers who speak English are solidly Liberal. However, because of the gross inequities of the electoral system, it won only seven seats—six in the predominantly working-class East End of Montreal and one in Saguenay. Premier Bourassa has promised a new electoral map before the next election.

Since the election, the PQ has been extremely active, certainly the most active party on the provincial scene. The PQ has consolidated its existing strength and expanded its grass-roots organization. It has a democratic structure comparable to that of the NDP, which permits a maximum number of people to become involved in the ordinary administration of the party. Numerous local associations maintain full-time propaganda offices, while the central organization operates out of headquarters on Christophe Colomb street in north-central Montreal. The party's own publishing house, Les Editions du Parti Québécois, produces a continuous stream of books, pamphlets, programs and manifestos which are sold commercially in most newsstands and bookstores. Books like the PQ's economic manifesto "Quand nous serons vraiment chez nous" (When we will truly be at home) often crop up on the bestseller lists.

The seven-man Péquiste delegation in the National Assembly acts and sounds as if it were the official opposition and contributes more to the quality of debate than either the Créditiste or Unité-Québec parties. However, the Péquiste presence is not felt only in parliamentary debate. Because of the nature of the party and its militants, it has a pervasive effect on all social institutions. Péquistes tend to be active in community organizations, unions, Caisses Populaires, citizens' committees, student organizations, even sports and leisure groups.

What do you think?

1. *What kind of people do you think support the PQ? What professions do they follow? Where do they live: in the city or in the country? What are their political and social ideals?*
2. *Why is it "crucial" for the PQ to maintain a "positive" image?*
3. *How realistic do you think the PQ's confidence in its ability to win over a majority of Quebec voters is? Why?*
4. *To what extent do affairs like the "Brinks episode" affect election results, in your opinion?*

17. THE CRÉDITISTES

The Social Credit party is known as the Créditiste party in Quebec. In an article written for the Toronto Star, *February 5, 1973, Peter Desbarats examines the Créditiste phenomenon. (Reprinted with permission* Toronto Star.*)*

It was a packed convention in the crudest sense. Membership cards at $2 each were all that almost 6,000 people required to enter the convention and vote for a new leader of the Social Credit party of Quebec this weekend. But the convention was also packed with power—the kind of people-power that the other parties only talk about.

They came to Quebec in hundreds of cars and buses from the farms and villages of Gaspé, Beauce and the Eastern Townships, from the mining and mill towns of northern Quebec, and this time, for the first time in large numbers, from the workers' districts in the east end of Montreal. They filled a hockey arena and overflowed into an exhibition hall.

In the gloomy exhibition hall, where dark masses of people voted and watched a huge television image of the convention projected through the tobacco smoke, the feeling of raw political energy was as hot and thick as the atmosphere. Everyone sensed intuitively that there was enough power here to affect the future of governments in Quebec, in Ottawa, and perhaps even the future of Canada. Where did it originate?

Some of the old farmers at the convention could recall forty years of Social Credit in Quebec. But most of that history belongs in the Old Testament of the movement, when its members wore white berets and believed that Social Credit was conceived overseas in the mind of Major Douglas, born in the election of William Aberhart in Alberta, and protected in Quebec by the Virgin Mary. It was only about ten years ago that Réal Caouette put away his white beret, stood before a blackboard and began to talk on television. In 1962, he came out of the bleak northwestern frontier of Quebec to win twenty-six federal seats. In 1970, against Caouette's advice, another car dealer from his own town of Rouyn-Noranda took the party into Quebec politics only a few weeks before a provincial election. Camil Samson won 12 per cent of the vote and 12 of the 108 seats in Quebec's National Assembly. A year ago this month, Samson was deposed as leader. There has been enough bitterness and confused wrangling about the leadership since then to have destroyed a dozen ordinary parties. But Social Credit has thrived on discredit. In the federal election last October, Caouette's party made its first significant gains in French-speaking Montreal.

This was the potent political instrument, fashioned from the poverty, discontent and conservatism of the Quebec farmer, worker and small businessman, motivated by an almost religious zeal, that was placed this weekend in the hands of a 45-year-old radio hot-liner and former member of the Pearson cabinet in Ottawa. "However," wrote Claude Ryan of *Le Devoir* last month, contemplating this possibility, "Monsieur Dupuis, thank God, isn't yet on the point of becoming premier of Quebec."

But Yvon Dupuis has become important. Despite the fury of many "true créditistees" at his election, and the likelihood of a split in the party, Dupuis with his personal following in Montreal is bound to move Social Credit into a new stage of development in Quebec. This is what every other party is thinking about today. The Union Nationale opposition in Quebec, dwindling away to less than half the current strength of Social Credit in rural Quebec, may face the choice between coalition or annihilation. With Dupuis leading Social Credit into east-end Montreal, René Lévesque and his Parti Québécois may be in trouble.

What do you think?

1. (a) *From what sectors of society are the Créditistes drawn? What parts of Quebec do they come from? Compare them to the members of the Parti Québécois.*
   (b) *How do you think the economic and cultural unrest in Quebec has affected these people?*
   (c) *Explain why the Créditistes seemed to be winning support from these people.*
2. (a) *What was the "new stage of development" for the Créditistes? How did this threaten the Parti Québécois?*
   (b) *Why was the Union Nationale threatened by the Créditistes?*

18. THE UNION NATIONALE

Peter Desbarats, one of Canada's most distinguished journalists, has become well known for his perceptive commentaries on Quebec affairs. In this article, "Who Can Resurrect the Union Nationale," published by Saturday Night, March 1971, *Desbarats analyses the role of the Union Nationale in Quebec politics. (Reprinted by permission of Peter Desbarats.)*

The party which first assumed power in Quebec in 1936 under the late Maurice Duplessis has received a bad press in English-speaking Canada almost from the beginning. Duplessis' nationalist position made him unpopular in the rest of Canada during the Second World War, when he was defeated temporarily by the combined might of federal and provincial Liberals. In the 1950s, he became anathema to progressive elements in other provinces because of his ruthless persecution of Communists and Jehovah's Witnesses. After his death in 1959, and the return of the Liberals to power in Quebec, a widely publicized government investigation scandalized English-speaking Canadians with revelations of large-scale patronage under the Union Nationale.

Eventually it became impossible for English-speaking Canadians to understand why Quebec voters had kept the Union Nationale in power for more than twenty years. The reason, of course, was that the party responded to needs in Quebec which were little understood by outsiders. Some of these needs were reactionary; for example, the need of the province's English-speaking business establishment to maintain a poorly educated, underpaid and docile proletariat. But there were many genuine political and social needs which the party responded to: The need for a political organization within which French-speaking Quebeckers could feel completely at home; the need for a party which would at least give the appearance of standing up to the rest of Canada; the need for a political organization that could take progressive measures slowly while re-assuring the bulk of an extremely conservative population that it was zealous in defending traditional values. All these needs were met to some degree by the Union Nationale in the years between the end of the Second World War and the beginning of the Quiet Revolution.

The death of Duplessis in 1959 started a rapid decline in the fortunes of the party. It's now evident that the Union Nationale's surprising upset victory over the Lesage Liberals in 1966 was merely a temporary reprieve. A combination of Liberal over-confidence and careful grassroots organization by the late Daniel Johnson produced electoral victory for the Union Nationale but no sense of direction. The adroit Johnson, with an assist from De Gaulle, was able to create an illusion of movement while the province, in fact, stood still in order to catch its breath and evaluate the many reforms of the early 1960s. When Johnson died in 1968 his successor, Jean-Jacques Bertrand, was unable to conceal the party's essential aimlessness.

This became clear during the campaign leading up to the election of April 29, 1970. Faced with a strong separatist party and leader, Quebec Liberals committed themselves to a much clearer federalist position than Jean Lesage had taken in the early 1960s. The onus was on the Union Nationale to respond. But the campaign merely illuminated the differences between Bertrand, whose personal position was fairly close to the Liberals', and more nationalist members of his cabinet, like Jean-Guy Cardinal and Marcel Masse.

Despite these difficulties, the Union Nationale managed to salvage 20 per cent of the vote, enough to give it seventeen rural members in the National Assembly and the role of official opposition. The role has been claimed by the Parti Québécois on the strength of its 24 per cent share of the total vote but the Union Nationale's moral right to its official position is reinforced by the twelve per cent share of the vote which went to the Créditistes' twelve members. In many respects, the concerns of the Union Nationale are identical with those of the Créditiste voters in the less developed and more conservative areas of the province.

"It's difficult to see where the Union Nationale can fit into the structures of Quebec today," concluded Professor Quinn. "If you're a federalist, you vote Liberal. If you're a separatist, you support the Parti Québécois. And I suppose if you're an ultra-conservative, you can always go to the Créditistes."

But there is one characteristic of the Union Nationale which the Liberals in Quebec have never acquired and which the newer provincial parties haven't consolidated in their own structures at this stage. It's the characteristic that I had in mind at the beginning of this article when I called the party a "unique Quebec political institution"; I suppose that as good a word as any to describe it is "accessibility." Most journalists who have covered recent Union Nationale and Liberal conventions have been struck by it—the atmosphere of élitism which stifles Quebec Liberal gatherings compared with the truly popular atmosphere that enlivens the Union Nationale even in its most depressing moments. This doesn't mean that the party is democratic in its workings. But the astonishing fact is that the party of the old authoritarian Duplessis is the only party, with the possible exception of the Créditistes, where all classes except the urban élite feel at home, where the ordinary guy feels that he belongs.

If the convention in Quebec City on June 19 is to be the last important gathering of the Union Nationale clan, I can't help but regret it. And I know that I won't be able to help enjoying the occasion itself, despite all my "finer" political instincts. I'm afraid that the older I get, the more I suspect the right-minded intellectual politicians (while accepting them as a necessary evil) and the more I admire, also with reservations, the pragmatic ones who go after limited objectives. The Union Nationale has always been a party of the latter, and its disappearance in Quebec would mean a significant loss of stability throughout the province's whole political system for some time to come.

What do you think?

1. (a) Why do you think the Union Nationale retained power in Quebec for such a long period of time?
   (b) Why do you think the Union Nationale went into a decline in the sixties?
2. Why is Desbarats concerned about the disappearance of the Union Nationale removing stability from the Quebec political scene? Do you agree with him? Why or why not?

19. THE LIBERALS

In an article in the Toronto Star *of June 24, 1971, staff writer Robert McKenzie described the rise of Robert Bourassa to the leadership of the Quebec Liberal party, as well as the approach that party intended to take to federal-Quebec relations and to Quebec's problems. (Reprinted with permission* Toronto Star.*)*

The dream [of the federal Liberal party] was to have a premier in Quebec city who would faithfully mirror the policies of the Trudeau administration, ushering in a new era of harmonious federalism featuring a strong degree of central direction from Ottawa.

The first moves toward making the dream come true were made

in August, 1969, when forces representing Ottawa interests pressured former premier Jean Lesage into resigning the Quebec Liberal leadership.

With a Quebec Liberal backbencher named Jean-Paul LeFebvre carrying the axe, a campaign was undertaken to squeeze Lesage into resigning and bring in Regional Development Minister Jean Marchand, one of Trudeau's closest friends, as Quebec Liberal leader.

Lesage duly resigned, referring to "intolerable" but unnamed pressures, but the campaign to bring in Marchand collapsed.

Of the three men running for the leadership—Robert Bourassa, former justice minister Claude Wagner and the late Pierre Laporte—two were eliminated almost automatically.

Laporte's nationalist background, although muted in latter years, ruled him out. Wagner's reputation for authoritarianism made him anathema to the *Cité Libre* clique surrounding Trudeau. (This was before October, 1970, and the War Measures Act.)

(*Cité Libre* was a post-war nationalistic magazine edited by Trudeau and Gérard Pelletier, now secretary of state.)

That left Bourassa, then only 36, with three years' experience as opposition financial critic. The Ottawa Liberals had doubts about him. He had come close to teaming up with former Liberal minister René Lévesque to form the Sovereignty-Association movement which later blossomed into the separatist Parti Québécois.

Bourassa was out in front in the leadership race, with the support of Lesage and much of the party hierarchy. He won easily and went on to pull off a surprisingly strong election victory: 72 of the Quebec National Assembly's 108 seats.

The new premier's platform was 100,000 new jobs in 1971 and "profitable federalism," meaning an end to ultimatums and tantrums towards Ottawa, and more cash, industrial subsidies and budgetary benefits in return.

It also meant a "reasonable" approach to constitutional negotiation in which, Bourassa said, he would prove his case with "well-prepared dossiers" and succeed where his predecessors had failed.

What do you think?

1. *What were the Ottawa Liberals looking for in a new Quebec leader? Why did Robert Bourassa win their support?*
2. *(a) Who in your opinion would be likely to vote for Robert Bourassa's Liberals and why?*
   (b) How would you distinguish Liberal supporters from supporters of the Parti Québécois? the Créditistes? the Union Nationale?

20. THE 1970 QUEBEC ELECTION

On April 29, 1970, a provincial election was held in Quebec. The election was regarded by many observers as being of crucial importance in determining not only whether Quebec was really serious about separatism, but also how "progressive" Quebeckers wanted the social policy of their government to be. The results of that election are included below. What do you think these results reveal about the two issues mentioned above?

	1970		1966		1962	
Union Nationale	563,331	(20)	948,928	(41)	900,817	(42)
Liberals	1,298,386	(45)	1,099,435	(47)	1,205,253	(57)
Parti Québécois	645,488	(23)	—		—	
Créditiste	336,602	(12)	—		—	
National Democratic Party	4,479		—		—	
Others	15,814		276,466	(12)	30,711	(1)
TOTALS	2,864,100		2,324,829		2,136,781	

FINAL PARTY STANDINGS BY SEATS IN THE QUEBEC LEGISLATIVE ASSEMBLY

Liberals	71
Parti Québécois	7
Union Nationale	16
Créditiste	13

What do you think?

1. How do you explain the difference between the number of parties contesting the 1966 and 1970 elections? In your opinion, what does this reveal about the Quebec political scene between the years 1966 and 1970? Account for this.
2. (a) What percentage of the vote went Union Nationale in 1966? In 1970? To what party do you think the UN lost these votes? Why?
   (b) What percentage of the vote went Liberal in 1966? In 1970? Why did the Liberal vote stay solid?
   (c) Explain what happened to the "Others" between 1966 and 1970.

3. What did the results of the 1970 Quebec provincial election reveal about—
   (a) The strength of separatism in Quebec?
   (b) The opinion of Quebeckers about a "progressive" social policy in their province?
4. Compare the percentage of the popular vote won by the parties with the percentage of the seats won by them in the Legislative Assembly. What do you notice? How can you account for this?

(Reprinted by permission of *The Globe and Mail,* Toronto.)

21. FLQ MANIFESTO, OCTOBER 1970

A few months after the April 1970 provincial election in Quebec, the FLQ, a separatist group advocating revolutionary and extra-parliamentary means for achieving their goals, kidnapped James Cross, a British trade commissioner and a few days later Pierre Laporte, the Quebec minister of labour, thus plunging the country into a series of dramatic events which came to be known as the October Crisis.

Below is the FLQ manifesto which appeared during the 1970 October Crisis. For a period of time, the publication and distribution of this material was illegal. Arthur, the student newspaper at Trent University, published the Manifesto in October of 1970.

The Front de Libération du Québec is not a messiah, nor a modern-day Robin Hood. It is a group of Quebec workers who have decided to use all means to make sure that the people of Quebec take control of their destiny.

The Front de Libération du Québec wants the total independence of Quebecers, united in a free society, purged forever of the clique of voracious sharks, the patronizing "big bosses" and their henchmen who have made Quebec their hunting preserve for "cheap labor" and unscrupulous exploitation.

The Front de Libération du Québec is not a movement of aggression, but is a response to the aggression organized by high finance and the puppet governments in Ottawa and Quebec (the Brinks "show," Bill 63, the electoral map, the so-called social progress tax, Power Corporation, "Doctors' insurance," the Lapalme boys . . .).

> The money power of the status quo, the majority of the traditional teachers of our people, have obtained the reaction they hoped for: a backward step rather than the chance for which we have worked as never before, for which we will continue to work.
> René Lévesque, April 29, 1970.

We once believed that perhaps it would be worth it to channel our energy and our impatience, as Réne Lévesque said so well, in the Parti Québécois, but the Liberal victory showed us clearly that that which we call democracy in Quebec is nothing but the democracy of the rich. The Liberal party's victory was nothing but the victory of the election riggers, Simard-Controni. As a result, the British parliamentary system is finished and the Front de Libération du Québec will never allow itself to be distracted by the pseudo-elections that the Anglo-Saxon capitalists toss to the people of Quebec every four years. A number of Quebecers have understood and will act. In the coming year Bourassa will have to face reality: 100,000 revolutionary workers, armed and organized.

*   *   *   *   *

Production workers, miners, foresters, teachers, students and unemployed workers, take what belongs to you, your jobs, your determination and your liberty. And you, workers of General Electric, it's you who make your factories run, only you are capable of production; without you General Electric is nothing.

Workers of Quebec, start today to take back what is yours; take for yourselves what belongs to you. Only to know your factories, your machines, your hotels, your universities, your unions. Don't wait for an organizational miracle.

Make your own revolution in your areas, in your places of work. And if you do not make it yourselves, other usurpers, technocrats and others will replace the iron fist of the cigar smokers which we know now, and all will be the same again. Only you are able to build a free society.

We must fight, not one by one, but together. We must fight until victory is ours with all the means at our disposal as did the patriots of 1837–38. (Those whom your sacred church excommunicated to sell out to the British interests.)

From the four corners of Quebec, those who have been treated with disdain, the lousy French, and the alcoholics will vigorously undertake combat against the destroyers of liberty and justice. We will banish from our state all the professional robbers, the bankers, the businessmen, the judges and the sold-out politicians.

We are the workers of Quebec and we will go to the end. We want to replace the slave society with a free society, functioning by itself and for itself. An open society to the world.

Our struggle can only be victorious. You cannot hold back an awakening people. Long live Free Quebec.

Long live our comrades who are political prisoners.

Long live the Quebec revolution.

Long live the Front de Libération du Québec.

What do you think?

1. *What was the reaction of the FLQ to the 1970 provincial election in Quebec? Why?*
2. *During the October Crisis it was said that although the majority of Quebeckers did not approve of the FLQ's methods, many Quebeckers did sympathize with their grievances and many of their goals. Do you feel that this position is a logical one? Why?*

22. PRIME MINISTER TRUDEAU ON THE PROCLAMATION OF THE WAR MEASURES ACT

Pierre Trudeau spoke to the people of Canada at the height of the FLQ kidnapping crisis in October 1970. The occasion was the invocation of the War Measures Act, an already existing statute, by the federal government, a move which later created considerable debate. Why? (Reprinted by permission of Prime Minister Pierre Elliott Trudeau.)

The governments of Canada and Quebec have been told by groups of self-styled revolutionaries that they intend to murder in cold blood two innocent men unless their demands are met. The kidnappers claim they act as they do in order to draw attention to instances of social injustice.

But I ask them whose attention are they seeking to attract. The government of Canada? The government of Quebec?

Every government in this country is well aware of the existence of deep and important social problems. And every government to the limit of its resources and ability is deeply committed to their solution. But not by kidnappings and bombings. By hard work.

And if any doubt exists about the good faith or the ability of any government, there are opposition parties ready and willing to be given the opportunity to govern. In short there is available everywhere in Canada an effective mechanism to change governments by peaceful means. It has been employed by disenchanted voters again and again.

Who are the kidnap victims? To the victims' families they are husbands and fathers. To the kidnappers their identity is immaterial. The kidnappers' purposes would be served equally well by having in their grip you or me, or perhaps some child.

Their purpose is to exploit the normal, human feelings of Canadians and to bend those feelings of sympathy into instruments for their own violent and revolutionary ends.

   * * * * *

To bow to the pressures of these kidnappers . . . it would be as well an invitation to terrorism and kidnapping across the country. We might well find ourselves facing an endless series of demands for the release of criminals from jails, from coast to coast, and we would find that the hostages could be innocent members of your family or of your neighborhood.

   * * * * *

If a democratic society is to continue to exist, it must be able to root out the cancer of an armed, revolutionary movement that is bent on destroying the very basis of our freedom. For that reason the government, following an analysis of the facts, including requests of the government of Quebec and the city of Montreal for urgent action, decided to proclaim the War Measures Act. It did so at 4 A.M. today, in order to permit the full weight of government to be brought quickly to bear on all those persons advocating or practising violence as a means of achieving political ends.

The War Measures Act gives sweeping powers to the government. It also suspends the operation of the Canadian Bill of Rights. I can assure you that the government is most reluctant to seek such powers, and did so only when it became crystal clear that the situation could not be controlled unless some extraordinary assistance was made available on an urgent basis.

The authority contained in the act will permit governments to deal effectively with the nebulous yet dangerous challenges to society represented by the terrorist organizations. The criminal law as it stands is simply not adequate to deal with systematic terrorism.

The police have therefore been given certain extraordinary powers necessary for the effective detection and elimination of conspiratorial organizations which advocate the use of violence. These organizations, and membership in them, have been declared illegal. The powers include the right to search and arrest without warrant, to detain suspected persons without the necessity of laying specific charges immediately, and to detain persons without bail.

These are strong powers and I find them as distasteful as I am sure do you. They are necessary, however, to permit the police to deal with persons who advocate or promote the violent overthrow of our democratic system. In short, I assure you that the government recognizes its grave responsibilities in interfering in certain cases with civil liberties, and that it remains answerable to the people of Canada for its actions. The government will revoke this proclamation as soon as possible. . . .

What do you think?

1. *Ten prominent Quebeckers, including René Lévesque and Claude Ryan issued a statement after the proclamation of the War Measures Act saying that dealing with the emergency was solely a provincial responsibility.*
   (a) *Why do you think they issued this statement? What do you think of their position and why?*
   (b) *Why do you think the federal government intervened in the October Crisis? What do you think of this intervention and why?*

23. PUBLIC REACTION

The Toronto Star published on December 12, 1970, a poll conducted by the Gallup Poll of Canada on the popular reaction to the imposition of the War Measures Act. (Reprinted by permission of the Canadian Institute of Public Opinion.)

"In general, do you approve or disapprove the government's action in bringing in the War Measures Act to handle the FLQ crisis, with the promise that it would be replaced shortly with special legislation to give the government the temporary powers it needs?"

	Approve	Disapprove	Undecided
Canada	87%	6%	7%
English-speaking	89%	5%	6%
French-speaking	86%	9%	5%
Other ethnic groups	79%	5%	16%
Public school education	81%	5%	14%
High school/technical	89%	6%	5%
University	89%	7%	4%

What do you think?

1. Compare the English-Canadian figures to the French-Canadian figures. What do you notice? Account for this.
2. (a) Why do you think some people disagreed with the invocation of the War Measures Act?
   (b) If the same question were given to the same group of Canadians today, do you think the figures would be the same? Why or why not?

24.   HIS TRUE COLOURS

(Reprinted by permission of the *Halifax Chronicle-Herald*.)

This cartoon appeared in the Halifax Chronicle Herald, *October 7, 1970.*

What do you think?

1. (a) *How would Parti Québécois supporters react to the cartoon? Why?*
   (b) *How widespread do you think this attitude was and is in English Canada? Why?*
2. *How do you think the October Crisis affected the Parti Québécois "image" in Quebec? In English Canada? Why?*

25. FLQ INTELLECTUAL RENOUNCES VIOLENCE

Charged with incitement to crime for his role in the October Crisis, a former associate of Prime Minister Trudeau, Pierre Vallières, had gone into hiding to evade trial. Vallières had provided the intellectual leadership for the FLQ and the rationale for their revolutionary, terrorist activities. But in December of 1971 he renounced violence as a means to win the independence of Quebec, and urged his colleagues in the FLQ to throw their support to the Parti Québécois. Vallières explained his conversion in a manuscript sent to Le Devoir, *which published the statement on December 13, 1971. (Reprinted by permission of* Le Devoir.)*

Pierre Vallières, the Quebec revolutionary leader, has decided to sever all links with the Front de Libération du Québec (FLQ) and considers the Parti Québécois as the only real alternative to the party in office, and as "the main strategic political force in the Quebec people's struggle for liberation."

Pierre Vallières is doing more than breaking with the FLQ. He is exhorting the "felquistes" (members of the FLQ) and their supporters to put an end to the action which began in 1963 and culminated in the October 1970 crisis.

After a vigorous analysis of the present political situation, the action of the FLQ and the dynamics of the Quebec liberation movement, the author of *White Niggers of America* concludes that the action of the FLQ has become in fact the "pretext and opportunity" sought by the government to crush the real strength of the liberation movement, which lies in the Parti Québécois, local branches of the trade unions, and the citizens' committees.

Vallières writes: "But if I accept this responsibility—incumbent on me for more than one reason—for publicly denouncing armed aggression, and at the same time, affirming the necessity for the FLQ to scuttle itself as a group, acronym and myth, as a "terrorist threat," and as theory and practice, I nevertheless have no power of decision over the "felquistes," no mandate to speak on their behalf, and no trick up my sleeve to prevent anyone, including the police, from using the three letters *FLQ* for any purpose whatsoever."

Thus the most brilliant leader of the Quebec revolutionary movement has evolved towards a fundamental realignment. A member of the 1966 "felquiste" faction, imprisoned for more than four years, a political writer, the favourite scapegoat of many in the government, a revolutionary symbol, still sought by police, Vallières a few years ago was advocating armed aggression as the only means of liberation for Quebec.

Vallières emphasizes that the "contents" of independence are defined at the basic level in the trade unions, citizens' committees and local "pequiste" (members of the Parti Québécois) organizations—and that these contents must "combine with the political action of the Parti Québécois (the people's party). . . ."

Tackling the burning issue of armed confrontation and electoral contest, Pierre Vallières writes: "In Quebec, there is no doubt that armed agitation has nothing to do with the armed struggle, which is a mass struggle. The FLQ has taken part in armed agitation, it has never committed itself to armed struggle, because in Quebec the mass struggle can use the electoral process, and does so effectively. It cannot simultaneously use the electoral process and armed force, since the mass struggle cannot be bicephalous and bistrategic without denying its own nature. In the nature of things, therefore, the armed struggle of the masses and the electoral struggle of the masses cannot coexist."

At the root of Vallières' realignment we find the October 1970 crisis. On this subject he synthesizes: "The important lesson of October 1970 is the following: the government feels and knows itself to be threatened principally and first of all not by the FLQ, of whose real importance it is well aware, but by the converging activity of the Parti Québécois, the trade union locals and the citizens' committees, a political activity which springs from a radical position because it aims objectively— and more and more consciously—at the dissolution of colonial and imperialist relations which benefit the Anglo-Canadian middle class, its American masters and the fragmentary élites which form the consumptive francophone business class. . . ."

According to Vallières, the government seeks more and more openly a confrontation which would give it the opportunity of crushing the Quebec liberation movement.

"The October 1970 crisis," writes Vallières, "provided the government with an opportunity for a full-scale rehearsal of this classic scene, at a time when the organization which, by its actions, had triggered off the crisis, possessed no means of sustaining a lengthy offensive against the government, nor of offering the people of Quebec strategy and arms which would have allowed them to resist repression. . . ."

And he goes on: "Had it not been for the combined action of the PQ, the workers' committees and all the progressive forces in Quebec— the FLQ would have gone down in history bearing the odious responsibility for having offered the exploiters of the Quebec people an un-dreamed-of opportunity for dealing them a blow which could well have proved fatal."

What do you think?

1. "The FLQ has taken part in armed agitation, it has never committed itself to armed struggle, because in Quebec the mass struggle can use the electoral process, and does so effectively." Why do you think Vallières had changed his views regarding the value of the electoral process between the time of the provincial election and his writing of this article?
2. What effects did the October Crisis have on the FLQ? Why?

26.   LABOUR ERUPTS

On April 11, 1972, Quebec labour's "Common Front," composed of three large Quebec trade unions—the Confederation of National Trade Unions (CNTU), the Quebec Federation of Labour (QFL) and the Teacher's Corporation—decided to go for an all-out general strike against the province's public sector, involving hospital workers, civil servants, teachers, engineers, jail guards, hydro workers and other government workers. The strike was called when negotiations with the provincial government reached an impasse. On April 21, the eleventh day of the strike, the Bourassa government brought down Bill 19 which permitted the government to impose a settlement upon the unions after one month's negotiation, and banned public strikes for a two-year period. The Common Front failed to retain its soli-darity in the face of the threat of Bill 19 and the union leaders ordered their members back to work. However when the Big Three, Marcel Pépin of the CNTU, Louis Laberge of the QFC and Yvon Charbonneau of the Teachers' Corporation were sentenced to one year in jail for contempt of court on May 4 and jailed May 9, Quebec labour arose again to protest their sentences. The result was the most widespread and most spontaneous movement of dissent that Quebec had ever experienced.

This selection, an editorial from the November 4, 1971, issue of *the* Toronto Star, *describes the radicalization of Quebec labour following the* La Presse *strike of October 1971. Many observers maintained that the* La Presse *strike was the catalyst for the general strike of the following spring. (Reprinted with permission* Toronto Star.*)*

For months before October, English Canadians indulged in melancholy speculations that "something" would happen that month in Montreal. They were anticipating some dramatic commemoration of the kidnap crisis and War Measures Act of one year ago. Now they are talking as though the moment has safely passed, but they are wrong. What happened in Montreal at the end of October was a manifest change in the political comportment of working men, something less traumatic than a kidnapping but nonetheless real.

Think of the change in Louis Laberge. If, one year ago, you had pictured him under a hail of stones on a barricade, knowing Montrealers would have laughed. For Louis Laberge is president of the Quebec Federation of Labor. In his modest style and function, he has often seemed the precise French-Canadian counterpart of David Archer, amiable figurehead of Ontario labor. But Louis Laberge has now led 10,000 workers to a police barricade, heard the thump of a nightstick on flesh and the terrifying roar of the motorcycle charge. He has shared a platform with revolutionary Michel Chartrand and FLQ lawyer Robert Lemieux and urged a "Common Front" against a "dictatorial city regime and an unjust economic system."

What happened to Louis Laberge happened to thousands of his members. The massive demonstration against Mayor Jean Drapeau last Friday night was staged not by youthful separatist zealots but by workers "radicalized" after the Power Corporation's lockout at its newspaper *La Presse* and Drapeau's police moves to protect the corporation's property. The Power group, largely English owned, has a vast web of interests in Quebec media: it is as resented there as American-owned media would be here. But it was not the Power Corporation itself, rather what Mr. Laberge calls "the inhuman savagery" of the troopers defending it that led him to declare his 250,000 member federation will never be the same again.

Quebec unions, it seems, are in the process of a dramatic switch to socialism. The Confederation of National Trades Unions, Catholic by origin and—before the Common Front—a rival of the Laberge group, has adopted a "socialist manifesto" to the left of the Waffle's. Socialism will dominate Mr. Laberge's convention later this month. It hasn't happened overnight. For months locals of international unions, angered by "sweetheart" contracts and payments to Washington, have been deserting to more militant national unions.

The background to all this is the highest unemployment in Canada. About 25,000 workers have been laid off in plant shutdowns this year.

Quebec's economic prospects are worsening. Marcel Pépin, leader of the national unions, reflects that "there is no place for the worker in the present economic system."

For the first time in history, middle-of-the-road industrial workers are burying their rivalries to join teachers, students and intellectuals in broad political aims. This is the long-awaited "happening." This fall the entrenched authorities face not the frantic desperadoes of an FLQ cell but the solid ranks behind Messrs. Laberge and Pépin. To them, the alliance of Drapeau at city hall, Robert Bourassa in the National Assembly and Pierre Trudeau in Ottawa, the alliance that engineered the War Measures Act, appears a hostile wall of power, offering no loopholes and no promise of a better life.

Unless English Canada understands this tension, which will inevitably influence coming encounters between Quebec and the federal government, all the social and fiscal demands, it will succeed only in intensifying the fermenting social pressures in Montreal. It is not a sure thing that Mr. Bourassa can or will do anything to ease these tensions. What is certain is that lack of understanding in English Canada can only make them worse.

What is meant by?

"Waffle"
" 'sweetheart' contracts"

What do you think?

1. *Explain why the radicalization of the trade-union movement in Quebec occurred. Does this radicalization appear to you to be an inevitable trend? Why?*
2. *What do you think the relationship between the PQ and the radicalized trade union movement in Quebec is? Why?*
3. *"What is certain is that lack of understanding in English Canada can only make them worse." Why?*

27. ONLY IN QUEBEC

Dennis Braithwaite is a columnist who writes for the Toronto Star. *In this column, published May 16, 1972, Braithwaite provided his opinion on the significance of the general strike in Quebec. (Reprinted with permission Toronto Star.)*

One thing the revolutionary ferment in Quebec has accomplished is to provide proof, if further proof were needed, that Quebec, indeed, is not a province like any other.

Nowhere else in Canada could such events occur. Even during the most violent demonstrations of the depression, the relief camp riots and the "March on Ottawa" from the West, there was never any question of workers' leaders seizing control of radio stations, shutting down metropolitan newspapers or launching a massive propaganda campaign demanding the overthrow of the capitalist system.

Quebec is different; Quebec, as it emerges from its long colonial sleep, is more like a modern industrial European state—France, say, or Italy—than what it has been heretofore, a backward, agrarian, cleric-ridden province of a largely underdeveloped dominion.

Quebec, let us face the fact, is a nation; possessing its own distinctive language, flag, culture, common law, customs, quasi state church, a long history, a number of indigenous political parties supported by universally accepted xenophobic myths, superstitions and prejudices.

28.   THE 1973 QUEBEC ELECTION

On October 29, 1973, Quebec again went to the polls with the four parties contesting for the victory. Polarization around the independence issue seemed more acute than in 1970. Below are the results of this election and an analysis of them by Robert McKenzie which appeared in the Toronto Star, *October 30, 1973. (Reprinted with permission* Toronto Star.)

	Percentage of Vote	Number of Seats
Liberals	54	102
Parti Québécois	30	6
Union Nationale	5	0
Créditiste	11	2

It will be tempting for Canadians to view yesterday's Quebec election as proof of a decline of the Quebec separatist movement. But the facts are to the contrary. If Premier Robert Bourassa's Liberals won such an overwhelming victory, it was because of the collapse of the Union Nationale and Créditiste parties, and not because of any weakening in separatist strength. In fact, the Parti Québécois advanced from the 23 per cent of the popular vote it won in the 1970 Quebec election to 30 per cent yesterday. This is somewhat more than the 4 or 5 per cent gain René Lévesque's top strategists were talking privately of making, when the election was announced.

Before writing the separatists off on the basis of yesterday's landslide win by Bourassa, one or two things should be kept in mind. Although it emerged from the election with only six or seven seats, the Parti Québécois now is the Official Opposition in the Quebec National Assembly. It is, in fact, the only opposition force left in Quebec, the Union Nationale having been eliminated completely and the Créditistes reduced to an amazing two seats. This means that Quebec has virtually returned to the two-party system and the Parti Québécois almost certainly will be the only viable alternative to the Liberals in the 1977 Quebec election.

The separatists suffered a couple of crushing blows, with the personal defeats of Lévesque, parliamentary leader Camille Laurin, and such heavyweights as economist Jacques Parizeau and former Quebec government mandarin Claude Morin.

But the Parti Québécois has shown tremendous resilience to such setbacks in the past. Professor Jacques-Yvan Morin, the international law expert elected in Montreal-Sauve, has stature equal to Laurin's, and union lawyer Robert Burns, one of the party's most effective parliamentarians, has been re-elected. It may be questioned, with such a slim reward in terms of seats, if the party has sufficient momentum to keep it going four years until another election. No doubt the election results will induce a wave of apathy among the 110,000 paid-up members the party claimed at the close of the campaign.

Perhaps there will be new acts of terrorism committed by young persons who despair of ever seeing Quebec achieve national sovereignty by the democratic process. But the danger of the Parti Québécois falling apart in the next four years is greatly diminished by the disintegration of the other opposition parties.

What do you think?

1. *In what way do the results of the 1973 election qualify the conclusions you drew from a careful analysis of the Quebec election in 1970? Why?*
2. *What are the future implications of the fact that the Parti Québécois obtained 30 per cent of the popular vote, about 38 per cent of the Francophone vote, but only 6 out of 110 seats?*
3. *What do you think would be the effect on Quebec politics and on Canadian politics if the PQ gave up its "sovereignty" platform and further emphasized its social democratic platform?*

4. What is the relationship, if any, between the Quebec election results and the future of the federal government's bilingual programme across Canada?

29.   VICTORIA CHARTER: THE ISSUES

*The seventies have been characterized by political turmoil in Quebec.
Moreover, there have been attempts at the national level to resolve
Quebec's position in Confederation.*

*How do the economic and cultural ambitions of the province of
Quebec affect the political relationship between Quebec, the other
provinces and the federal government? To what extent must a
Quebec government bear in mind the political situation in Quebec
when negotiating at the federal-provincial level?*

*The constitutional talks held at Victoria, B.C., in June 1971, provide
an excellent opportunity to examine these questions. Journalist
Anthony Westell outlined the issues at Victoria in the* Toronto Star,
June 12, 1971. (Reprinted with permission Toronto Star.)

The chances are a little better than fifty-fifty that Prime Minister
Pierre Trudeau and the provincial premiers will break through to a major
agreement on the constitution at their three-day meeting in Victoria next
week.

What this means in stark fact is that the question of whether
Canada can hold together or is doomed to disintegrate is probably going
to be decided in Victoria next week.

The federal government and the provinces have been negotiating
for three years to try to agree on a new constitution which will make
Canada a happy homeland equally for French- and English-speaking
citizens. Now they have reached the moment of decision.

Trudeau and most of the premiers realize that there can be no more
delays, no more bland communiques. At Victoria there must be decisions.

(1) If the conference can agree on the basic elements of a new
constitution—the charter for a new confederation—Canada will be on the
road to cooling the crisis of national unity which has been escalating for
ten years. Many detailed problems will remain to be settled, but at least the
Quebec government will be committed to the belief that solutions are
possible within a united Canada.

This would remove much of the debilitating uncertainty of recent
years in which successive Quebec governments have withheld full commitment to federalism while seeking concessions from Ottawa.

(2) If there is no substantial agreement at Victoria, no one can
be sure what will happen—but it's not likely to be good. The federal

government has made a major effort over several years to win agreement on the constitution and has no contingency plan to cope with failure.

The English-speaking provinces have been growing weary of the long-drawn-out negotiations, and seem in no mood to make a major new effort; some western premiers have indicated that they will not be interested in attending further meetings if Victoria is inconclusive.

In Quebec, a failure would be a victory for the separatists. They have always said that Canada cannot be redesigned in such a way as to satisfy the aspirations of the French-Canadian people, and they would have been proved right.

So it is not sensationalist to emphasize the deadly seriousness of the conference next week. Canada really will be at stake.

The first major debate is likely to be over language rights. Under the BNA Act, the rights of the English language in Quebec are protected, but there is no guarantee for French minorities in other provinces.

At the opening constitutional conference in 1968, the eleven federal and provincial governments reached a consensus that "as proposed by the Royal Commission on Bilingualism and Biculturalism and as a matter of equity, French-speaking Canadians outside of Quebec should have the same rights as English-speaking Canadians in Quebec."

The idea was to encourage French Canadians to regard the whole of Canada, and not just Quebec, as their homeland; to assure them they are full citizens in Canada and that wherever practicable, education and public services would be available in their own language.

There was never any suggestion that all Canadians should be bilingual. The concept is that government services and schooling should be available in French where any substantial number of French-Canadians live, and in English wherever any substantial number of English-Canadians live. In practice, this is mainly of importance in Quebec, Ontario and New Brunswick, which each have substantial English and French populations.

Ontario seems to be the main stumbling block. While the province is making good progress in improving services in French—practical bilingualism—it does not want to be tied down to precise guarantees.

Premier William Davis probably fears a backlash, particularly from ethnic groups who regard themselves as neither French nor English, if he makes too many promises. Several western premiers have much the same political doubts.

It is now being argued also that Quebec has lost interest in bilingualism anyway, and that it won't help to placate the nationalists if Ontario and the other provinces do guarantee French language rights.

This is true to a certain extent. Quebeckers are now more interested in protecting and promoting French in their own province, by making it the language of work and education, than they are in extending it to other provinces. Quebec is the centre of the French-Canadian culture—

the way of life—and that's where the main battle must be fought. But this is not to say that the rights of the French language outside Quebec are of no importance. The proposal to guarantee bilingual rights in the English-speaking provinces has always been more of a symbolic gesture toward Quebec—a gesture of partnership to French Canadians. So Ontario's quiet good works are not enough. You cannot write good intentions into the constitution. There has to be a precise form of words.

The B and B Commission proposed to broaden Section 133 which now protects English rights in Quebec to guarantee French rights in Ontario and New Brunswick. The federal government would like to see that happen, but will probably settle instead for a declaration of the equal rights of English and French languages and minorities in the new constitution.

The argument will be over the exact wording of the declaration, over the breadth and timing of the guarantee which Ontario should give its French-speaking citizens.

The second major issue at the conference will be control of social policy. Just as Quebec feels that it must protect French to preserve its culture, so it insists that it must be able to control social policy in order to develop its own particular style of community life and social organization.

The federal government now controls most social programs, paying family allowances, mailing out pension cheques, influencing welfare priorities by controlling the purse string, operating manpower policies, and so on. There is a good argument to be made in fact that Ottawa is in many ways encroaching on provincial jurisdiction.

Quebec, however, is not demanding to take control of all these federal programs.

But it is insisting that federal schemes should fit into its general framework of social policy. In other words, Ottawa can continue to administer (and pay for) the social security schemes as long as they don't run counter to Quebec's priorities.

The federal government has largely accepted this argument on the practical level. There is agreement that most of the programs can be integrated, and Ottawa offered this week to get over the remaining practical hurdle by changing its legislation to make it possible for provinces to use federal welfare funds to finance their own guaranteed income plans, if they so choose.

The difficulty is that Quebec wants more than a pragmatic arrangement by this federal government which could, after all, be changed by the next government in Ottawa. It wants recognition in the constitution that it has primary jurisdiction in social policy—that is, that its wishes and laws have precedence over those of Ottawa.

The federal government won't yield this guarantee. It might accept that the present Quebec government would use the power with common sense, allowing Ottawa to administer national plans, but the next provincial government, after all, might cut the federal government right out of the social picture in the province.

If the provinces had primary jurisdiction and exercised it to exclude Ottawa from operating social security plans, the federal government fears it would find itself unable to set national standards, to redistribute wealth or to control the revenues with which to manage the economy.

So the argument at Victoria will be what to put into the constitution concerning control of social policy. Is there a form of words which will satisfy Quebec and yet not tie federal hands?

What do you think?

1. *According to Westell, what were the two major issues at the Victoria conference? Of these two which do you think was the most crucial and why?*
2. *"Just as Quebec feels that it must protect French to preserve its culture, so it insists that it must be able to control social policy in order to develop its own particular style of community life and social organization." What are "social policies"? Why do you think Quebec feels that control of social policies is necessary for preserving and developing its own special character?*
3. *Do you agree with Anthony Westell's assessment of the importance of the Victoria conference?*

30. THE SIGNIFICANCE OF VICTORIA

Toronto Star *staff writer Robert Mackenzie analyses the reasons for Quebec's rejection of the Victoria charter in an article appearing in the* Star, *June 15, 1971. (Reprinted with permission* Toronto Star.)

The federal government, apparently feeling Bourassa was mainly interested in "dollars-and-cents" gains to boost investment and unemployment, meanwhile promoted a package deal to bring the three-year-old constitutional negotiation to a rapid conclusion.

Part of the Ottawa power play appears to have been based on the calculation that the Bourassa government would drop most of its constitutional demands for "primacy" in the field of social affairs if administrative steps were taken to help Quebec mesh its proposed social programs with those of Ottawa.

This is the key area that explains the failure of the June 14 to 16 summit conference of Ottawa and the provinces in Victoria, B.C.

The constitutional charter proposed at the close of the Victoria conference, if anything, increased the powers of the federal government— rather than Quebec—in the field of social security.

It left the way open for Quebec to control a number of social programs but gave no guarantee that Ottawa would turn over the fiscal or financial equivalent in terms of the funds needed to run them.

Whatever the near-term advantages which may have been offered to Quebec behind closed doors, the deal was clearly unacceptable to Claude Castonguay, Quebec's social affairs minister and probably the strongest figure in the Bourassa cabinet.

By saying no, Bourassa averted the resignation of Castonguay and possibly that of his communications minister, Jean-Paul L'Allier.

He cut short a mounting protest movement by a "common front" of labor unions and nationalist societies which could have easily degenerated into violent demonstrations beginning today, on French Canada's national holiday, Saint-Jean-Baptiste Day.

At the same time, he robbed the Parti Québécois of an opportunity to mount a massive publicity campaign against him as a "traitor" who had sold out Quebec's rights to Ottawa.

In the same stroke, Bourassa has altered his basic slogan from "profitable federalism" to "decentralized federalism."

This clearly differentiates him from the "centralized federalism" of Prime Minister Trudeau and its robs Gabriel Loubier, new leader of the opposition Union Nationale party, of his basic platform.

Bourassa, in effect, may be trying to broaden his base to appeal to many of the non-separatist nationalists who still might have been tempted to vote for the badly faltering Union Nationale.

The truth is that, for federalists in Canada, there is no alternative to Bourassa on the horizon. What Bourassa loses, the Parti Québécois is likely to win.

So whether the Trudeau administration likes Bourassa or not, they are stuck with him. Removing Jean Lesage as opposition leader was one thing. Getting rid of a young premier, with a strong degree of public support—and no one in sight to replace him from within his party—is quite another.

On the longer term, Bourassa is still in trouble, however.

Although winning new constitutional powers for Quebec was only part of his "profitable federalism," it was an important part.

How can Claude Castonguay put into effect his proposed integrated social security program unless he wins the constitutional powers to do so?

Likewise, how can Quebec Labor Minister Jean Cournoyer win control of the manpower field, as he wants to, if constitutional negotiations are at a standstill?

And what chances does Communications Minister L'Allier have of negotiating Quebec control over communications, including cable TV, in this climate?

Will Bourassa really succeed in reviving constitutional talks in the near future through a series of meetings with Ottawa and other provinces?

Few observers here take this prospect seriously. The impression is that Bourassa simply doesn't want to admit the constitutional review process is completely deadlocked because this would give grist to the mill of the Parti Québécois.

Is it thinkable that Prime Minister Trudeau will reverse the strong centralizing tendencies which are his hallmark and which he confirmed at Victoria? Few people here think so.

And, if he doesn't, what are Castonguay, Cournoyer, L'Allier and some of their colleagues going to do?

These are the real questions being asked here in the wake of the Victoria fiasco.

What do you think?

1. According to Mackenzie, why did Bourassa and the Quebec cabinet reject the Victoria charter?
2. "What has Bourassa risked by saying no? Certainly not as much as he would have risked by saying yes."
   (a) What were Bourassa's risks in saying yes?
   (b) What were his risks in saying no?
   (c) Do you agree with Mackenzie that saying no was safer for Bourassa than saying yes? Why or why not?
3. How would the failure of the Victoria charter affect English-Canadian attitudes towards Quebec? Why?
4. Was the fact that the Victoria charter failed to win agreement sufficient evidence to believe that there would be no further constitutional negotiations in Canada? Why or why not?

Outside Quebec

You have read that the source of the crisis in French-English relations in Canada lies within the province of Quebec. In what ways does the provincial crisis in Quebec become a national crisis?

Part of the answer lies in the fact that many groups outside the province of Quebec are either directly affected by federal policies designed to resolve the French-English issue or are apprehensive about what Quebec's ambitions mean for them.

Who are the Canadians outside Quebec most affected by the

French-English issue? Where are they located? What are their attitudes towards Quebec? How will their views affect the future course of French-English relations in Canada?

In the Capital

The federal government's policy on bilingualism has been a subject of heated debate ever since 1965, when the Royal Commission on Bilingualism and Biculturalism first suggested, among other things, that all federal services should be available in both official languages, that the federal civil service should be equally accessible to both French and English Canadians, and that certain districts in Canada should be declared "officially bilingual." The government's policy, based on the B and B Commission's recommendations, has received a mixed reaction in the various regions of Canada, but nowhere has the controversy been more heated than in Ottawa, the nation's capital.

Why has Ottawa become a focal point for the debate over bilingualism? How does the Ottawa reaction compare with the reaction from other parts of Canada? Why are decisions made about the Ottawa area crucial for the future of the bilingualism programme?

31. LANGUAGE BACKLASH

In this article published in the Montreal Star *June 3, 1972, journalist James Stewart reports on the bitter division over the language issue in the federal civil service. (Reprinted by permission of the* Montreal Star.)

The Alkenbrack file is about three inches thick, contains the outrage of hundreds of civil servants over bilingualism, and on the whole is about as good a specimen of English backlash as you're likely to find in any one place.

The letters in the file come from all parts of Canada. They add up to something approaching a civil service revolt against the federal government's program to bilingualize the public service and give the French and English languages equal status in all its institutions.

The program has really just begun. The goal of equal opportunities and equal services for French-speaking Canadians is still years away.

Yet already the language policy has caused bitter resistance among public servants and staff associations. They see their careers threatened, the merit system of promotion abandoned, by what many of them, apparently in all seriousness, call the French takeover of Ottawa.

In the past few months they've poured out their anguish to Douglas Alkenbrack, a Conservative member of parliament from eastern Ontario, who for one reason or another has become the champion and confidant of the unilingual English-speaking public servant.

In his first annual report the Commissioner of Official Languages, Keith Spicer, wrote that it was perhaps inevitable that in Ottawa the climate surrounding bilingualism should be far from serene.

"After all, in this administrative capital, bilingualism is no distant matter of theory, it concerns jobs and careers right now."

His report contains a number of examples of the tension that built up so rapidly over bilingualism in the civil service.

(File No. 58 tells of a personnel officer in the Health and Welfare Department who tore up a form filled out by an employee in French, and made disparaging remarks about the language.)

The commissioner suggested in his report that everybody involved, working in "informal harmony," ought to be able to relieve a good deal of the anxiety raised.

That was before Doug Alkenbrack began spilling some of the contents of his file, talking about shattered morale, corruption of policy, even the danger of fist fights in, of all places, Statistics Canada, over rapid advancement of Francophones.

"He didn't wake up to the situation until I brought it out," says Mr. Alkenbrack of the language commissioner. "Now he's backing me up."

He notes that Mr. Spicer is now warning against over-zealous implementation of bilingualism in the public service and has called for special efforts to assist "the casualties of the linguistic revolution."

Douglas Alkenbrack is a stocky, plain-talking lumberman of 59 who swears he will "continue to fight this government and its minions on the issue of imposed bilingualism."

He is the Progressive Conservative member for Frontenac-Lennox and Addington which, according to the 1971 census, contains 61,668 people, of whom 743 are of French mother tongue.

He says civil servants have come to him because they are afraid to take their complaints through ordinary channels. As one of the few opposition members of parliament in the Ottawa area, he is both able and willing to say what civil servants want to hear:

"Thousands of careers have been affected, many of them cut short by layoffs, demotions and loss of promotions," Mr. Alkenbrack said in the House of Commons a few months ago.

"The official languages program has already been corrupted and has become outright French Canadianism," he said. "What we are dealing with now is not bilingualism but a more sinister move, a move to promote the use of one language in every area of federal activity."

Specific cases of injustice caused by language policy are hard to find, in the Alkenbrack file or elsewhere. But the file reflects the sense of fear and potential injustice that permeates the service, and that has been recognized by government, opposition parties, the Public Service Commission, civil service unions, and the Commissioner of Official Languages.

The incipient revolt threatens not only the program for bilingualism in the civil service. It also threatens the more basic but still shaky concept of Canada as a multicultural community with two official languages.

Prime Minister Trudeau went out West bearing the message that Quebecers couldn't be expected to identify with a government that didn't speak their language. Accept bilingualism, he said, to prevent separatism and keep Canada together.

The message that runs through the Alkenbrack file and through the mail of many a member of parliament is rather different: Fight bilingualism. Make it an issue and you'll win the next election.

In other words, the language problem is a political one. And it is general, rather than specific. An individual with a complaint can take it to the boss, or use the grievance procedure of his union, or go to the language commissioner, the linguistic ombudsman.

But few of them do that, even though Mr. Spicer has invited public servants to bring their complaints to him and says that "absolute discretion protects a public servant who might fear reprisals. . . ."

They do not make specific complaints because they know that what is happening to them, for the most part, is legal. It's government policy. The Official Languages Act declares French and English to have equal status, equal rights and privileges.

They don't like the law and they don't like the way it is being implemented. But it is the law. They know that, and they feel there is no use seeking administrative redress to a political injustice.

The file contains very few certifiable cases of damaged careers. Not one letter writer says, "I was fired because I couldn't speak French," though several say they quit because their lack of French blocked promotion.

Others tell about doing a job for months in an acting capacity, and then being denied even the right to compete for the permanent job because bilingualism is required.

The laments come from all over Canada, from practically every department or agency. Some of them are simple expressions of insecurity as a result of language policy; others are raw statements challenging the kind of Canada the present government is trying to make.

"I thought the French were defeated on the Plains of Abraham."

"Why don't they all go back to their lily pads?"

"I'm a former Liberal poll captain in Toronto but I'm going PC because I'm fed up with the French Mafia in Ottawa and fed up with being force-fed in French."

Doug Alkenbrack doesn't go along with that sort of thing. Groups like the Canadian Loyalists, he says, are too far right for his liking.

"I'm not a bigot," he says. "I speak French, and my wife is a French teacher in Napanee. I have no desire to be a rabble-rouser or to stir up trouble. I just want to see that there is fair play and that the public service operates on the merit system."

"The public service is not a vehicle for promotion of culture or language. It's a vehicle for administering the country and if its efficiency is destroyed that would be a very bad mistake."

The use of the English language in this part of the world, says Mr. Alkenbrack, is a condition of survival. That applies as much to Montreal as it does to the little town of Flintan, in his riding, where he went to school.

He remembers French being spoken in Flintan in his youth but no longer. "Last year I attended the funeral of the last French-speaking person there. Charles Brochu. The French names are still there, but not the language. . . . I can deplore that, the town is culturally poorer with only one language, but that's what happens. It's inevitable, an incontro-vertible process. The same thing will happen in Montreal, though it may take centuries."

What do you think?

1. *Discuss the following statements, made in Mr. Stewart's article:*
    (a) *"In his first annual report the Commissioner of Official Lan-guages, Keith Spicer, wrote that it was perhaps inevitable that in Ottawa the climate surrounding bilingualism should be far from serene."*
    (b) *"Fight bilingualism. Make it an issue and you'll win the next election."*
    (c) *"The public service is not a vehicle for promotion of culture or language."*

32. BEYOND BILINGUALISM

Quebec journalist Claude Lemelin wrote the following editorial for Le Devoir, *July 21, 1972. (Reprinted by permission of* Le Devoir.*)*

When hard pressed, the best tactic is to attack. This is just what Prime Minister Trudeau chose to do Wednesday when he told those persons unhappy with his linguistic conversion of the federal civil service that progress had not been rapid enough over the last four years and that the pace had to be stepped up during the coming years.

Let us all rejoice that the Trudeau government plans to encourage even more the promotion of Francophones within the government machinery. The separatists can always say that Mr. Trudeau is helping to initiate Quebeckers in the various skills required for the successful running of a sovereign state; those unconditional federalists can still continue to hope along with Mr. Trudeau that the extension of bilingualism in Ottawa will be enough to drown the separatist fish.

As for the other Quebeckers—and there are still some who have attached themselves to neither camp—they will be pleased to see that the Liberal team plans to continue its attack on the root of intolerance which gnaws away at the political conscience of the Anglophones, and to gradually correct injustices which have accumulated and become institutionalized over the past centuries.

The Anglophones are aware that the Trudeau government has often been clumsy in its political management of bilingualism. It has been unreasonably aggressive and disturbing, through its "coast-to-coast" measures, to the people of the most solidly Anglophone village, without in as much making any significant contribution to solving the linguistic problems of Quebec. But they also know that the measures adopted since 1968 have barely scratched the surface of English unilingualism in Ottawa; that the proportion of Francophones in the higher levels of the civil service has barely increased, that the prickly problem of designating functional bilingual districts has not yet been settled, and that Francophone work units have scarcely begun to be established.

But we should not doubt for a minute Mr. Trudeau's sincerity. The bitterness he let show the other day and which is felt by his advisers deserves our sympathy.

For four years these men have been tackling the inertia and often the resistance of one of the most polished bureaucratic systems in the world; what has been won since 1968 as regards bilingualism was often done so by force. And it cannot be denied that the Liberals, in order to put forward this policy, have taken electoral risks. Let us add that if the bilingualism programmes in the federal public services had been received more enthusiastically in Quebec, if they had coincided with a decline in the separatist feeling in this province, perhaps it would have been easier for the Liberals to increase the rhythm with the least political risk. And the English Canadians would then have been more willing to swallow the bitter potion, knowing that it would effectively restore Canadian unity.

But this could not be so, as we have often emphasized since the 1968 election, not because the independence of Quebec is inevitable and that any attempt to maintain the political integrity of Canada, under any form, is necessarily doomed to fail, but rather because the political, economic and cultural alienation of the Francophones in respect to Canada has attained such proportions that the mere remedy of bilingualism cannot fully cope with it, and also because the aspirations of the Franco-phones have evolved after their discovery that, although a minority in Canada, they form a clear majority in Quebec, and that the dream conceived of for them three-quarters of a century ago by Henri Bourassa, and taken up by Mr. Trudeau, cannot be allowed to keep them in check.

What can be done about it? Bilingualism came fifty years too late. It is not useless; it is insufficient.

What do you think?

1. *"Bilingualism came fifty years too late. It is not useless; it is insufficient." Discuss.*
2. *M. Lemelin is not opposed to the idea of a bilingual federal service, but he does feel that it is insufficient to the task of preserving Canadian unity.*
   (a) *What reasons does he give for this position?*
   (b) *Does M. Lemelin feel that it is "too late" to preserve national unity? Why do you or do you not think so?*
   (c) *What initiatives do you think M. Lemelin would suggest that the federal government take, in addition to the bilingualism policy, to help preserve Canadian unity? What would his arguments be in support of these suggestions?*

French Minorities

French-speaking Canadians are not confined to the province of Quebec. More than one million Canadians outside Quebec are of French-speaking origin. These so-called "French minorities" have been the source of considerable debate. Why?

What problems do the French minorities share with the Québécois? What problems are unique to them? What are the attitudes of these groups towards Quebec's ambitions? What are the attitudes of the Québécois towards these groups?

Decisions made about the French minorities will be of considerable importance in determining the future of French-English relations in Canada. Where do you stand and why?

33. CAN FRENCH CANADA SURVIVE OUTSIDE QUEBEC?

Journalist Valerie Miner Johnson wrote the following article on the situation of French Canadians outside Quebec. Ms. Johnson's article appeared in Saturday Night, November 1972. *(Reprinted by permission of Valerie Miner Johnson.)*

Somewhere in the suburbs which web around Vancouver survives the French-Canadian village of Maillardville. It survives in the street signs: Cartier Avenue, Laval Square, Charland Avenue. In the local establishments: Le Foyer, La Boucherie Dansereau, La Caisse Populaire. In the Opportunities for Youth project: La Maison Maillardville. And in the churches: Notre Dame de Lourdes; Notre Dame de Fatima. Four thousand Canad*iens* live in Maillardville, twelve miles from downtown Vancouver. A profitable place for a quaint tourist town.

But Maillardville offers no gourmet restaurants or weaving shops or woodcarving studios. Maillardville is not a western St.-Jean-Port-Joli. The people are not peddling culture; they are trying to preserve it. Although they have salvaged some signs and symbols of their *Canadien* heritage, they, themselves, are gradually becoming Anglicized. Men work at the Crown Zellerbach Mill; women shop at the Safeway; children graduate from *les écoles* into Centennial High School. And almost everyone has adopted the English pronunciation of the village. Maillardville is becoming Mallardville.

Maillardville, British Columbia. Sturgeon Falls, Ontario. Cheticamp, Nova Scotia. Almost one million French Canadians live in the "English provinces"; 20 per cent of all *Canadiens* live outside Quebec. They are *"les autres"*—caught between two languages and lifestyles, invisible to both Quebeckers and Anglos. *Les autres* descend from pioneer Acadians as well as from the West's *coureurs de bois*. Today they make up one-third of New Brunswick's population; they number 482,045 in Ontario alone. They are scattered throughout each province and territory in rural areas and in small towns—like Maillardville.

Their alienation from the English language and the Protestant ethic follow the classic French-Canadian complaints. Their isolation from their Quebec cousins is more subtle: rooted in historical friction and contemporary debate about separatism. Most feel more allegiance to *"la Patrie"* than to *"la Belle Province."* *Les autres* are neither Canadian nor Quebeckers. They are immigrants in their native land. Their history is forgotten. Their traditions are lost in daily life. Their language is ignored in official contacts. Their schools are unsupported. According to one Maillardville citizen, "We're not treated like second class citizens. We're not treated like citizens at all."

Maillardville residents can write to the federal government in French, but they must request the stamps in English from the unilingual postal clerks. They can listen to CBC in French, if they can afford an FM radio. They can borrow French books from the Vancouver City Library, from the "foreign languages" section. Such are the ironies of

Canada's bilingualism which manifests itself in grocery stores and not in courtrooms. The frustrations extend from Newfoundland to the Yukon and expand as time goes by.

* * * * *

Les autres consistently reach lower occupational and income levels than English Canadians. In Toronto, they make an average annual income of $1,093 less; in Ottawa, they make $1,496 less. Jean Guy Bruneau explains in the Franco-Ontarian daily, *Le Droit:* "One only has to be aware of the high degree of assimilation in Ontario, and even in Quebec, to realize how large groups of French Canadians have rejected, whether (consciously) or not, their language and culture for material or financial reasons. Flocks of people questioned at random in the streets answer with brutal frankness: 'You don't eat books, you eat bread.' Who can blame them?"

* * * * *

"Le drainage" is a *Canadien* term for the Anglicization of their communities, generation by generation. Today one-third of Franco-Ontarians and one-half of Franco–Nova Scotians no longer speak French. Various cultural and recreational organizations create a buffer zone between the French patrimony and the English daily life. But what is membership in *Les Fédérations des Femmes Canadienne-Françaises* compared to the omnipresence of English in the shopping centres, business offices, courts and schools?

* * * * *

The identity of the minority and the majority is precisely the distinction between life for Quebeckers and for *les autres,* according to Roger Albert, president of the *Fédération des Franco-Colombiens* in Maillardville. "We look on things in a different way—necessarily. In Quebec, the French-speaking Quebeckers outnumber the English. Here in B.C., the English look upon us as a thorn in their sides and they have a hard time understanding why we should have any rights. It's two completely different worlds for the Quebeckers and for us."

Many of *les autres* complain that French-speaking Quebeckers look down on them, criticizing the *joual* of their language and the Anglo camouflage of their culture. Western *Canadiens* say Quebeckers don't even recognize their existence. Albert is not bothered by any of this discrimination. "If a *Québécois* says I don't speak French properly, that's too bad. I say, 'That's what I am.' I don't feel inferior at all. In fact, I've been accused of arrogance."

If Albert is not arrogant, he is at least forthright. His voice is loud; his tone is tough; his words are uncompromising. At twenty-six, he speaks with the idealism of his fellow students at Simon Fraser University as well as with the authority of his previous work and travels. He is assertive in his trenchant mannerisms and in the determined flair of his wardrobe. Albert always seems to be in a rush, even when he's sitting still. For instance, there was the time he decided to give his class-mates a seminar on French Canadians. . . .

"At least in Quebec, they have French history. Here there's virtually nothing." He told them that the French exceeded the British in B.C. before the gold rush, that the first provincial newspaper was French. He described the Plains of Abraham as "a strategic retreat," adding that the battle is still being fought by Francophones. When the students asked what he wanted, he demanded hospital care in French. He demanded French schools. "And you know what they said to me then? They called me 'a stupid Frenchman.' Actually, this happens to me quite often. I've been told to 'speak white,' to 'go back to Quebec.' "

Albert has no intention of going back to Quebec. Like many of *les autres,* he is rooted outside Quebec, rooted in his province's geography and in his family's traditions. As one Maillardville woman explained, "Those mountains are pretty big. A lot of us have never been east of them." Besides, Albert says he feels more Acadian than Quebecker (his father is from Acadia). "It's a completely different identity. Not only were the Acadians exploited by the Anglos, but they were ostracized by Quebec, too. In Acadia, with the deportations, migrations and the physical isolation from Quebec, they retained the intonations and the expressions of sixteenth-century French. And the music is altogether different. More folklorish, more sentimental. I don't feel *Québécois.*"

*   *   *   *   *

Assimilation is one prediction for the future of the Maillardvilles across Canada. The other solutions are separatism and bilingualism.

Most of *les autres* look at the future with measured optimism. They are encouraged by the changes wrought through the B and B Commission and they are sustained by the tenacious *devoir du ras* described by Moreau. André Chenier declares: "The French is a stronger culture in some ways. After all, we're up against two hundred twenty-two million English-speaking people on this continent. Look how long we've been able to maintain our culture. When you substract the English Canadians from that number, I think you can see how easy it would be for us to overcome them if we didn't have the Americans to contend with."

Separatism would be as much of a defeat to *les autres* as assimilation. Some object more strongly than their Anglo counterparts because separatism would lose more for them, such as the little federal support they now receive. [There are] doubts that separatism would create a mass migration of Franco-Albertans back to Quebec. "You can't say, leave your roots of three generations and go. Our identity is more than a language. It's the land and the way of living."

Chenier explains, "French is a resource to everyone. We need help from the English to sustain this culture. But it's their resource too. People shouldn't talk about it as a problem—'the French problem.' It's no more a problem than the lakes and the trees and the mines are a problem. It's there for everyone to benefit from and to protect."

Maillardville: it isn't a tourist town; perhaps it is a resource. A French village in *British* Columbia. "Maillardville doesn't have any official status," says Roger Albert. "It's recognized by the post office, but not by the phone company. It's not a district or a town or a municipality. Maillardville is a state of mind."

What is meant by?

"Anglicized"
"joual"

What do you think?

1. *What is the distinction between the term "French Canadian" and the term "Québécois?" Why is this distinction important?*
2. *"Les autres are neither Canadians nor Quebeckers." Why?*
3. *What attitudes do les autres have towards English Canadians? Towards the Québécois? How do these two groups feel about les autres? Give reasons why the three groups feel about each other the way they do.*
4. *What problems do les autres share with the Québécois? Where are their problems different? Why?*
5. *How do les autres feel about separatism? Why?*

34. TIRED OF BEING LEFT OUT

For the most part, French Canadians living in the Maritimes are descended from the original Acadians and consequently see themselves as somewhat separate and distinct from the Québécois. A young Acadian from New Brunswick spoke out during the Canadian Union of Students' seventh seminar "A New Concept of Confederation" held in 1965:

As a French Canadian from New Brunswick, I would like to say that the young French Canadians outside of Québec are tired of being left out every time somebody is discussing the rights of the French Canadians as a nation. Why is it that those who question us always limit it to the political lines which make the province of Quebec? If we speak of the rights of a nation, you can't stop at an imaginary line which was drawn by accident or by history. If you speak of the rights of the French-Canadian nation, it should extend to the French Canadians who live outside of Quebec and are just as French Canadian as people in Quebec are. This is the thing that the young French Canadians outside of Quebec are speaking for now.

What do you think?

1. (a) *How do you define "nation"?*
   (b) *How does the speaker in the above passage define nation? Compare his definition with your own.*
   (c) *Do you feel that the French-Canadian "nation" is represented by the province of Quebec or by all French Canadians living in Canada? Why?*
2. *Why does one's definition of "French-Canadian nation" influence the option that we might choose for resolving the French-English issue in Canada?*
3. *Do you think that it is contradictory to speak of a French-Canadian "nation" existing at the same time as a Canadian "nation"? Why?*

35. PORTRAIT OF A TROUBLED TOWN

In the fall of 1971, Sturgeon Falls, a town of seven thousand located near North Bay, Ontario, was the scene of a serious controversy concerning the educational rights of the French minority. The following article "The School That Split a Happy Town in Two" appeared in the Toronto Star, *August 24, 1971. (Reprinted by permission of Press News Ltd.)*

Sturgeon Falls Secondary School is a rambling, flat-roofed modern structure at the far north of Main Street. Last year it had 550 English-speaking students, from homes in Sturgeon Falls, and 1,300 French-speaking students. . . . The school is well equipped but overcrowded. The largely English-speaking Nipissing School Board, responsible for Sturgeon Falls since the regionalization of Ontario school boards in 1969, proposed to overcome the shortage of space by building a $2,200,000 addition to the existing school.

In June, Dr. Roger Gervais, the short, fiery Main Street dentist who represents separate schools on the Nipissing board, and L'Association, claiming support from 680 taxpayers in Sturgeon Falls, demanded that the plan for a new wing be scrapped. For $100,000 more, they suggested, the board could build a new school for Anglophone children on land it already owned.

They could settle it all in the holidays, Dr. Gervais urged. They could end three years of chaos—the pinprick frustrations of teaching the same courses in two languages, the student demonstrations ("On veut notre école") and boycotts, the agitation among 100 teachers, the high drop-out rate, the impossible administration by a triumvirate of bilingual principal, French- and English-speaking vice principals. They could then hope to hire a principal—the last one quit and "who'd want to sit on top of this barrel of powder?" They could have two schools, each with its own special character.

The Nipissing trustees, most of them North Bay men, were not convinced. A new high school might cost considerably more than $2–300,000. Chairman Dave Doney, a North Bay lawyer, worried about operating costs. The English-speaking school population would, he forecast, settle down at 300—hardly a "viable" unit.

But the trustees set up a "fact-finding committee." Seventeen of the twenty-two briefs it received favored a new school. But when the fact-finders reported to the Nipissing board at an open meeting in North Bay last night, their plan—similar in essentials to L'Association's demands—was immediately stalled. Two other committees of the Nipissing board had produced, out of the blue, a rival scheme. This called for the creation of a new school district of West Nipissing and East Sudbury, a district that would contain two French and one English high school.

French-speaking students at last night's meeting shouted in fury. After all the delay . . . a new deadlock, inflaming passions again, reviving the talk of a student strike next month.

Throughout the controversy, the English minority has been careful not to stand in open opposition to the demand for two schools. "We aren't fighting them on the French school issue," says [one English parent]. "But we're dealing with a public high school. How can you push one portion of the public out of a public high school?" If they are pushed out, he insists, their children must be given facilities in every way equal to those they have lost—classrooms, workshops and all. The Abitibi mill, which pays $111,000 to North Bay in education taxes, insists it does not oppose the second school. But it nonetheless warned the Nipissing board that any tax increase could jeopardize the company's marginally profitable operation at Sturgeon Falls. . . .

The English feel rejected and hurt. Perhaps defensively, they have built the mixing of language groups into their community pride. . . .

In his one statement on the school crisis, Mayor John Valiquette denounced "the incomprehensible position that the French- and English-speaking students of our town cannot walk together in the same halls, eat in the same cafeterias and take their athletic training in the same gymnasium, while receiving their secondary education in the language of their choice. . . ." In this view, it is L'Association's insistence on "separateness" that is dividing the young people in the town. In [one French-Canadian teacher's] view "It's the frustrations of the present school producing another generation with the old hatreds. I can see it happening. We don't want to stop the kids going to dances together, or divide the Kiwanis. That's ridiculous."

But in the classroom, he argues, every student must be able to pose questions and receive answers in his own tongue. He should be able to act in a school play, write in a school newspaper, participate in the full range of activities outside the classroom, in his own language. Because of their English courses and the English milieu around them, the Francophone children of Sturgeon Falls will always be bilingual. The secure ambiance of a French high school could arrest a years-long decline in the quality of spoken and written French in the area, slow down cultural assimilation. . . .

In Sturgeon Falls, Dr. Gervais dates the ferment back to 1968, when well-intentioned Ontario legislators passed Bill 141 to guarantee Francophones the right to instruction in their own tongue wherever classes of twenty could be assembled. It did not guarantee them their own schools, saying only that "a board *may* establish and maintain secondary schools"; that is why all the Francophone appeals to Queen's Park have been passed back to North Bay.

Bill 141 raised the expectations of Franco-Ontarians. Queen's Park's subsequent insistence on local decision-making by a school board on which Francophones feel under-represented embittered the Sturgeon Falls quarrel. The Nipissing board must apply traditional criteria of economics and size to any question of building a school, group children according to their age even though chairman Doney has learned, "Grouping them according to language has a much higher priority among the French-speaking population."

What do you think?

1. *Identify the issue in the Sturgeon Falls crisis. Outline the French-Canadian arguments. Outline the English-Canadian arguments. Evaluate the arguments. Who do you feel has the stronger case and why?*

2. *(a) What are the advantages and disadvantages of leaving the protection of minority rights in Ontario to a strong central authority such as Queen's Park? A local authority such as the Nipissing School Board?*

   (b) Transfer this difficulty to the national scene. What are the

advantages and disadvantages of Ottawa protecting minority rights? The provinces protecting minority rights?

(c) Do you think the protector of minority rights should be a central authority or a local authority? Why?

3. Can the concept of "separateness," as espoused by L'Association d'Education de l'Ouest Nipissing, be fitted into the concept of a bilingual and bicultural Canada? Why or why not?

36.   POLITICAL HOSTAGES

Claude Morin, a political adviser for many Quebec governments, contributes frequently to Le Devoir. *The following article was written by M. Morin for the October 7, 1972 edition of* Le Devoir. *(Reprinted by permission of* Le Devoir.*)*

Some people believe that English Canada "would take its revenge," as it were, on an independent Quebec by further reducing the rights of French-Canadian minorities in the other provinces. In other words, the minorities would be treated as hostages. Overly recalcitrant Quebeckers are induced to believe that the rest of Canada could as well turn against their "brothers" outside Quebec boundaries if they push their concern for self-determination too far.

There are even French Canadians in other provinces who are spreading about such ideas. In doing so they are courting danger and should be aware of this. The Francophone Quebeckers are being forced to choose between the growth of their political autonomy (and hence their possibilities of self-assertion as a people) and the maintenance of partial and often extremely theoretical rights for minorities. If too much emphasis is placed on the supposed equation which would exist between the political status quo for Quebec and partial minority rights, the Quebeckers will certainly prefer to take care of themselves first of all.

In short, the French Canadians in the other provinces should avoid leaving the way open for this kind of blackmail and should resist being considered hostages. They have nothing to gain.

At present, the federal government has perhaps done the Francophone minorities of Canada a favour by stressing a bilingualism policy, yet it would be of consequence to learn to what degree it has thereby provoked an anti-French-Canadian backlash. Whatever the case may be, its arguments used to promote this policy were frankly often opportunist and tended to be erroneous. This policy was actually presented as a kind of independence insurance. In other words, it led people to believe far too readily that if Canada were to become more bilingual, Quebec would no longer aspire to independence.

Ottawa has never accepted and understood that Quebec objectives have been on a different level for several years, and has never explained this to the other provinces. Many English Canadians have consequently resigned themselves to bilingualism because they deeply believe that this new federal policy would henceforth keep Quebec placated. In all of this, there has been a serious misunderstanding, knowingly cultivated by Ottawa.

The rest of Canada will end up believing that the problem of bilingualism has been poorly expounded. This is why it is necessary to base this policy not on the illusory search for an independence insurance but rather on the respect of the fundamental rights of one of the founding peoples of Canada. Because, whether Quebec is in the Canadian federation or not, it is nonetheless true that French Canadians are still at the very origin of Canada. Here is a question which should above all hold the attention of French minorities.

Once again, we must not forget that Quebec is not seeking to isolate itself by becoming independent. Relations between Quebec and Canada should normally be rather close (since it is in the interest of the two states) so that the place of the French in these relations, and throughout Canada, will remain at least as important as it is now. What's more, there is no reason for the rights already acquired by the French Canadians in other provinces to be reduced should Quebec gain its independence. An increase in these rights on local and regional levels will therefore depend (as is already the case) on the vitality of the minorities themselves. It is not the presence or absence of Quebec in the federation which defines the position of minorities.

What is meant by?

"independence insurance"

What do you think?

1. (a) *What does Claude Morin mean when he uses the word "hostage" in connection with French minorities outside Quebec?*
   (b) *Why does Morin feel that the "hostage" concept is dangerous? Do you agree? Why?*
2. *"Ottawa has never accepted and understood that Quebec objectives have been on a different level for several years. . . ." What is the "different level"? Why is this "different level" significant for French minorities outside Quebec?*
3. *"It is not the presence or absence of Quebec in the federation which defines the position of minorities." Discuss.*

Regional Reactions

How has "English Canada" responded to the tensions created by a resurgent Quebec? How have those Canadians who are of neither French- nor English-speaking origin reacted to the national pre-occupation with relations between the two major cultural groups?

In this section you are encouraged to probe some of the attitudes expressed in the different regions of Canada about French-English relations and to examine the views of Canada's "third force," as those who are of neither French nor English extraction are often referred to.

How significant are these attitudes in determining the intensity of the debate over the French-English issue? Are these attitudes becoming more or less "progressive"? How will they affect the future?

37. WEARY FATALISM

Peter Desbarats, a well-respected commentator on Quebec matters, describes some attitudes he encountered while touring the Canadian West in an article published in the Toronto Star, *November 30, 1971 (Reprinted with permission* Toronto Star.*)*

Western Canadians regard Quebec today with an air of weary fatalism.

"At the moment, it's an attitude of . . . oh, not boredom but indifference after years of a fairly high level of interest," said Premier Ed Schreyer of Manitoba.

Then he paused, thought about it again and said, "No, indifference is the wrong word. It's an attitude of, well, you know, how long is this going to go on? Nothing too serious is on the horizon now and people are turning their attention to other things."

"Not for one second do I believe that their claims are right," insisted Mayor Tom Campbell of Vancouver. "Nevertheless, they've couched them in such a way that they have got a certain number of people in Quebec convinced.

"If the separatists can convince a majority of the people, what is Canada going to do about it? We've got to face reality. If this is the way Canada has to go, we'll have to accept it and live with it.

"It's a frightening thought," reflected Mayor Campbell, "and one that I certainly wouldn't have expressed ten years ago."

Most Western Canadians now discuss the independence of Quebec as a distinct possibility; but it would be wrong to assume from this that they really expect it to happen.

"I think that separation is something that is talked about but you just don't think it will ever happen," said a senior provincial civil servant in Victoria.

"Like: I'm smoking cigarettes, somebody is going to get cancer but it's not going to be me."

In the early 1960s, when I travelled across the West to report on the first public hearings of the Royal Commission on Bilingualism and Biculturalism, the question that came up again and again was: "What does Quebec want?" Now they say, "Let them separate!"

For the first few weeks of my recent tour, I took this to be a reflection of the same know-nothing attitude. But eventually I understood that it reflects a significant development of opinion in Western Canada.

The acceptance of the possibility of Quebec independence, discouraging as it might seem to a federalist at first sight, can be understood as the acceptance of Quebec's right to make up its own mind about its future. If this has happened, it means that the psychological relationship between Quebec and the four western provinces is on a much more "adult" level than it was ten years ago.

This is reflected in another current reaction that was never encountered in the early sixties: jealousy of Quebec.

"Maybe I'm a bit of a bigot or not properly informed," said the civil servant in Victoria by way of preamble, "but I'm slightly prejudiced against the attitudes of Quebec and the obviously special treatment that is being given to Quebec within Confederation."

In the early sixties it was fashionable among a certain urban elite in Western Canada to be sympathetic and "progressive" about Quebec. This attitude is now much less prevalent. Today there is substantial concern about such specific questions as the intensive recruiting of French-speaking Quebeckers for the federal civil service and the continued ability of Western Canadians to compete on an equal basis for civil service positions in Ottawa.

The whole process of "B and B" is still deeply resented in the West. Every bilingual sign on a federal institution is another goad in the old wound. Every time a Westerner flicks past one of the new French-language channels on his television set, he still gets a shock.

But there also seems to be an acceptance of all this, a grudging realization that the changes are permanent. It is clear that no further important advances in "B and B" are going to be possible in the near future; but it also seems evident that no one seriously proposes turning back the clock. In this area, the seventies will be a time for consolidation for the reforms of the sixties.

In the meantime, political leaders on the Prairies have been drawing some interesting practical conclusions from the power struggle between Quebec and Ottawa that has waxed and waned during the years of Quebec's "quiet revolution."

"It has struck me," said Peter Lougheed, the new premier of Alberta, "that many of the things that Quebec would like to see in terms of their jurisdictional and revenue-sharing responsibilities are almost exactly the feelings that I and my colleagues have.

"For example, there are certain things that we think can be done better at the provincial than at the federal level. The federal government is charging into these areas and trying to work on shared-cost programs, duplicating administrative efforts and doing it without consideration for the priorities of the provincial governments.

"This is what Quebec is concerned about," said Premier Lougheed. "Well, so are we. There is some common ground here.

"It's early to talk much about it but it's something that I'd like to explore, provided the Quebec cabinet is amenable to discussing it."

In Western Canada, the emotional attachment to Confederation is probably stronger than in any other part of the country. At least, people in the West keep telling you this. If this sentiment now accommodates an appreciation of Quebec's right to self-determination, and a desire to collaborate with Quebec in practical matters, it is certainly an advance over the patronizing attitudes of the early sixties.

What do you think?

1. *Why do you think Peter Desbarats, the author of the preceding reading, would write an article dealing with specifically western attitudes towards Quebec? Do you think that writing about western attitudes as distinct from attitudes in other parts of Canada is a valid procedure? Why or why not?*
2. *According to Desbarats, how have western attitudes towards Quebec changed since the sixties? Account for this change.*
3. *Why do you think that "B and B" is or is not more deeply resented in the West than in other parts of the country?*

38. ONTARIO: A UNIQUE RELATIONSHIP

The remarks of Ontario Premier William Davis about the province of Quebec were quoted in Le Droit, *June 23, 1973. (Reprinted by permission of* Le Droit *and Premier William G. Davis of Ontario.)*

(. . .) Ontario and Quebec enjoy a unique relationship that goes back to the historical roots of Canada. Together, our two large provinces constitute the foundation of a strong and powerful industrial future.

The premier of Quebec and I have held several meetings to discuss matters of mutual interest and count on continuing this program of discussion, particularly in the fields of education, culture and governmental cooperation.

As you know, our province's French-speaking population is both substantial and widespread. Ontario has approximately three-quarters of a million Francophones living mostly in the Ottawa Valley and also in the central-north and south-west regions.

You will understand then that Ontario has particularly strong and natural reasons for having an active interest in bilingualism and in Ontario-Quebec relations.

In the first two sections of the 1969 Ontario-Quebec agreement on cooperation and exchanges in education, culture and government administration, the two governments have declared their commitment to the question of language rights.

In Ontario the government has undertaken a program to reinforce and improve bilingual services which are offered in response to the legitimate needs of Francophone citizens of this province. The policy of the government is to wish for a continued and progressive effort to improve public services offered in Ontario.

To develop the exchange and cooperation programs included in the 1969 agreement, the Ontario-Quebec Permanent Commission was created. This commission has already held seven meetings and launched numerous programs.

We intend to support the work of the Ontario-Quebec Permanent Commission in the years ahead with the confidence that its activities can only lead to a greater understanding between our two provinces.

On this day when all French Canadians are united to celebrate their existence and cultural vivacity, the people of Ontario wish to express their most sincere wishes for an ever-growing cooperation and friendship.

What do you think?

1. *Do you feel that Premier Davis's remarks reflect Ontario attitudes towards French Canadians and towards Quebec? Why or why not?*
2. *How does the presence of so many Franco-Ontarians in Ontario affect the attitudes of English-speaking Ontarians towards French Canada in your opinion?*

39. TENSION IN MONCTON

Journalist John Carroll wrote the following article describing certain events in Moncton, New Brunswick, which revealed the tension in French-English relations there. Mr. Carroll's article appeared in the

Globe and Mail, *Toronto, March 1, 1972. (Reprinted by permission of John R. Carroll.)*

With a population of approximately 47,000, of which 35 per cent is of French descent, Moncton almost exactly parallels the French-English percentage in New Brunswick as a whole and is not greatly in excess of that of all Canada. Thus Moncton could be a proving ground for the federal drive for greater bilingualism and biculturalism in progress in Canada. Until recently, there was no apparent French-English issue, but in recent years it has surfaced and raised anxieties. Demands have been made for bilingualism in the civic administration. And as the demands have grown in intensity, vehement opposition has been expressed by some English-speaking residents.

The agitation began in 1968, during a boycott of classes at the French-language University of Moncton by students protesting higher tuition fees. About 1,200 U of M students, together with students from the French-language Vanier High School chanting "En français," demonstrated at City Hall and a delegation appeared before a regularly scheduled meeting of council. Mayor Leonard C. Jones refused to hear a submission in French, pointing out that all members of his council could understand English, whereas all could not understand French.

*   *   *   *   *

Later that night of February 16, 1968, a pig's head was placed on the doorstep of the mayor's home. Subsequently, two U of M students from Quebec pleaded guilty to a charge of disturbing the peace and were placed under a $500 bond to be of good behavior for eight months. . . .

Things remained dormant until this January when the National Film Board production *L'Acadie, l'Acadie,* relating the events of 1968 and 1969, was shown on the CBC French-language network and, a couple of weeks later, in abbreviated form on the English network. The film sparked reaction. Some English-speaking citizens saw it as a provocation, the students mounted some minor demonstrations. Mayor Jones was the target of threatening and obscene telephone calls and a bomb threat. Moderation was urged by both sides, but some Anglophones expressed opposition to any portent of bilingualism. They saw bilingualism as a plot to make Moncton a French-speaking city and to give Francophones the inside track for civic jobs.

On February 15, fears of this nature were raised at a Moncton council meeting when four communications supporting bilingualism and/or establishment of a committee to study the cost and feasibility of a program of bilingualism in municipal government were discussed. Opposing communications were from the Canadian Loyalist Association, and in the form of a petition signed by 2,464 citizens urging against bilingualism on the ground of the increased costs to taxpayers.

Baptist Minister Rev. Myron O. Brinton told council that rightly or wrongly many English-speaking Monctonians believed "the French are taking over." The seeds for open conflict were being sown with the demand for bilingualism and "its concomitant, biculturalism," he said.

Outside the council chamber, about fifty U of M students gathered and, chanting "En veux français" and singing the Marseillaise, tried to gain entry and disrupt the meeting. More students gathered in the street outside.

Mr. Brinton, perhaps with the demonstrating students in mind, spoke of a "rabble element" creating a situation "a step removed from violence." Both English and French had lived together in peace in Moncton despite the history of conflicts between the two peoples, but now "agitation, propaganda and demagoguery" were driving a wedge between them. "This is bilingualism and biculturalism," he asserted.

*   *   *   *   *

The other side of the issue was aired by Ward One Councillor Stephen Campbell, whose ward to a large degree is French speaking, and Ward Three Councillor Leopold Belliveau, whose ward also has significant French-speaking representation. Councillor Belliveau, an Acadian, told council he believed an independent committee should be established to examine the question of bilingualism and this should be composed of three Francophones and six Anglophones. This committee would name its own chairman, hold public meetings and report to council within three months.

Councillor Campbell, a U of M professor, said the only reasonable course to follow was to establish such a committee to find out the facts. There was too much emotionalism and nobody really knew what bilingualism meant or what it would cost.

"Let's keep the French and English friends," he pleaded.

The council then voted on the motion: whether to take no action on the communications. The vote resulted in a 4–4 tie. With power to cast the deciding ballot, Mayor Jones then addressed the meeting.

He said there were several historic periods to the development of Moncton, starting with the Acadians from the early to mid-1700s. Then came Dutch, German and Welsh settlers. There were English connections through much of the development and in the present century the city's growth had been nurtured by the efforts of both English-speaking and Acadian elements, working in peace, love and harmony. "There are some Acadians, at least I have this impression lately," he said, "who would like to make Moncton an entirely French community. There are some . . . I seem to believe as a result of things that have happened to me, who believe they can force their will on others, with obscene messages, demonstrations to decision-makers in our city by the harassment of members of our family by threats of various nature. . . ."

Mayor Jones said that he did not believe this was the outlook of the majority of citizens. He felt no committee could function in the atmosphere of tension and coercion created by the demonstrators and, therefore, he was voting in favor of the motion to take no action.

During the course of this meeting and immediately after, five students were arrested by Moncton police. Following the conclusion of the meeting, a noisy demonstration and march took place on Main Street. Two nights later, about 2,000 citizens, not all students, and not all French speaking, marched in a silent procession to City Hall and a banner was burned and a coffin symbolically buried in actions intended to symbolize banishment of fear of bilingualism.

*   *   *   *   *

The dispute is not yet apparently a general cause of friction between the ordinary citizens. In the city's offices, workshops, clubs, taverns and other places of social interaction, the people of both groups get along without any apparent animosity, as they generally have for years. Nevertheless, the odd whisper of bigotry is becoming louder and more frequent. The Anglophone bewilderment is to be found in such utterances as: "It's stupid; they can all speak English. Why should we waste money on bilingual signs and all the rest?"

The Acadian anguish tinges this plaintive query of a French-Canadian barrister: "Do you think an Acadian can ever be elected mayor of Moncton?"

What do you think?

1. *"Until recently there was no apparent French-English issue, but in recent years it has surfaced and raised anxieties." Why was there no "French-English issue" in Moncton until recently? Why did this state of affairs change in your opinion? What is the significance of the fact that the agitation began with university students?*
2. *How do the attitudes of French and English towards each other in Moncton, New Brunswick, compare with the attitudes of French and English towards each other in Sturgeon Falls, Ontario (Pt. 3—The Contemporary Scene, Reading 35)?*
3. *Do you feel that attitudes towards French Canada vary from one Canadian region to another? If so, how can you account for the regional variations?*

40. THE THIRD FORCE

Canadians who are of neither French nor British extraction are frequently referred to as the "third force." Below are figures taken from
the 1961 and 1971 censuses which show the ethnic composition of
Canada and the change it has undergone since the turn of the century. (Reprinted by permission of Information Canada.)

CANADIAN POPULATION TRENDS

(Percentage)

	1901	1911	1921	1931	1941	1951	1961	1971
British	57	56	55	52	50	48	44	45
French	31	29	28	28	30	31	30	29
Third Element	12	15	17	20	20	21	26	26

Source: Canada Census, 1961, 1971.

ETHNIC COMPOSITION OF THE CANADIAN POPULATION BY PROVINCES
1971

(Percentage)

	British	French	Third Element		British	French	Third Element
Canada	45	29	26	Quebec	11	79	10
British Columbia	58	4	38	New Brunswick	58	37	5
Alberta	47	6	47	Nova Scotia	77	10	13
Saskatchewan	42	6	52	P.E.I.	83	14	3
Manitoba	42	9	49	Newfound-land	94	3	3
Ontario	59	10	31				

Source: Canada Census, 1971.

What do you think?

1. Examine the statistics given in the two tables above.
   (a) Trace Canada's population "mix" from 1901 to 1961. What
       has happened to the British element? The French element?
       The third element?
   (b) Account for these changes.

(c) *Are these trends likely to continue? Why or why not?*
(d) *In what parts of Canada is the third element the strongest? Why?*

2. *How do these figures explain the attitudes expressed in the three preceding selections, if at all?*

41. THE THIRD FORCE IN THE WEST

This selection, taken from The Preliminary Report of the Royal Commission on Bilingualism and Biculturalism *(Information Canada, 1968), recounts the feelings of those Canadians who are of neither English nor French extraction, about the French-English issue. The commissioners noted that these feelings were strongest in the West. Why? (Reprinted by permission of Information Canada.)*

. . . the idea of Canada having a dual nature aroused fears among members of the other ethnic groups. The question was posed in Winnipeg: "Are we, west of the Ontario border, to be considered second-class citizens? We are a third of the population in this country . . . and should be considered equal citizens." "Is there some justification," asked a man in Sudbury, "for members of the other groups to be afraid of being caught in a power play, right in the centre (between the English and the French)?" Or, as stated in Kingston, is it true that "my freedoms are actually limited because my extraction is not from one cf the so-called founding races?"

This fear that other ethnic groups might be forgotten in the developing dialogue between Canadians of French and British origin was coupled with a strong affirmation of their importance to Canada. On several occasions this was expressed by an over-estimation of their numbers, as by the Winnipeg speaker who said: "We are the third element of the population of this country, of which I think our proportion today is almost one-third."

We were reminded of the prominent role which men and women from Germany, the Ukraine, the Scandinavian countries, Holland, Poland and elsewhere had played in the settlement of the West. In many communities, we were told, a vigorous sense of cultural identity persists. A Saskatchewan lawyer wrote in a letter to the Commission: "The Dominion government . . . settled the different immigrant nationalities in little island groups with the result that we have large areas which are bilingual. They (the immigrant groups) speak the language of their respective fatherlands and English. Some of the older generations speak nothing but their native tongue."

This picture of non-French, non-British Canadians as pioneers contrasted sharply with the tendency of some participants at the regional

The procession grows longer—and sillier.

August 2, 1965: The Laurendeau-Dunton commission to investigate biculturalism and bilingualism in Canada. (Reprinted by permission of the *Halifax Chronicle-Herald*.)

meetings either to ignore them or to think of them only as recent immigrants. The term "New Canadian," which was used so often, did not satisfy the desire for distinctive recognition which was felt especially by Ukrainian Canadians, whose grandfathers had been among the first to plough the open lands of the Prairies. For those Canadians of German descent whose ancestors came to Nova Scotia or Ontario in the eighteenth century, the expression, "New Canadian" was even more inapplicable. The desire of these groups to be seen as a special element in Canadian life was strongest on the Prairies. Elsewhere, solidarity with English or in some cases French Canada, was more often emphasized.

What do you think?

1. *What are the members of the "third force" afraid of? Are these fears justified?*
2. *"The desire of these groups to be seen as a special element in Canadian life was strongest on the Prairies."*
   (a) Why do these groups see themselves as a "special element"?
   (b) Give reasons why this desire is strongest on the prairies.
3. *What image of Canada would do justice to the presence of these varied ethnic groups?*

4

The Historical Perspective

The Quiet Revolution

In 1960 the Quebec Liberal party, led by Jean Lesage and dedicated to reform, won a stunning victory in the provincial elections over the Union Nationale, the party of the late notorious Maurice Duplessis, premier of Quebec, except for a brief wartime period, for twenty-five years.

The 1960 Liberal victory has become in many Canadian minds the symbolic beginning of the Quiet Revolution. Yet in many ways the election was merely the culmination of a period of intense self-examination on the part of Quebeckers, prompted by the vast changes undergone by their society since World War II. Industrialization, urbanization, technological advance and the growing popularity of twentieth century ideologies, had created in Quebec a conflict between traditional French-Canadian values rooted in an agrarian, semi-feudal past, and the new values generated by rapid modernization. The result was a desire to redefine French Canada's place in Canada.

If the Quiet Revolution represented the victory of the "new" over the "old," what was the "new"? Why did the turbulence in Quebec spill over into the federal sphere, to the extent that the very unity of Canada was questioned?

In this section you are encouraged to probe these questions by examining the early years of the Quiet Revolution. What was it a revolution "against"? What was it a revolution "for"? Is it still with us?

1. THE ASBESTOS STRIKE

During the late forties and early fifties, Quebec was shaken by a series of bitter, prolonged and often violent strikes. In his book written about the 1944 asbestos strike, La Grève de l'Amiante (1970), Pierre Elliott Trudeau analysed the significance of the labour unrest. (Reprinted by permission of Editions du Jour, Montreal.)

For fifty years the phenomenon of the industrial revolution created problems in the province of Quebec which always remained without a very real answer; and the conservatism which impregnated our social ideas equally characterized the official attitudes towards the problems that a new world created in the realms of intellect, religious experience, artistic expression, economic structures, political reform, etc.

However, the Second World War—that interrupter of tradition—had begun the state of awakening which has been mentioned above. In divers sections of the population and in many branches of human activity, individuals and groups were engaged in elaborating new forms. But these forces were never united as a cohesive group and there was a great danger that with the end of the post-war period, these scattered forces would once more be submersed by the relentless return of tradition. It is well that a large-scale social disorder, but confined to Quebec society, occurred so that the isolations could be overcome and which could furnish a rallying point. The asbestos miners' revolt against an authoritarian company and government—at the precise moment when the traditional reflexes ought to have encouraged obedience and submission to the recognized symbols of command—appeared like the responsibility of all those who believed it necessary to establish on liberty their faith in the future. The asbestos struggle arrived as the crystallization point in a saturated liquid. The province of Quebec had to come out dressed in new forms.

What do you think?

1. *Why would World War II create "a state of awakening" in Quebec?*
2. *(a) "The asbestos struggle arrived like the crystallization point in a saturated liquid." Explain how this scientific simile sums up Pierre Trudeau's assessment of the significance of the asbestos strike.*
   (b) Do you feel that there has been any event in recent Quebec labour history which could be compared to the asbestos strike? (See Pt. 3—The Contemporary Scene, Readings 26 and 27.) Why or why not?

2. THE TIMES ARE CHANGING

André Laurendeau, whose death in 1968 deprived French Canada of one of its most articulate spokesmen, was the editor of Le Devoir and one of the original commissioners for the Royal Commission on Bilingualism and Biculturalism. The following editorial was written by Laurendeau for the June 27, 1953, issue. (Reprinted by permission of Le Devoir.)

One of my friends has lived abroad for several years. When he returned here he was conscious of modifications in the atmosphere. He said:

> But what has happened to French Canadians? When I left, it was language, traditions, and survival that were spoken of. They were what interested people. Now they are hardly spoken anymore, and I have the impression that they interest no one.

It is true the climate has changed. We practice oratorical patriotism much less. Certain clichés already well worn out for ten years have almost disappeared and when one hears them one smiles spontaneously as at old-fashioned dress. Does this signify profound changes? Or is it modesty, fatigue, or indifference?

The most important source I believe is restlessness, at least among those who are reflective. We have been knocked silly by the Industrial Revolution. We are still completely upset by it.

We are living through a time of reflection. We are meditating over the new conditions of our life, not in the manner of hermits in the desert or of philosophers in their cells, but from day to day, as we are touched by events. And we are testing ourselves in new spheres.

So we are speaking less of language, of tradition, and above all of *la survivance*. We are preparing ourselves to live in conditions which the age creates, to tackle problems which the old responses will no longer solve.

The most immediate problem of all is the economic one. Abbé Groulx, at the Club Richelieu on Thursday, called to mind in a very full account, reproduced entirely in *Le Devoir,* that the history of our economic life remains to be written.

It would be, it seemed to him, a history painful enough to read. . . . It would say that since 1760 we have been behind. We have been lacking that which is essential to an economy: a tradition of large businesses and the formation of large funds of money for capital. The problem has worsened in proportion as enterprises have become larger and more important. We have ended up convincing ourselves that big business necessarily eludes us. We have too often limited our ambitions to establishing and then selling, at a mediocre profit, small and medium-sized businesses.

"Well," says Abbé Groulx, in a felicitous aside, "the populace, and not just the populace, will lean fatally towards the culture where they make their living."

The historian brought to mind the two judgments held for two centuries by two men as little alike as is possible. Premier Papineau described the scene in Quebec in 1828: "They (the English) in Quebec have the energy and the necessary wealth to prosper." Durham in his famous report noted that the majority of the wage-earners "are French and in the employ of English capitalists." Write instead "Anglo-American capitalists" and the phrase remains appropriate for 1953.

But the times are changing. Today a large section of the intellectual and the active among French Canadians are scarcely interested in creating French-Canadian capitalists. They discard, by hypotheses, the present forms of capitalism. They believe in cooperation and in trade unionism and in political action stemming from these two movements. When they come almost to the end of their thinking, they wish to entrust to the state of Quebec, reformed of course, the administration of major natural resources. Fernand Dansereau has noted in a study published a few weeks ago that a nationalism that is new and probably unconscious animates these minds.

What do you think?

1. (a) Why did Laurendeau think the economic issue was the most important for French Canadians? Do you think that French-Canadian nationalists feel the same way today? Why?
   (b) How did Laurendeau propose to attack the economic problem? Compare his proposals to the solutions being proposed in Quebec today.

3.   ATTACK ON EDUCATION

Quebec's traditionalist educational system was often blamed for the province's economic troubles and for the poor position of French Canadians in the economy. In 1962 an electrifying attack on the Quebec school system was made by a Roman Catholic priest, Frère Untel, in a little book called The Impertinences of Brother Anonymous *(1962, trans. by Miriam Chapman). (Reprinted by permission of Harvest House Limited Publishers, Montreal.)*

Take a look at history, my friend. When the Department was set up, a century ago, the object of the authorities was to dodge two perils, protestantism (permit me that word; it's awkward but it's clear) and anglicization. No fault to be found with that purpose; it was valiant and legitimate, but just the same, it was tricky. The aim was not to strive for a goal, it was to avoid a precipice. They knew where not to go but they hadn't fully decided where to head for. Our present discomfort began right there; the Department was a dodging machine, an escape tunnel. We have never succeeded in disposing of that inherited confusion, in getting out of that blind alley. Incompetence and irresponsibility are the bastards engendered at the beginning by Madam Confusion and her pimp Misdirection.

A typical result of this incompetence and irresponsibility is the public secondary course. Everything about it has been improvised, programs, textbooks, teachers. Public opinion demanded public secondary education. They were sold the label, pasted on an empty bottle. The trouble was not due to evil intentions, but to muddle and false starts. They tried to play two tunes at once without ever making up their minds what to play. For one thing, they wanted to save the private secondary schools, considered the national reserve for the priesthood, and for another thing they also wanted to satisfy public opinion. The Department has been busy and efficient on the institutional side, the classical colleges; it has passed all too lightly over the academic side, the public secondary schools. The proper solution required that they should distinguish (notice how neatly I use the imperfect subjunctive) once for all between these functions. They chose to fiddle about and improvise. Primary teachers were hoisted into the secondary schools with no qualifications except their years of service in the primary grades, with no training, no textbooks, no programs.

The primary grades, where the real purpose of the Department comes close to coinciding with the one they proclaim, have long been the object of all its solicitude. Things don't go too badly there. One sign of this solicitude is that the normal schools for girls, which prepare the majority of primary grade teachers, are numerous and scattered all over the province, while until recently there were only two normal schools for men, one in Quebec and one in Montreal. The teaching brothers were expected to fill the gaps.

Only by hard struggle have these teaching brothers extracted permission to do a little improvising of their own, to cook up a sort of boys' secondary course. If the Department had wanted to spoil any chance of setting up such a course, it could hardly have acted any differently. The academic side does not interest the Department. Mind you, our faultfinding applies only to the present secondary course. We would like nothing better than a real one.

The incompetence of the Department emerges clearly from the mess of programs in which we flounder. Their irresponsibility shows up in that, never being definitely committed to anything, they can always retreat, change things round, contradict themselves, while none of us can ever find out who is truly responsible. When a man is accountable only to God the Father who is in Heaven, he can afford to take a few liberties with temporal history. It is dangerous, but not everyone has the imagination to perceive that. We live in a surrealist world.

*   *   *   *   *

The Department is a machine so regimented, so centralized, that it is impossible to find anyone responsible for anything. Everything is filtered through veils. The bits of information that are passed out to us are so finely screened that you never know where you are going, if indeed you are going anywhere.

The exercise of authority in the province of Quebec is the practice of witchcraft. In politics we have the Negro-King. For everything else, we have the witch doctors. They reign by virtue of the fear and mystery they wrap around themselves. The farther away they can keep themselves, the more mysterious they are, the more often things can fall on us suddenly, the better, for then events can appear to come directly from God-the-Father, like the thunder in the days before Franklin. From time to time an inspector, very secretly, after exacting a promise that we won't tell, gives us quite unofficially a hint of some change to come. In the end we are informed at the same time as our pupils.

What is meant by?

"the Department"
"classical colleges"
"Negro-King"

What do you think?

1. *What were the complaints of Brother Anonymous against the school system?*
2. *According to Brother Anonymous why was education in such a bad state? Who was responsible?*
3. *By implication what do you think Brother Anonymous would claim had to happen in Quebec before changes could be made in the educational system? Why? Has this happened? Defend your answer.*

4.   CITÉ LIBRE

In 1950 a small magazine founded by Gérard Pelletier and Pierre Elliott Trudeau appeared on the Quebec scene establishing itself quickly as a journal of considerable note in social and intellectual reform circles. Cité Libre was to be an important influence on the thinking of Quebec progressives in the fifties. The following passage, written by Trudeau for the June 1950 issue of the magazine, illustrates the tone and spirit of the journal. (Reprinted by permission of Pierre Elliot Trudeau.)

"But we have preserved the language and the faith of our fathers. That is something positive."

That is a lie which illustrates very well how we have confused quantity and quality. Our language now has become so poor that we no longer realize how badly we speak it . . . our faith, so tenuous, has ceased to be apostolic. . . .

There are not many ways out of our quandary. We must stop trembling at the thought of external dangers, stop fortifying our traditions by sullying what is opposed to them, and consider by what positive actions we can uphold our beliefs.

We want to bear witness to the Christian and French fact in America. So be it. But let us sweep away all the rest. Let us submit to methodical doubt all the political notions of past generations; the strategy of *survivance* no longer serves the flourishing of the City. The time has come to borrow from the architect the style that is called functional, to scrap the thousand past prejudices that clutter up the present and to start building for the new man. Let us throw down the totem poles and violate the taboos, or better yet let us consider them as non-existent. Let us be coldly intelligent.

What do you think?

1. *What is Trudeau proposing in this passage? Why?*
2. *What do the word "functional" and the phrase "coldly intelligent" tell you about the philosophy of Cité Libre? In general has the reform movement in Quebec been characterized by this philosophy? Defend your answer.*

5. HYDRO QUEBEC

One of the major moves made by the Liberal regime was the nationalization of Quebec's electrical resources. In his book The Nationalization of Electric Power *(1962), Paul Sauriol argues the case for Quebec control of that industry. (Reprinted by permission of Harvest House Limited Publishers, Montreal.)*

Hydraulic energy is a natural resource and, as such, is the property of the province; because this resource is in the hands of private enterprise, Ottawa is able to impose a considerable tax on profits deriving from a provincial asset.

Over a fifteen-year period, Quebec has consistently struggled to obtain a more equitable share of the income tax which Ottawa began to seize on such a large scale during the war. Nationalization of electricity would allow the province to recover the huge federal portion of the millions annually levied on profits deriving from Quebec power.

We are engaged in a constitutional and fiscal battle where the autonomy of the province is at stake; also involved are the religious, cultural and social values which it is Quebec's mission to safeguard for the greater good of French Canada. We are letting tens of millions of dollars slip through our fingers, millions we could easily recover. And no revolution is required: the example has been set by other provinces, particularly Ontario. Unlike Quebec, the other provinces have no objection to federal grants in provincial fields such as education; they have no need to protect their fiscal system to defend a religious and cultural minority; they do not feel their rights encroached upon by Ottawa's fiscal and constitutional acts of aggression. We have only to follow their example.

We have more than our share of American capital invested in our hydraulic power resources; at the same time, we have no control over electric production operated by Canadian capital, because it is almost entirely in the hands of English-Canadian capitalists.

In this important branch of the Canadian economy where Canadian capital is deeply entrenched, French Canada faces double foreign domination, double economic occupation. Our inferiority is still more pronounced, because in several other provinces, including Ontario, electricity is publicly owned and is free from the drain of profits and income taxes.

Nationalization of the commercial sector of the hydro-electric industry would help us to correct another handicap which stems largely from our economic dependence. This is the absence of French Canadians from managerial positions in large companies, which makes it very difficult for us to train competent executives. The situation is understandable, and the outlook need not be too pessimistic, provided we take steps to remedy it.

What do you think?

1. *What reasons did M. Sauriol give for nationalizing Quebec's electrical power resources?*
2. *Why do you think Ontario had a publicly owned electrical utility years before Quebec did? How "revolutionary" would the idea of nationalization have been to the average Quebecker in 1962 and why?*

6. HAVE I GOT IT STRAIGHT?

This cartoon by Jan Kamienski was published in the Winnipeg Tribune *in 1964. It was during the Lesage government that Quebec began to aspire to a special place within Confederation. (Reprinted by permission of Jan Kamienski.)*

What do you think?

1. What is the cartoonist trying to say?
2. Why do you think or not think that this cartoon depicts a particularly "western" viewpoint? Have western Canadian attitudes changed since 1964?

7. THE POWER OF THE STATE

René Lévesque, now the leader of the Parti Québécois, was one of Premier Lesage's most dynamic cabinet ministers. (It was Lévesque who oversaw the nationalization of Quebec electricity.) In an interview for Le Devoir, *July 5, 1963, Lévesque told why he supported the idea of a strong government. (Reprinted by permission of* Le Devoir.*)*

It is especially necessary for us to use the economic power of the State as we are one of Canada's "have not" minorities. The private sector of our economy is too weak to provide us with the "rocket-launchers" that can blast us off the ramp of our debilitating poverty. Our principal "capitalist" for the moment—and for as far into the future as we can see—must therefore be the State. It must be more than a participant in the economic development and emancipation of Quebec; it must be a creative agent. Otherwise we can do no more than we have been doing so far, i.e., wait meekly for the capital and initiative of others.

. . . It is we alone, through our State, who can become masters in our own house.

What do you think?

1. *Explain the nationalization of Hydro Quebec in light of Lévesque's remarks.*
2. *How, with his theory of the state in mind, could Lévesque go from a federalist position to a separatist position? Have his views on the role of the state changed? (See Pt. 5—The Future, Reading 9.)*
3. *To what extent was this enlarged role for government anticipated by the reformers of the fifties?*

8. THE APOSTOLATE

The exuberant confidence of the early years of the Quiet Revolution is described in these next two readings. The first is from Thomas Sloan's book The Not-So-Quiet Revolution, *published in 1965. (Reprinted by permission of McGraw-Hill Ryerson Ltd., Toronto.) The second is from Peter Desbarat's work* The State of Quebec, *also published in 1965. (Reprinted by permission of The Canadian Publishers, McClelland and Stewart Limited, Toronto.)*

(a) For when we talk of the Quebec of the mid-sixties we must forget many of the preconceptions, valid enough in their time perhaps, that still clutter our thinking. Today's Quebec is no longer a folklore society of colourfully dressed old farmers and woodsmen dancing around the wood stove to the tune of the fiddle, with the women and children clapping hands in the background, all under the benevolent eye of the kindly old curé in his black smock. It is no longer primarily a landscape of picturesque villages dominated by great church steeples; it is no longer a priest-ridden, lawyer-ridden, nostalgia-ridden piece of would-be pre-revolutionary France. It is no longer a land of rustics singing Alouette. To various degrees these still exist, but they are no longer typical. Their significance is steadily disappearing. The folklore culture still exists, and as such still has its place. But Quebec is no longer the folklore province.

Of course tradition remains, coexisting with the express train of revolution. Those who prefer the old ways of thinking, acting, making money and spending it still carry on their existence in the schools, the Church, in business and on the farms. Though they count as individuals, and sometimes in politics, the brutal fact is that they no longer count as a vital social force in the new Quebec. They are in Quebec, but no longer of it. The future of Quebec belongs to the students, the young professionals, the engineers, doctors, scientists, teachers, lawyers, businessmen, farmers and union members who are no longer willing to live in a backwater.

(b) The new Quebec is, psychologically at least, more akin to the New France of the early days than to the Quebec of the more recent past. With its sudden release of energies and acceptance of change and experiment, it has more in common with the colony that was the stage for exploits of the *coureurs de bois* and the explorers than it has with the ingrown, tradition-bound Quebec of the nineteenth and early twentieth centuries, ruled by politicians who were timid outside and all too often brazenly corrupt inside the province. Now timidity has faded in the face of self-assertion, and the traditionally exclusive stress on political issues is giving way, especially in the younger generation, to a realization of the overriding importance of economic issues, as opposed to the barren if picturesque strife of political personalities.

"In France right now the young men have to sit and wait. I imagine it's the same in English Canada. But in Quebec the whole structure is changing. You don't feel compressed into a pattern, you feel that the collectivity is open to suggestion."

"This, not separatism, is the real challenge—to build this province in the way that the people want it."

Another young civil servant summed it up by saying, "There's no handbook here in Quebec."

And another, "It's sort of an apostolate."

Quebec must be the only place in North America in 1964 where the civil service seems as glamorous as the Foreign Legion, where a dynamic director-general of buildings and equipment for a department can be known as "Flash Gordon" to his contemporaries.

"I had ten close friends in my law class at the University of Montreal and not one of them is working for the big firms on St. James Street," a young civil servant said proudly.

"Two are working, like myself, for the province. Another is a professor of criminal law in the Congo. One is in the labour movement. Another is working for the World's Fair. All of us are doing something useful."

What do you think?

1. *Explain the significance of the following statements taken from the two readings above.*
   (a) *"They are in Quebec, but no longer of it."*
   (b) *"There's no handbook here in Quebec."*
   (c) *"It's sort of an apostolate."*
2. *Would you say that the growth of the Parti Québécois was an inevitable product of the "younger generation's" belief in the overriding importance of economic issues? Why or why not?*

9.   A NOTICE TO THE PEOPLE

In the early weeks of March 1963 three Canadian Army establishments in Montreal had been bombed with Molotov cocktails. The mysterious letters "FLQ" had been painted on the walls before the bombings. The following day the FLQ published its first notice to the people identifying itself.

NOTICE TO THE POPULATION OF THE STATE OF QUEBEC

The Quebec Liberation Front (FLQ) is a revolutionary movement of volunteers ready to die for the political and economic independence of Quebec.

The suicide-commandos of the FLQ have as their principal mission the complete destruction, by systematic sabotage, of:

a) all colonial (federal) symbols and institutions, in particular the RCMP and the armed forces;

b) All the information media in the colonial language (English) which hold us in contempt;

c) all commercial establishments and enterprises which practise discrimination against Quebecers, which do not use French as the first language, which advertise in the colonial language (English);

d) all plants and factories which discriminate against French-speaking workers.

The Quebec Liberation Front will proceed to the progressive elimination of all collaborators with the occupier.

The Quebec Liberation Front will also attack all American cultural and commercial interests, natural allies of English colonialism. All FLQ volunteers have on their persons during acts of sabotage identification papers for the Republic of Quebec. We ask that our wounded and our prisoners be treated as political prisoners in accordance with the Geneva Convention on the rules of war.

INDEPENDENCE OR DEATH

THE DIGNITY OF THE QUEBEC PEOPLE DEMANDS INDEPENDENCE

QUEBEC'S INDEPENDENCE IS ONLY POSSIBLE THROUGH
SOCIAL REVOLUTION

SOCIAL REVOLUTION MEANS A FREE QUEBEC

STUDENTS, WORKERS, PEASANTS, FORM YOUR CLANDESTINE
GROUPS AGAINST ANGLO-AMERICAN COLONIALISM

What do you think?

1. *Read the "notice" carefully. Compare the FLQ of 1963 and the FLQ of 1970 (Pt. 3—The Contemporary Scene, Reading 21). Account for any similarities or differences in attitude, goals, techniques that you note.*
2. *Could a group like the FLQ have come into being unless a phenomenon like the "Quiet Revolution" happened as well? Explain your answer.*

10. ENGLISH-CANADIAN IGNORANCE

French-Canadian writer Solange Chaput-Rolland and her English-Canadian friend Gwethalyn Graham published their correspondence concerning the situation in Quebec in a book called Dear Enemies *(1964). This letter of Mme Rolland's is dated December 20, 1962. (Reprinted by permission of The Macmillan Company of Canada Limited, Toronto.)*

Moved by a rather naive desire to be useful, I went into the vast English-speaking world to talk about the current upheaval in Quebec. I left Montreal a French-speaking Canadian, and I came back a French

Canadian, furiously determined to remain just that, in the face of no matter whom or what. I had been curious and anxious to discover the reality of Canada as a whole, but I hadn't found it and here is why.

I won't go into details about the itinerary of my trip; I would need a guide book to recall all the places I visited. However, I did visit more than fifty Canadian cities and towns. I often found myself with fellow-members of the press, radio, and television, and I had the great pleasure of rubbing shoulders with painters, sculptors, and writers. It seems to me, therefore, that I have a genuine "sampling" of Canadian citizens among my memories. Once back in Quebec, I went on remembering the wonderful welcome everyone had given me, but I am still suffering under the conviction that English Canada has absolutely no interest in the awakening of French Canada or in our struggles, our history, or our reality. Between you and us there is a gap of cordial misunderstanding, free of any animosity but also lacking any real will to make even a gesture of friendship, one towards the other. Beyond Winnipeg, for example, the very existence of Quebec becomes a sort of myth, a folklore of trappers and traders. Please don't think I am exaggerating; between one city and the next I was constantly obliged to rewrite my lectures, to change my speeches so as to talk not about revolution in Quebec, but literally about the fact that Quebec is there.

*   *   *   *   *

Scarcely two years ago, some English newspapers in Quebec, the *Star* and the *Gazette,* for example, were still systematically ignoring the reality of French Canada. Reading them, one could have sworn that Quebec was an English province! Today they are making a real effort to pay some attention to us, but we haven't the slightest illusion about this sudden interest in our problems. What makes us suddenly attractive to your compatriots is our nationalization of electricity, our almost miraculous industrial development, and our astonishing possibility of becoming in less than ten years one of the most prosperous provinces in Canada. We are no longer the poor relations of Confederation; we are no longer employees to be exploited or poverty-stricken citizens to be tolerated; we have become a force to be reckoned with. So "Bravo, French Canada; you are suddenly wonderful and we love you." And what I say to you is . . . zut! I listen to your politicians extolling our merits, recognizing our vital role in the history of our national identity. Your businessmen suddenly discover ours and are astonished by their industrial intelligence. All this is good, fine, but it reeks of political capital—this anxiety, which is a little too recent, not to lose a promising market in the future by committing more blunders. Yes, Gwen, zut it is!

What do you think?

1. *"I left Montreal a French-speaking Canadian and I came back a French Canadian. . . ."* What is the difference between the two? Why did this happen to the author? Would this be likely to happen today? Why or Why not?

2. *". . . between one city and the next I was constantly obliged to rewrite my lectures, to change my speeches so as to talk not about revolution in Quebec, but literally about the fact that Quebec is there."* How can you account for this? How and why do you think Mme Rolland would have changed her views since 1962?

11. BICULTURALISM, A SIDE ISSUE

In 1963 the Liberal government in Ottawa appointed a Royal Commission on Bilingualism and Biculturalism to inquire into the relationship between Canada's two "founding" cultures and to probe the source of the crisis between them. This selection consists of René Lévesque's reaction to the B and B Commission. Lévesque was still a cabinet minister in the Lesage government at this time. His remarks were quoted in the July 5, 1963, issue of Le Devoir. *(Reprinted by permission of* Le Devoir.)

QUESTION: What do you expect of the famous enquiry into the state of the two nations and cultures in Canada, and into the means of giving them equal status and recognition—in short, what do you think of what is generally described, by that grating, newly-coined term, as "biculturalism"?

ANSWER: As defined by its terms of reference, the enquiry at best only promises to bring one possible benefit: a greater respect for, and a wider use of, French in the federal government departments and in the services controlled by the central government. This is not negligible, but it is obviously minor. However, there is also a risk of misplacing the proper emphasis, which could be very dangerous. We must not mislead others into believing, nor end up by convincing ourselves, that "biculturalism" is a basic goal or value.

It is infinitely more important to make Quebec progressive, free, and strong, than to devote the best of our energies to propagating the doubtful advantages of biculturalism. Moreover, if French culture is to spread, if the French language is to be respected, that will depend above all on the vigour, on the economic and political importance, of Quebec. These must become and must remain our first concern, by far our most decisive and constant preoccupation.

What do you think?

1. How do you think the creation of the B and B Commission was received in English Canada, judging by Mme Rolland's letter?

The Duplessis Era

Maurice Duplessis, premier of Quebec from 1936 to 1939 and from 1944 to his death in 1959, gave his name to a whole collection of certain values and attitudes in Quebec. During the Duplessis era, "Duplessis-ism," or some version of it, provided for many outside Quebec their only impression of French Canada.

Duplessis came to power when he assumed leadership of the Union Nationale, a new coalition party created in 1935 from the Quebec Conservative Party and Action Libérale Nationale, a reform-minded political group whose social ideas appealed to a Quebec electorate hard struck by the depression. However, once premier, Duplessis eliminated the radicals in his coalition and governed Quebec with an economically and socially conservative philosophy. By carefully cultivating the rural voter and by making Ottawa a scapegoat for French-Canadian nationalism, Duplessis was able to retain power in Quebec despite his conservative and uninventive policies. During this period Quebec became caricatured as a backward, rural, priest-ridden society whose people were ignorant, suspicious and parochial.

How does this image account for some of the attitudes and beliefs expressed by some English Canadians? How would it frustrate and annoy French Canadians?

12. ABBÉ GROULX

The urbanization and industrialization of Quebec proceeded quickly following World War I, heightening nationalist feeling, not only because the traditional French-Canadian way of life was threatened, but also because so much of the developmental capital came from English-Canadian or American sources.

The new nationalism of the post-war period spoke through L'Action francaise, a journal first produced in January 1917. Father Lionel Groulx was the unofficial leader of the new movement. Groulx believed that race and religion were the foundation of a nation. His aim was to instil pride in French Canadians for their history and language and to build up a strong national character based on tradition and a French-Canadian "mission" in North America. It was

Groulx's type of parochial nationalism that politicians like Duplessis were to exploit.

These selections are from the writing of Lionel Groulx. The first is taken from the January 1921 edition of L'Action francaise, *the second from* L'œuvre de l'abbé Groulx *edited by Olivar Asselin and published in Montreal in 1923.*

(a) It is possible to sum up our whole credo in this brief phrase: We want to restore the fullness of our French life. We want to recover, to recapture in its entirety the ethnic type which France left here and which five hundred years of history have moulded. We want to draw up again the inventory of our moral and social strengths, an action which itself prepares these things for their development. This ethnic type we wish to free from its foreign overgrowth so that it may develop by itself, intensively, the original culture. We want to bind to it the new virtues acquired since the conquest, and to preserve it above all through intimate contact with its historical life sources. We want to afterwards allow it to go in its own regular and unique way. It is this rigorously characterized French ethnic type, dependent on history and geography, with ethnic and psychological birth rights, which we want to continue and upon which we place our future hope. A people, as with all that grows, can only develop that which is already in itself, can only develop those powers which already have a living seed.

(b) Race is of all historical factors the most powerful and the most fundamental. Believed to be disinherited, it will surface after centuries to lay claim to its immortal right. Race transforms without being transformed. More than all unifying forces, save that of religion, it determines the political, economic, social and intellectual life of a nation.

What do you think?

1. *Abbé Groulx was profoundly disturbed by the modernization of Quebec and the threat to traditional values that it posed. Is this fear evident in these passages?*
2. *Why do you think Groulx was preoccupied with history and race? What connection did he see between race and nation? How would you describe the type of nationalism that Groulx represents? What parallels are there between this phase of French-Canadian nationalism and that of the 1960s and 1970s?*

13.   A TYPICAL FRENCH CANADIAN?

This selection has been taken from the Toronto Star *of November 11, 1944. How would you describe the writer's attitude towards French Canadians? (Reprinted with permission* Toronto Star.)

Though Pierre lives well, it costs him little in cash. For $20 a month he can buy sugar, tea and shoes for his family. That's because he is his own provider.

Pierre's needs are satisfied from the land on which he lives and from the stream that flows past his strip.

Pierre Turnotte is typical of the French-Canadian farmers who know of no other home than the Isle d'Orléans. Pierre is rearing his family of ten children in a whitewashed stone house that was new 250 years ago.

Nine miles down river from Canada's ancient city of Quebec, the St. Lawrence river forks, to join again forty-two miles nearer the Atlantic. This fork in Canada's mightiest river has made an island, the Isle d'Orléans, and on this island live Canadians whose French customs are as firm as the cobblestones in Quebec's lane-like streets.

On the Isle d'Orléans no English is spoken. Their carts are styled as they were when Montcalm battled Wolfe. Their houses have been standing since New France was new. Tractors? Oxen drag wooden plows that till the fertile fields. Some modern farmers boast a horse.

Pierre, like his friends, is happy. Maybe he is behind the times . . . perhaps he has never ridden a street car or been nearer to a train than to hear its "toot." Pierre eats, is comfortable and does not know what it is to want because the sweat of his brow and the fertility of his land supplies everything.

"Voilà," says Pierre as he beams with French pride on his forty acres on the Isle d'Orléans. "Elle est bonne."

In his earth-floor cellar Pierre has stocks of food that make his basement look like a wholesale warehouse. Potatoes, not bagged—dumped carefully in a corner—will last him until next fall, the next crop. Beets and carrots and cabbage are ready for the table. In his barn large leaves of tobacco hang to dry. When dry, these leaves will be cut and Pierre will puff his pipe contentedly this winter.

Even the shirt Pierre wears was grown on his land. He has seven sheep and each spring they are sheared. The wool is washed and spun and dyed. Both Pierre's older daughters received their education in the Catholic convent a few miles down the twisting road that snakes through Pierre's farm. At the convent they learned to operate a loom and when cloth is to be made Marie Antoinette or Candide take it to the convent where they may use the loom.

Starting early in the spring, Pierre taps his maple trees, his sugar. Then he shears his sheep and the wool may be used for anything from sox to table cloths. Planting is his biggest job because it must be a big crop. For this he got his two sons out of the army. They are big boys, typical of the race that thrives on the Isle d'Orléans. Daniel is 23 and Gabriel is 25.

Besides vegetables, Pierre grows strawberries and raspberries. He gathers hay to feed the cattle that supply him with his milk and cream and butter. In the winter, he kills a steer for beef. He may kill more than one hog a year. In the winter there is always salt pork in the pork barrel.

Pierre likes to show his friends his home, each room separately and each room sparkling in gleaming cleanliness. The floor is new; Pierre laid it. He does most of the carpentry even to making the stiff-backed chairs that rim the parlor wall like a precision squad. Pierre did not make the beds. They were hewn from maple logs by Pierre's grandfather many years ago. But the sheets were made by Pierre's wife and the pillows were chucked to overflowing with fine feathers from Pierre's chickens.

Pierre has only three other interests outside his forty-acre patch. They are his church, his market business in Québec on Friday (Friday, not Saturday is market day in Québec) and the school board. Pierre is a member of the village school board, even though his daughters were—and will be—educated in the convent. A few years ago Pierre was an alderman at Ste. Famille. The job took too much time. Pierre was needed at home.

What do you think?

1. *If this typifies the view of French Canada held by English Canada, what were the implications for relations between the two? Why?*
2. *How did the style used by the author of this excerpt enhance the impression that he wanted to give about Pierre?*

14.   THE THREE PILLARS OF POWER

Leon Dion, in an article "The New Regime" (The Globe and Mail, Toronto, January 1962) described the bases of Duplessis' political power. (Reprinted by permission of Leon Dion.)

A first pillar of power Duplessis sought and found in a Machiavellian alliance with U.S. and Canadian capitalists. In this he continued and intensified the policy of his predecessor, Alexandre Taschereau. However this was a period of intense industrial development and social evolution; what might have been considered before as an aristocratic disdain for economic matters was rapidly transformed into an open conspiracy against the people of Quebec. The province, blessed with abundant natural resources, became a target for capitalist investments. All doors to free economic exploitation being kept open by Duplessis himself, financiers and entrepreneurs reciprocated by an occasional gesture of gratitude and affection: Under the table, they made a token gift of a few thousand dollars, or they contributed "commissions"—not, of course, to be spent for the welfare of the people of Quebec, but to be taken over by the treasurer of the party, in order to finance the next elections and permit the smooth operation of a shameless patronage.

A second pillar of Duplessis' power consisted in his success as a demagogue. To the people, especially in rural districts, he appeared as a great and trustworthy leader, speaking their own language and giving expression to their own prejudices and emotions. Until the end came for him, his personal prestige over the common people suffered no eclipse. To them, he was a big and loving father.

A third pillar of power Duplessis found in the political machine which he had built but whose operation he handed to men he trusted, like J. D. Bégin and above all Gerald Martineau. After the 1956 election the population of Quebec finally became aware that it was being ruled by an all-powerful political machine. So strong was this machine, indeed, that the Union Nationale might have triumphed over Jean Lesage's team on June 22, 1960, even without Duplessis, if Premier Antonio Barrette and the political boss of the party, Martineau, had not become estranged.

During the Old Regime of Maurice Duplessis, no law was enacted officially abrogating the political and civil rights which are enjoyed by all Canadian citizens. But the friends of the administration benefited from occult protection while its opponents found all privileges and opportunities closed to them. Sometimes the law was harsh toward social groups and institutions which supposedly contained subversive elements, such as the labor unions, for example. The right of expressing one's opinions was not abrogated either. Since the regime was not grounded on any ideology whatsoever, it had no system of ideas to impose upon the population.

Ideas and opinions inimical to the regime, in general, were not banned; they were considered with suspicion, of course, but above all they were simply branded as "leftist" or "Communist" and as such put under the severe ban of a poorly educated public opinion.

Duplessis was shrewd enough not to interfere directly with *Cité Libre, Le Devoir,* Radio-Canada and so on. But he saw to it that those who wrote or spoke in or through the mass media should be prevented from exerting any appreciable degree of influence. By various devices, and through direct pressure exerted on private institutions, the Old Regime had in the end succeeded in establishing a climate of fear and a feeling of impotence which extended to all and everybody, except to a few who were courageous enough to speak in a time during which only cheers or silence was rewarding.

The leitmotif of provincial autonomy which won to Duplessis so many partisans and friends, even among Anglo-Canadians from outside Quebec, was only a void and negative concept to him. It was periodically reshaped in order to suit electoral purposes. But the sad fact was that, in this case, Duplessis put into practice what he preached. Thus the population of Quebec was prevented from benefiting from many federal progressive policies in the fields of social security and welfare, and especially in education. Instead of trying to find ways of adjusting the provincial rights and prerogatives and federal policies which may have been technically derogative of the constitution while they indisputably answered urgent needs, he stubbornly clung to a purely negative attitude, which was electorally rewarding while it left our teachers and our institutions in a desperate position.

What is meant by?

"demagogue"
"inimical"

What do you think?

1. According to Dion what were the secrets of Duplessis' success? In each case explain how these devices kept Duplessis in favour with the Quebec voter.
2. What was Duplessis' attitude towards French-Canadian nationalism? Why do you think this approach was successful with Quebec voters, especially in the rural areas?
3. Pierre Trudeau has written that democracy in Quebec is a "frail flower." To what extent is this statement supported by evidence in this document?

15.   VIGNETTES

In his book The True Face of Duplessis (1960), Pierre Laporte describes some incidents characteristic of Maurice Duplessis. (Reprinted by permission of Harvest House Limited Publishers, Montreal.)

Duplessis was horrified at the thought of change—not only in his immediate circle but in the provincial administration as well. Born in the last quarter of the nineteenth century, he apparently lived through the tremendous industrial changes of the past fifty years without being influenced by them in any way. He did adopt a timid program of social welfare, but his odd manner of striving to make it as ineffectual as possible clearly indicates that he moved forward in this field against his true wishes.

This reactionary attitude sometimes led to almost incredible statements.

During a press conference—somewhere around 1950—the question of job classification and trade unions came up. Duplessis could not swallow the development. "When I was young and the plumber came to repair a stove pipe," he said, "he did not complain if we also asked him to fix a kitchen chair at the same time."

*   *   *   *   *

Duplessis knew how to be fierce when necessary. He never drew back an inch in the face of a threat to grab from him that which he desired more than all else in the world: the great power he enjoyed as provincial government leader. At Shawinigan, in the St. Maurice constituency, he once declared that if the voters re-elected a member of the Opposition, a bridge needed for the heavy local traffic would not be built. They were warned. And when they elected a Liberal Opposition member anyway, the bridge was not built while Duplessis was alive.

In Verchères County, Duplessis said during a political meeting in 1952: "I warned you not to elect a Liberal candidate. You did not listen to me. Unfortunately your riding did not receive any of the grants, the subsidies that could have made it a happier place in which to live. I hope you have now learned your lesson and that you will vote against the Liberals this time."

*   *   *   *   *

Verchères riding, in the Montreal area, discovered what it can cost to elect a Liberal. Until 1956 its secondary roads remained in a lamentable condition. A priest had to ride a tractor for over five miles to reach the parish church of St. Amable. A physician was unable to get to a patient because the roads were impassable. So it was no surprise when the farmers of this riding declared, on the eve of the 1956 provincial election: "We have shown our friendship for Arthur Dupré (Liberal) by electing him in 1944, in 1948, and in 1952. This time we are going to vote for new roads." Dupré was defeated . . . very probably because of Duplessis' implacable logic.

What do you think?

1. What was your reaction to these incidents? Why?

16.   THE BLACK KING

Why did Duplessis' actions and philosophy receive very little criticism from the English-language press in Quebec? In his celebrated "Theory of the Black King," André Laurendeau provided one answer. The article was first printed in Le Devoir, *July 4, 1959. (Reprinted by permission of* Le Devoir.)

The British have political astuteness. They rarely destroy the political institutions of a conquered country. They hem in the black king but they allow him some illusions. They permit him on occasions to cut off heads, if it is the custom in that country. One thing would never strike them and that is to expect that black king to conform to the high moral and political standards of the British.

It is necessary to ensure that the black king cooperate and protect British interests. This cooperation assured, the rest is less important. And if the puppet king violates the rules of democracy? . . . One should know not to expect better of a primitive. . . .

I am not attributing these sentiments to the English minority of Quebec. But things occur as though some of their leaders believed in the theory and practice of the black king. They excuse Duplessis and the native leaders of Quebec for things which they would not tolerate from their own.

This tendency can readily be seen in the Legislative Assembly. It was seen in the last municipal election. It has just been confirmed in Quebec.

The result is a backward step for democracy, a regime more un-contested than arbitrary, an unceasing collusion of Anglo-Quebec finance with which the politics of this province are more than rotten.

What do you think?

1. *How valid do you think Laurendeau's theory of the black king was?*
2. *Is his analogy between Duplessis and a black king a fair one? If not, is his thesis still good?*

Imperialism and Defence 1880–1950

In the late nineteenth and early twentieth century the British Empire and British imperialism were at their most powerful. Referring to relations within an empire—between mother country and colonies —imperialism is a word which is frequently misused because too often it is used only with reference to the attitudes of the imperial power. In fact, many times, the colonies were just as much, if not more, enraptured with the imperial spirit, the spirit of Empire.

The Canadian response to late-nineteenth-century, early-twentieth-century imperialism contributed greatly to the complexion of many issues facing Canada today. This is especially true for the issue of French-English relations, since French Canada and English Canada were often deeply divided over the question of Canada's relationship with England. The reasons for this division are not hard to find. The difficulty lies in assessing the impact that this division, often a bitter one, had on creating the attitudes of French and English Canadians in the following years.

In this section you will examine three major events which revolved around the issue of Canada's relationship with England: the Boer War, the Naval Question, the 1917 Conscription Crisis, and a fourth, the Conscription Question of 1942–44, which included many of the same issues as the first three. What *was* the position of the opposing groups in each of these crises and why? Why was imperialism an important factor in determining the positions of French and English Canada on these defence questions? Did these positions change over the years? Can you see any connection between the tension created by these events and the feelings of today?

The Boer War

In the 1870s the Boer republics of Transvaal and the Orange Free State fell under British control, but were allowed to retain republican status and local self-government. However, the discovery of gold and diamonds in these Dutch-speaking territories attracted British immigration and investment. Since British imperial sentiment had become a potent force by the 1890s, there was pressure to incorporate the Boer republics into a federation dominated by Britain's Cape Colony. When British nationals in the Boer-held territories complained of ill treatment at the hands of the Boers, there was pretext for war.

Joseph Chamberlain, the British Colonial Secretary at that time and an ardent imperialist, inquired about the possibility of Canada's sending troops to South Africa. Laurier, the Canadian prime minister, faced a difficult decision which involved not only the issue of Canada's relations with Great Britain but also the issue of French-English relations in Canada. His compromise solution was that one contingent (later followed by another) would be raised and equipped in Canada but would be paid by the British government and would be incorporated into the British army.

Why did the Boer War arouse tension between English Canadians and French Canadians? Did the principles involved in this controversy appear in later events?

17.   A PLEA FOR CANADIAN NON-INVOLVEMENT

Dominique Monet, Liberal member from Laprairie and Napierville, rose in the House, March 13, 1900, to second a motion by Henri Bourassa. (Reprinted by permission of Information Canada.)

This title of Canadian satisfies my pride and ambition. I am a Canadian; I am not French, I am not English, but I am Canadian, not for the sake of France, nor for the sake of England, but I am a Canadian, loving this country, because it is the land of our forefathers, who were Canadians. I love this land because it has been opened up and developed by our own forefathers, Canadians, whose labours and blood have made her what she is today, the finest, as she is the freest, colony in the world. But, it is because I want to defend inch by inch the bulwark of our political liberties, the bulwark of our political freedom, from any further encroachment, that I rise again to support and second the motion of the hon. member for Labelle (Mr. Bourassa). As a matter of fact, it embodies the very essence of the Liberal democratic school to which I belong. In this motion lies the very fundamental principle of responsible government. It indicates that after God, the sovereign will of the people is the source of all authority and of all legislative action. Here is the motion which I have seconded:

That this House insists on the principle of the sovereignty and the independence of parliament as the basis of British institutions and the safeguard of the civil and political liberties of British citizens, and refuses consequently to consider the action of the government in relation to the South African war as a precedent which should commit this country to any action in the future.

That this House further declares that it opposes any change in the political and military relations which exist at present between Canada and Great Britain unless such change is initiated by the sovereign will of parliament and sanctioned by the people of Canada.

What is meant by?

"sovereign will"
"sovereignty"

What do you think?

1. *Why did M. Monet support the Bourassa motion?*
2. *Why were men like M. Monet accused of being disloyal by some English Canadians? What do you think of these accusations and why?*

18.   WE ARE MORE CANADIAN THAN YOU

Joseph Israel Tarte was at this time minister of public works in the Laurier Cabinet and Liberal party organizer in Quebec. In this letter to John Willison, the editor of the Globe, Toronto, dated November 28, 1900, Tarte explains the French-Canadian position.

The French-Canadian population do not belong, if I may speak that way, to the same civilization as their fellow-countrymen of English origin. The French genius is not the same as the Anglo-Saxon genius. We are French, you are English. Would you permit me to add that we are Canadians to the fullest extent of the word while, on many occasions, you are more British than Canadians. If there is any trouble in the future, the trouble will come out of that difference.

The reluctance of the French Canadians to taking part in the Transvaal war had for its cause the earnest desire of the French population not to be involved in continental European conflicts. Mr. Spender was perfectly right when he wrote that the French Canadians "do not like the war, but they love the British rule." Is it not our right not to love that infernal war in South Africa? And why should we be accused of disloyalty because we don't like the war? We think that in minding our own business we could be a very happy people. The English and the French of this continent would very soon become close friends if there was a real, genuine national sentiment.

What do you think?

1. *What reasons does Mr. Tarte cite for French Canada's desire for Canada's not participating in the war? What do you think of these reasons and why?*
2. *If French Canadians loved British rule, should they have supported Canadian participation as British subjects? Why?*
3. *". . . we are Canadians to the fullest extent of the word, while, on many occasions, you are more British than Canadians." Was Tarte correct? Why?*

19.   WE HAVE BEEN CHILDREN LONG ENOUGH

This is a summary of a speech made by Colonel Denison to the Canadian Military Institute. It is taken from Denison's book, The Struggle for Imperial Unity *(1909). (Reprinted by permission of The Macmillan Company of Canada Limited, Toronto.)*

Continuing, Colonel Denison said it could not be gainsaid that the question was one of vital importance to the whole empire, and Canadians were as much interested as any of Her Majesty's subjects. The Dominion had not fully and properly appreciated her responsibilities as part of a great empire. If Canada was an independent nation of six millions of people it would have to support a standing army of 40,000 men, besides reserves of 200,000 or 300,000. "Is it right," he asked, "that we should all the time be dependent upon the home Government and the British fleet for protection? Is it fair that we should not give any proper assistance? What kind of treatment would we have received from Washington in the Behring's Sea business or in reference to this Alaskan question if we had not had behind us the power of the Empire?"

Such a course was not only selfish but impolitic and foolish. In his opinion not only should one contingent of 1,500 men be offered in the present crisis, but another 1,500 should be immediately got together and drilled so as to be ready in case of emergency. No one could tell where the thing was going to end, and reserves might be expected in the beginning. Other great nations envied the power of Britain and would be ready to seize the opportunity if the Empire was in a tight hole. Therefore they should be prepared, not only to send one contingent and have another on hand ready for the call, but should be in a position to relieve the garrisons at Halifax and Esquimalt, allowing the regulars to be added to the forces in the field. "We have been children long enough," he concluded; "let us show the Empire that we have grown to manhood."

He then moved that "the members of the Canadian Military Institute, feeling that it is a clear and definite duty for all British possessions to show their willingness to contribute to the common defence in case of need, express the hope that in view of impending hostilities in South Africa the Government of Canada will promptly offer a contingent of Canadian militia to assist in supporting the interests of our Empire in that country."

What do you think?

1. (a) How did Denison justify the action of the British in South Africa? Compare his views to those of Joseph Israel Tarte in the reading preceding this one.
   (b) Why was it important for Denison and Tarte to comment on the morality of the war?
2. (a) What did Denison feel were Canada's responsibilities to Britain? Why?
   (b) How did his views differ from Tarte's? Why?
3. In your opinion do Denison's arguments effectively answer those put forward by French-Canadian spokesmen? Why?

20.   LAURIER: CEMENT CANADIAN UNITY

This selection is an excerpt from a speech made by Sir Wilfrid Laurier in the House of Commons, March 13, 1900.

My hon. friend dreads the consequences of our action in sending out a military contingent to South Africa. Let me tell him from the bottom of my heart that my bosom is full of the hopes I entertain of the beneficial results which will accrue from that action. When our young volunteers sailed from our shores to join the British army in South Africa, great were our expectations that they would display on those distant battlefields the same courage which had been displayed by their fathers when fighting against one another in the last century. Perhaps in more than one breast, there was a fugitive sense of uneasiness at the thought that the first facing of musketry by raw recruits is always a severe trial. But when the telegraph brought us the information that such was the good impression made by our volunteers that the commander in chief had placed them at the post of honour, in the first rank, side by side with that famous corps, the Gordon Highlanders; when we heard that they had justified fully the confidence placed in them, that they had charged like veterans, that their conduct was heroic and had won for them the encomiums of the commander in chief and the unstinted admiration of their comrades of those famous troops, who had faced death upon a hundred battlefields in all parts of the world—is there a man whose bosom did not swell with pride, the noblest of all pride, the pride of pure patriotism, the pride of the con- sciousness of our rising strength, the pride of the consciousness that that day the fact had been revealed to the world that a new power had risen in the west.

Nor is that all. The work of union and harmony between the different elements of this country is not yet complete. We know by the unfortunate occurrences that took place only last week that there is much yet to do in that way. But there is no bond of union so strong as the bond created by dangers shared in common. Today there are men in South Africa representing the two branches of the Canadian family, fighting side by side for the honour of Canada. Already some of them have fallen, giving to the glory of their country the last full measure of devotion. Their dead bodies have been laid in the same grave, there to rest to the end of time in that last fraternal embrace. . . . Can we not hope—I ask my hon. friend himself—that in that grave shall be buried the last vestiges of our former antagonism? If such shall be the result, if we can indulge that hope, if we can believe that in that grave shall be for ever buried all our past division, the sending of the contingents would be the greatest service ever rendered to Canada since Confederation. These are the motives which guided us; these are the thoughts which inspired us; they ought to commend the heart and mind of my hon. friend, knowing him as I know him, and in my judgment, they should induce him not to press further this motion.

What do you think?

1. *"But there is no bond of union so strong as the bond created by dangers shared in common." How accurate was Laurier's assessment of the effects of the Boer War?*
2. *Compare Laurier's views on the role of the Boer War in unifying Canada with those of Joseph Israel Tarte (Pt. 4—The Historical Perspective, Reading 18). Account for the difference.*

The Naval Issue

By 1909 England and Germany were engaged in a naval arms race which had been prompted by the creation of the dreadnought class of battleship. Britain, claiming that she needed financial help in order to keep abreast of Germany, appealed to her colonies for assistance. In Canada, the question was whether to make a direct contribution of money to the British Admiralty or to build a Canadian navy which would be placed under British direction in the event of war.

Laurier chose the latter course, placing before Parliament in 1910 plans for the creation of a Canadian navy consisting of five cruisers and six destroyers. However Laurier's proposal was not popular with a large section of English and French Canada and the controversy became an issue in the 1911 federal election.

Why did the idea of building a Canadian navy to be under the control of the British Admiralty in time of war for Imperial defence create tensions between English and French? What other ideas were proposed? What did each group see as the issue? What do you think the issue was?

21. TWO VIEWPOINTS

The first document is an editorial from a Liberal paper, the Manitoba Free Press *of August 23, 1909, which supported Laurier's policy. (Reprinted by permission of the* Winnipeg Free Press.)

The second editorial here appeared in The Sentinel and Orange and Protestant Advocate, *October 21, 1909. What was the Orange*

Lodge? What was its attitude towards French Canada and why? (Reprinted by permission of The Sentinel and Orange and Protestant Advocate.*)*

(a) Canada will establish her own fleet.

While in the beginning of things, Canada will have to avail herself of the expert knowledge and experience of British naval officers and engineers, the objective is a fleet built in Canada, manned by Canadian sailors, officered by Canadians.

This fleet from the outset will be paid for, owned and controlled by the people of Canada through their government at Ottawa. Its particular duty will be to guard the shores of Canada and to protect the trade routes across the Atlantic: but, in the event of war, it would be available for any service in any part of the world in the larger interests of the Empire. It will never pass from the control of the people of Canada except temporarily for particular reasons and with the consent of the Canadian government.

This is the naval policy of Canada. The present Dominion government is pledged to it. The Dominion Parliament has supported it unanimously. It has recently been affirmed in London by the Canadian delegates to the Imperial Defence Conference, and has been accepted with cordiality by the British government and the British people.

The only critics are a group of Canadian Conservative newspapers who cannot appreciate or appraise the strong feeling of nationality now throbbing in Canada, a spirit which is the guarantee of Canada's future greatness as one of the nations of the British Empire.

The cause of Imperialism in Canada secured an important advance when the federal government consented to the establishment of a Canadian navy. . . . Among English-speaking Canadians it is cause for gratification that to this extent at least our obligations to the mother country have been recognized.

(b) It must be clear, however, to any man who studies the situation, that infinitely better results would be secured by devoting the same amount of money to making additions to the home fleet than any attempt to organize a Canadian navy under the control of the federal government. There must be grave doubts as to the effectiveness of several independent fleets co-operating on any critical conflict. A naval force under the command of one staff which has been organized and trained for combined action will surely act with greater harmony and effectiveness against an enemy. The duplication of fleets means duplication of energy and financial resources. The cost of administration alone would be excessive for the results aimed at and a greater probability that the anticipated results would not be attained.

If Canada had suffered in the past from any lack of interest on the part of the Imperial authorities there would be some ground for the establishment of a Canadian navy. But there has been no time in the history of Canada when the whole fighting force of the British navy was not at our disposal. It is only fair to assume that this would be our experience in the future. . . .

If Canada contemplated separation from the Mother Country the case for the building of a Canadian navy would be unassailable. But there is no prospect of any change in our political conditions. In the last hundred years Imperial sentiment has never been as strong as it is in Canada to-day. It is fair to assume, therefore, that we have settled the question of our future political relations and intend to remain a portion of the British Empire. That being the case, we are unable to discover any valid reason why a new force should be organized on this side of the Atlantic.

What do you think?

1. *Summarize the arguments in these two editorials. Which argument is the "imperial" argument? Why?*
2. *Which argument do you find the most convincing and why?*
3. *Why do you think English Canada was divided over the issue of the navy?*

22. LOYAL CANADIENS REJECT NAVAL BILL

The Nationalist party was a French-Canadian political party formed by Bourassa after he split with Laurier over the Naval Bill. The Nationalists participated in the 1911 federal election, combining with the Conservatives in Quebec to defeat Laurier.

This resolution was passed by the Nationalists in St. Eustache on July 17, 1910. Bourassa included it in his pamphlet, Why the Naval Act Should Be Repealed *(Montreal, 1902).*

We, citizens of Canada, loyal subjects of H. M. King George, we declare ourselves ready to defend with our blood the soil of our country and the rights of the British Crown in Canada, as our fathers did in 1776 against the British subjects of His Majesty, in 1812 against the armies of the American Republic, and as we did in 1885 against our fellow-citizens in rebellion.

Firm in our belief in the greatness and efficiency of the principles of decentralization and self-government, which have been for half a century solemnly proclaimed and acknowledged by both the authorities of Great

Britain and Canada, we are opposed to any new policy, the result of which would be to draw us into distant wars, foreign to Canada, so long, at least, as the self-governing colonies of the Empire shall not enjoy with the mother country, and upon an equal footing, the sovereign power and authority which control the Imperial army and navy, treaties of peace and alliance, foreign relations, and the government of India and of the Crown Colonies.

We sincerely believe that such a policy of centralization and apparent imperial unity, in the accomplishment of which the new naval law is but an initial step, will generate within the Empire misunderstanding, rivalries and conflicts which will threaten the peace and unity of the numerous countries and peoples of all races that are now so proud of their loyalty to the British Crown.

Having never been in the past a case of conflict for Great Britain and the Empire, we believe that a policy of peace and of moral and material development is necessary to Canada, to her growth and unity, and, thereby, to the glory and safety of the Empire.

Free citizens of a democratic country, we claim the right to express openly our sentiment upon this question, as well as upon any other that may affect the fate and the interests of Canada.

We acknowledge the right of the majority of the Canadian people to determine a new course in our relations with the other parts of the Empire, provided such a step is taken in full knowledge of its consequences.

But we protest against any attempt to withdraw such a ponderous problem from the free consideration of the Canadian people at large, and of any of its various groups.

We disavow the declarations made in Toronto in December last by Hon. Alexander Castongueau, provincial minister of public works, by which he callously contended that the people of Quebec were ready to accept blindly any policy of national defence for the Empire and we blame the members of the government and of the legislature of this province, who by their vote, on the second of June last, sanctioned those declarations.

We blame the federal government and the majority in Parliament who have imposed on Canada the new navy legislation, thrown our country in the vortex of militarism, erstwhile so emphatically denounced by Sir Wilfred Laurier, threatened the peace of Canada, and misappropriated for the construction of murderous weapons and the preparation of bloody wars millions destined to the development of our agriculture and means of transportation.

We censure as well the attitude of Mr. Borden and those of his followers who have urged the adoption of a no less nefarious policy.

We maintain that Parliament had no right to pledge the future of Canada to a policy which has never been submitted to the people upon whom shall fall the tribute of blood and the load of military taxation.

We approve unreservedly of the courageous and straightforward conduct of Mr. Monk and the few members of Parliament who, faithful to their trust, have demonstrated the dangers of that policy, and claimed for the people of Canada the right to express their will before their representatives bind them to such heavy obligations.

What do you think?

1. *Why did the gathering at St. Eustache oppose the Naval Bill?*
2. *Judging by the two preceding editorials from the* Manitoba Free Press *and* The Sentinel and Orange and Protestant Advocate, *and by the Nationalist resolutions, had attitudes hardened between 1900 and 1911? Support your answer with evidence.*

The Conscription Crisis of 1917

While at the Imperial Conference in London in 1917, Conservative Prime Minister Robert Borden had been persuaded by the General Staff that conscription was necessary to keep the Canadian Corps, decimated by the heavy casualties of trench warfare, up to strength. Accordingly Borden announced, in June 1917, the Military Service Bill, authorizing the conscription of all single men between eighteen and sixty years of age.

Laurier was vigorously opposed, saying that Canada had already made the maximum effort by fielding 424,000 men from a population of eight million. He felt that conscription would split the country while contributing little to the war effort. Bourassa and his Nationalist party were also vehemently opposed, having by mid-war concluded that Canada should remain neutral during European wars. Public opinion in Quebec became extremely agitated with the passing of the bill in July 1917. The English-Canadian backlash was almost as violent.

Never before had Canada witnessed such bitterness, mistrust and hatred. The election of 1917 showed the extent of the country's division: Laurier's Liberals won sixty-two of Quebec's sixty-five federal seats while gaining only twenty in the rest of Canada.

What was the issue that divided French and English over conscription? To what extent can the attitudes of Quebec in later years be traced to the trauma of 1917?

23. BORDEN'S POSITION

In this extract from the House of Commons Debates *of June 11, 1917, Prime Minister Borden stated the issue as he saw it. (Reprinted by permission of Information Canada.)*

I desire to point out that this enactment is based upon the principle, which is as old as the principle of self-government, that while the state owes to its citizens certain duties, the citizen also owes corresponding duties to the state. To the citizen the state assures protection and security of his person and property, the enforcement of law and orderly government. To the state, each citizen owes a duty of service, and the highest duty of all is the obligation to assist in defending the rights, the institutions and the liberties of his country. I desire to express my profound conviction that there never has been, and there never will be, an occasion when that duty could be more manifest, more urgent, or more imperative than at the present time.

What do you think?

1. (a) *Do you think the state has a right to conscript its citizens for military service? Why or why not?*
    (b) *Do you think a citizen has a right to refuse to serve? Why or why not? Under what circumstances do you think a citizen can refuse, if you feel he can?*
    (c) *Do you feel a minority, or a group, of people has the right to seek collective exemption from conscription? Why or why not?*
2. *How do you think a French Canadian would have answered Borden's argument?*

24. LAURIER'S POSITION

The first reading here is an excerpt from a speech made by Sir Wilfrid Laurier in 1914 in which he outlined his views on the war and Canada's place in it. Laurier's speech was reported in The Canadian Annual Review *(Toronto: Castell Hopkins, 1915). The second document was a speech made on November 4, 1917, during the election campaign. Laurier here makes clear his position on conscription (*The Canadian Annual Review, *1918).*

(a) "I affirm it with all my power" he declared, "that it is the duty of Canada to give to Great Britain in this war all the assistance that is in the power of Canada. The reason is that this war is a contest between German institutions and British institutions. British institutions mean freedom, German institutions mean despotism. That is why we as Canadians have such a vital interest in this war." His final appeal was personal and powerful:

"I have fought for justice, for tolerance and for freedom as God gave me to understand justice, tolerance and freedom. This has been the aim of my life, and I think that the attitude which I take at the present time is fashioned after the model I set for myself. I am an old man but rather than in this war see Belgium, France and England dismembered and Germany triumph, I pray that God will not let me see that day. But it is not my death that I am looking for. I am thankful to God that He has given me enough strength yet in my old age to be able to fight this battle. What is the duty of our young men? If I were a young man and I had the health which I have today and which I did not have when I was young, I would not hesitate to take the musket, and to fight for freedom, as so many of our fellow-countrymen are doing. I cannot do that now. But there is one thing I can do, I can use my voice, such as it is, in the great cause in which we all have such a supreme interest. This is the message that I bring to you upon this occasion. The peril is at present great. We must not rest under the misapprehension of false security. If we want to win, we must be worthy of freedom, we have to be prepared to fight for freedom."

(b) As to the present Military Service Act, my policy will be not to proceed further under its provisions until the people have an opportunity to pronounce upon it by way of a referendum. . . . It is a fact that cannot be denied that the voluntary system, especially in Quebec, did not get a fair trial. . . . It is no answer to say as is now often said that we must have conscription or "quit". . . . Australia rejected conscription and did not "quit." Australia is still in the fight under the voluntary system.

What do you think?

1. What was Laurier's attitude towards the war? How acceptable do you think his views were to French Canadians in 1914?
2. What was his attitude towards conscription? Did it conflict with his attitude towards the war? Why or why not?
3. ". . . the voluntary system, especially in Quebec, did not get a fair trial." Explain why Laurier said this.

25. BOURASSA ON THE WAR

Henri Bourassa, founder of Le Devoir *and a prominent political figure, was an ardent French-Canadian nationalist and deeply suspicious of any Canadian involvement in European conflicts.*

A French-Canadian army officer, Captain Talbot Papineau, wrote a letter denouncing the nationalist position on the war. This selection is a translation of Bourassa's reply to Captain Papineau which he published in Le Devoir *August 5, 1916. (Reprinted by permission of* Le Devoir.)

I had accepted, within reasonable limits consistent with conditions in our country, the free, independent intervention of Canada—free for the nation and free for individuals; but the government, the whole parliament, the politicians and the press of both parties have set out to systematically destroy this spirit of freedom. "Voluntary" enlistment is achieved by means of blackmail, intimidation and threats of all kinds. But above all, these people have taken advantage of the emotion aroused by the war to re-affirm, in its most intense and intolerant form, the doctrine of imperial solidarity, a doctrine which was fought and triumphantly repelled by statesmen in the past and by the whole Canadian people, until the occasion of the infamous war in Africa campaign, plotted by Chamberlain, Rhodes and the English imperialists with the manifest intention of dragging autonomous colonies "into the abyss of European militarism." No doubt you recall this expression—it belongs to your political leader, Sir Wilfrid Laurier. After allowing themselves to be swept along on the imperialist current in 1889, Mr. Laurier and the Liberal party had regained their self-possession and returned to the doctrine of nationalism. The naval panic of 1909 caused them to pass once more under the yoke of imperialism; the war brought about their complete enslavement; they joined forces with the Tories, the jingoists and imperialists of all shades to make Canada's intervention in the war a huge political manoeuvre and to ensure the triumph of British imperialism. You and your associate, like many others, echoed the changing policies of your party. I stood firm by the principles which I propounded as far back as the African War and which I have upheld unwaveringly until now. . . .

French Canadians comprise a far larger population of farmers who are also the fathers of large families, than any other ethnic group in Canada. Above all, they are the only group that is wholly Canadian, as a group and by virtue of the individuals that make up the group. The upheavals in Europe, even those in England or France, are foreign affairs as far as they are concerned. Naturally, their sympathies are with France and against Germany; but they do not think of themselves as French. European Frenchmen would not feel obliged to fight for Canada against the United States, Japan, or even Germany, if Germany were to attack Canada without threatening France's security.

English Canadians, apart from the *blokes,* comprise a considerable proportion of people who are still in the first stages of assimilation. A fairly large number, under the pressure of imperialist propaganda, still have not made up their minds whether they belong to Canada rather than the Empire, and whether the United Kingdom is not just as much their homeland as the Canadian Confederation.

As for the newcomers from the United Kingdom, they are in no way Canadian. Their only homeland is England or Scotland. They enlisted for the war in Europe in the same way that French or English Canadians would enlist to defend Canada against American aggression.

Hence it is completely accurate to say that this recruitment is in inverse ratio to the development of Canadian nationalism. The newcomers from the United Kingdom, who have provided a far bigger proportion of recruits than any other sector of the population, would have just as much right to accuse English Canadians of treason and lack of patriotism, as the latter would have to reproach the French Canadians with their low number of recruits.

What do you think?

1. *What do you think Bourassa's position during the conscription crisis was? Give his position on the war. When do you think Bourassa might support conscription and why?*
2. *Compare Bourassa's opinion about the war to Laurier's in the preceding readings. What do you notice? Would their different attitudes towards the war produce different attitudes on conscription? What would the differences be? Account for them.*
3. *"For many English Canadians, nationalism and imperialism were two sides of the same coin." Is this correct? Support your answer with evidence. How does Bourassa's letter support this statement?*

26.   PRESS OPINION IN ENGLISH CANADA

Three editorials from the English-language press in Canada follow. The first is taken from the May 31, 1917, issue of the magazine of the Orange Lodge. (Reprinted by permission of the Sentinel and Orange and Protestant Advocate.*) The second is from the* Manitoba Free Press, *July 7, 1917. The third is from the* Monetary Times, *December 14, 1917.*

(a) THE SENTINEL AND ORANGE AND PROTESTANT ADVOCATE

Whatever its faults may be, whatever bungles it has committed, there can be no doubt that the present government is wholeheartedly in favour of contributing all the resources of Canada to assist in achieving a peace with victory. These are circumstances which history will record as complete justification for any extraordinary steps that may be found imperative in order to continue Canada's participation in the war at its full strength. The time has passed for any further paltering with nationalism or pacifism. Academic views of a government's duty should have no weight on public policy today. To win the war is the one consideration that should govern those who are charged with the enormous responsibilities to administer the affairs of the country. Nothing else counts at this time. For if Britain dies, Canada cannot live.

(b) THE MANITOBA FREE PRESS

Of the division (second reading of the Military Service Bill, 1917), it may be said that it is the nearest approach to a straight split upon racial lines that the Canadian Parliament has ever known. Of the fifty-five votes against the measure, forty-three were cast by French-Canadian members. Of the one hundred and eighteen members voting for the bill, only five were French Canadians. The figures are eloquent as to whither we are drifting in Canada. Quebec has only to keep on insisting that her point of view must be honored as the only basis for national unity, to bring about in the near future a virtually solid English block in opposition to these pretensions. This lies at the end of the road we are now travelling; nothing is to be gained by pretending otherwise. This would be a catastrophe, but it is not to be avoided by the majority submitting to the demands of the minority. Even majorities have rights in this country. If there is to be a betterment in relations—which is much to be desired—it must begin by our French-Canadian friends displaying a reasonable regard for the feelings and convictions of their English fellow countrymen in this matter of the war.

(c) THE MONETARY TIMES

To-day, in our national crisis, Quebec alone, among all the provinces, stands more united than ever before. She knows what she wants:

(1) Withdrawal from the War.
(2) Bi-lingual schools everywhere.
(3) Weakening of the ties of British connection.
(4) Political control of Canada.

From the Ottawa River to Labrador and the Gulf a common purpose actuates Quebec in her determination to profit by the factional divisions of Canada and to impose her will upon all the people of Canada. Within the last few weeks Quebec has mobilized all her forces to dominate Canada under the unified leadership of Bourassa and Laurier. . . . With sixty solid seats Quebec is about to accomplish her designs. Bourassa, the real master and idol of Quebec, is in sight of his goal. To attain her purpose, Quebec has not scrupled to ignore British traditions and to suppress freedom of speech. So thoroughly organized is her campaign to prevent even the discussion of the war that Unionist candidates are prevented from holding public meetings throughout that province. The Unionist minority in Quebec are the victims of organized obstruction. To be successful in her determination to rule all Canada, Quebec has but to secure a few seats in each of the other provinces. United in her determination to quit the war, Quebec would compel a divided Canada to do likewise. By union only can the English-speaking people prevent this calamity.

What do you think?

1. *Explain the significance of the following statements. What do they reveal about English-Canadian opinion?*
   (a) "For if Britain dies, Canada cannot live."
   (b) "Even majorities have rights in this country."
   (c) "From the Ottawa River to Labrador and the Gulf a common purpose actuates Quebec in her determination to profit by the factional divisions of Canada and to impose her will upon all the people of Canada."
   Are similar sentiments ever expressed today? Support your answer.

The Conscription Question of 1942–44

When Canada entered the war both the Liberal and Conservative parties pledged themselves to co-operate fully with Britain but not to conscript Canadians, especially for service outside Canada. However, the full impact of the war created pressure on Prime Minister Mackenzie King to invoke conscription. In 1942 he held a national plebiscite asking if the country would release him from this no conscription pledge of 1939. English Canada voted 79 percent "yes" while Quebec answered 72 percent "no." These results made King even more reluctant about bringing in conscription. The principle of conscription for overseas service was accepted by the government, but only volunteers for overseas duty were sent. However, by 1944, public opinion and the senior military staff brought renewed pressure to bear on King. After several cabinet crises, King agreed to send conscripts overseas.

What is your opinion of the way King handled the second conscription crisis? How do you think the experience of 1917 influenced King's policy?

27.   KING INTERPRETS THE PLEBISCITE RESULTS

Prime Minister King announced the results of the 1942 plebiscite to the House of Commons on May 11, 1942, and gave his interpretation of them. (Reprinted by permission of Information Canada.)

The results of the plebiscite on April 27 are now all but complete. Although final official returns are not yet available, the most reliable figures indicate that on the question asked there were over 2,926,856 persons who voted in the affirmative, and over 1,618,730 persons who voted in the negative; in other words, 64 percent of the voters answered in the affirmative and 36 percent in the negative.

The total number of votes cast on the plebiscite is an impressive demonstration of the importance which the electors of Canada attach to giving to the government a free hand at a time of war.

The question on which the people of Canada were asked to express an opinion was—

> Are you in favour of releasing the government from any obligation arising out of any past commitments restricting the methods of raising men for military service?

By their vote, the people have decisively expressed the view that the government should be released from any such obligation. In other words, there no longer remains any issue which the government or members of parliament, because of past promises or pledges, are restricted from considering, discussing and deciding on its merits, in the light of what is best for Canada and for Canada's war effort.

The question in the plebiscite was of equal concern to all citizens of Canada. The result is a national expression of view on a national issue. It should be so viewed in all its aspects. In all of the provinces, and for that matter, in every constituency, affirmative and negative votes were cast. The vote was taken in a democratic fashion. It will be recognized throughout the country that, in a democracy, the will of the majority should prevail.

The vote in the plebiscite shows that the people generally recognize that the war has taken a course which was altogether unforeseen; that conditions wholly unexpected may yet arise; and that, in consequence, there should be no restriction upon the freedom of the government apart from its constitutional responsibility to parliament.

In the plebiscite, the electors were not called upon to vote for or against the government. The result, therefore, is not to be construed as a vote for any political party. In fact, the plebiscite was selected by the government precisely because it afforded the best known means of obtaining an expression of the views of the people on a specific question, regardless of political parties, or party considerations.

As, in some quarters, an effort has been made since the plebiscite to interpret the result as a mandate for conscription for overseas service, it is necessary for me to repeat that, in the plebiscite, conscription was not the issue. The government did not ask the people to say whether or not conscription for overseas service should be adopted. That was not the issue before the people. With respect to the issue of conscription, the result can only rightly be construed as leaving to the government and to parliament entire freedom to deal with that question on its merits.

What do you think?

1. *What interpretation did King give the results? What other interpretation was given to it?*
2. *How does the wording of the question given in the plebiscite show Prime Minister King's skill as a politician? In view of the ambiguity of the question in the plebiscite, why do you think King held the plebiscite?*

28. THE MAJORITY BROKE ITS WORD

On July 23, 1942, a French-Canadian M.P., E. P. Raymond, gave his own interpretation of the plebiscite results to the House of Commons. (Reprinted by permission of Information Canada.)

MR. RAYMOND: They are rights. There was a contract in 1867, and I dare anyone in this house or anyone outside it to cite one fact to show that the province of Quebec has not fulfilled all its obligations under the British North America Act. In the province of Quebec, French Canadians are the majority, and we have always fulfilled our obligations and always respected the rights of the minority. Unfortunately, however, I do not think the same can be said of all the other provinces.

In a democracy the majority should rule, but may I add that the majority should never abuse its powers, and when a pledge has been given by the majority to the minority it is sacred. In this case a most solemn pledge, so qualified by the Prime Minister, was given by the majority to the minority. Think of it! We are now asked to pass a bill to conscript men to go and fight for a broken pledge. It has been said that the government has been released from that pledge. That is not a fact. The government has not been relieved from its pledge because the pledge was given to the minority. I have only to refer to the compromise made in September, 1939. Mr. Lapointe, speaking in the name of the province of Quebec, said this, when war was declared. I am quoting from page 68 of *Hansard* of that date:

> The whole province of Quebec . . . will never agree to accept compulsory service or conscription outside of Canada. . . .
> Provided these points are understood, we are willing to offer our

services without limitation and to devote our best efforts for the success of the cause we all have at heart.

This is the condition which has been asked of the majority for our participation. It was agreed to, and the Prime Minister has said that it was the most solemn pledge that had ever been given to a group. When they say that the plebiscite has relieved the government from its pledge I say no, because the pledge was given by the majority to the minority, and the province of Quebec has voted almost unanimously against relieving the government from this pledge. But to-day we are asked in the name of national unity to relieve the government from its pledge when the population has refused to do so; and because the province of Quebec is refusing, some people treat the province of Quebec as a disloyal province. Since when has disloyalty consisted in asking someone to respect their pledge? Is it not the one who wants to violate the pledge that is disloyal?

I am not going to insist any more, but I wanted to say to the House before this bill passes that if it is passed it is passed at the price of a broken pledge.

What do you think?

1. (a) "The result is a national expression of a view on a national issue" (King, House of Commons Debates, May 11, 1942).
   (b) "The government has not been relieved from its pledge because the pledge was given to the minority."
   What is the difference between Mr. King's and Mr. Raymond's interpretation of the plebiscite? Whom do you agree with and why?

29. CANADA IN PERIL

In this speech, part of which is recorded here, W. S. Hanson, an M.P. from York-Sunbury, urged that the House support conscription (House of Commons Debates, July 23, 1942). (Reprinted by permission of Information Canada.)

We have been at war for nearly three years. For nine months of that period of time the war seemed to the people of Canada a very remote affair. Then came Dunkirk, when those of us who were following intensely the situation came to the realization that there was a great possibility that this war might be lost. Then came the period when Britain herself was in danger, when all that stood between us and a horde of Huns who might pour across the Atlantic Ocean was the British navy; when in fact and in deed our front line of defence was overseas, and when I thought, and all people who think as I do were driven to the conclusion, that the war must be kept away from these shores if it was humanly possible.

*   *   *   *   *

I appeal to my fellow citizens in this country of Canada, to my fellow members on all sides of this House, to Canadian men and women of whatever racial origin they may be, to unite to repel the common foe, because a nation divided against itself cannot stand. We should not allow ideas which have grown up upon erroneous premises over a period of years to blind us to the significance of present-day events and the potentialities of the immediate future.

Therefore, Mr. Speaker, my last word to the membership of this House tonight is this. No matter what our political differences may be; no matter what our opinions may have been on the war effort of this government in days gone by, when this nation is in as dire peril as I believe it is today, and when the united nations are in as dire peril as I conceive them to be, let us forget past differences, party politics and partisanship. Let us unite as never before so that we can say to our children and our children's children: when Canada was in peril, the Canadian people united.

What do you think?

1. *"We should not allow ideas which have grown up upon erroneous premises over a period of years to blind us to the significance of present-day events and the potentialities of the immediate future."*
   (a) *What is the significance of this remark?*
   (b) *To what extent do you think French-Canadian ideas in 1942 were moulded by the memories of 1917? Explain why you feel the way you do.*
2. *Why did Mr. Hanson emphasize the point that Canada's "front line of defence was overseas"? How do you think French Canadians would react to this argument and why?*

30.   IN THE WAKE OF EMPIRE

Mr. Liguori Lacombe, a French-Canadian M.P. from Laval–Two Mountains, spoke to the House about conscription on November 29, 1944. (Reprinted by permission of Information Canada.)

One last word. Since Canada has started participating in the war, we have lost all our prerogatives. We have reverted to century-old colonialism. Our country, thanks to the acts and errors of the government, is now trailing for good in the wake of the Empire to the great satisfaction of our partisans of colonialism. Let us hope that we may forsake this chaotic situation to unfurl at last a Canadian flag in an independent country, mistress of its own destinies. Whether we wish it or not, the deep reactions of the post-war period are bound to bring about the independence of Canada.

At last, because they have camouflaged the facts, the government who have willingly declared war must inevitably be led to conscription. Let them shoulder their dreadful responsibility in this matter, which they share with those who have refused to support the amendment I moved against participation in the war, on September 9, 1939. Their attitude at that time has been and still is the main cause of conscription. If, in 1917, a similar measure was a tremendous mistake, to use the expressions of the former minister of justice, it is doubly wrong today. The experience of the last war should have been a warning to the administration. The Canadian people, after seeing the economical structure of their country threatened, besides shouldering too heavy a burden of taxes and loans must, by the expressed will of their government, pay the blood tax. Such are the deferred, but dire results of the military and financial imperialism laid down as a creed by the very people who claimed they were opposing it.

Personally, I shall maintain the attitude I have taken, resolved to fight to the end against this unjustifiable measure.

What do you think?

1. "We have reverted to century-old colonialism." Why did Mr. Lacombe use this argument? Was its use legitimate? Why or why not?
2. How do Mr. Lacombe's remarks reveal the lasting effects of 1917?
3. (a) Compare positions taken and arguments advanced by the two sides in 1942-44 and in 1917?
   (b) Were the steps taken to solve the problem in 1944 more or less effective than those taken in 1917?
4. "The one thing we learn from history is that we learn nothing from history." To what extent does your study of these two conscription crises bear out this statement?

The Manitoba Schools Question, 1890–96

In the nineteenth century, religion played a much larger role in people's lives than perhaps it does today, and the tradition of religious instruction included in formal education was accepted uncritically. Since Canada was made up of a Protestant majority and a Roman Catholic minority, the educational rights of minorities had been a crucial issue in the Confederation debates. The same issue surfaced again several times in Canadian history in New Brunswick (1870–76), Manitoba, Alberta and Saskatchewan (1905) and Ontario (1917). The Manitoba case, which is perhaps the best known of these, illustrates clearly the political controversies surrounding the issue of minority education.

In the face of the political storm surrounding the 1870 Riel Rebellion in Red River, John A. Macdonald's Conservative government granted the tiny settlement provincial status. The new province, Manitoba, was given the same constitution as Quebec's, which included identical guarantees protecting minority rights. However, by the 1890s the population of Manitoba, with the large immigration from Ontario, had become largely English speaking and Protestant. In 1890 the Manitoba legislature abolished tax support for Catholic schools.

French Canada was outraged with the Roman Catholic leadership in particular. It appeared to French Canada that by the action of the Manitoba legislature, French minority rights were to be confined to Quebec alone. Quebec demanded that the federal government use its power of remedial legislation contained in the BNA Act, to repeal the Manitoba legislation. English Canada, influenced by such organizations as the Orange Lodge and the Protestant Protective Association, opposed any such resort to remedial legislation. Education became the major issue in the 1896 federal election, which Wilfrid Laurier, who opposed remedial action, won.

How did the 1870 Manitoba constitution interpret the nature of Confederation regarding biculturalism? How did the Manitoba legislature change this interpretation in 1890? Why did Wilfrid Laurier, a French Canadian, oppose remedial legislation? What was the significance of his victory for the future of French Canada in Confederation? How did the issue affect French-English relations at that time? To what extent has the issue, and its resolution, contributed to today's situation?

31. NOT A QUESTION OF SEPARATE SCHOOLS

Sir Charles Tupper, Conservative prime minister during this period, favoured the use of remedial legislation in the Manitoba case. Speaking during the debate on the Remedial Bill in the House of Commons, May 3, 1896, Tupper urged very strongly that the legislation be passed.

. . . no man . . . can read . . . the emphatic statements made by the Lords of the Judicial Committee of the Privy Council without arriving at the conclusion that the responsibility and the duty were transferred from the legislature and government of Manitoba and imposed on the central government of the Dominion and on the Parliament of the Dominion to legislate in respect to this case.

. . . no man who takes the trouble to examine this question can for a single moment consider that the question of separate schools is at issue at all. It is not a question of separate schools, it is a question of the constitution of the country. The progress and the prosperity and the future development of Canada depend upon that constitution being sacredly maintained, and that all the rights that are guaranteed under it, whether to the central or the provincial governments, shall be sacredly guarded.

No person can read this bill without seeing on the very face of it that it is not proposed that the government of Canada should take action under this bill, by the appointment of a board, or by the appointment of the superintendents, to guarantee that the [French] schools shall be of the same high character as that of the other schools in Manitoba, for, before all that is done, this bill provides, first, to invite the government of the province of Manitoba to take action: and it is only when they refuse, and when the unpleasant and disagreeable duty is forced by the Act of the Imperial Parliament upon the Dominion of Canada, that this government proposes, in the least degree, to interfere with this matter. And, as I say, the coercion does not come from the Dominion government. . . . There is a simple, a most easy and natural provision to meet the interests of these people whose consciences deprive them from the opportunity of making use of such schools in Manitoba as they are now taxed to sustain. Under these circumstances, the government have been compelled to adopt the policy which they have adopted. I need not say that they have adopted this policy in the face of great difficulty, because it is always an extremely unpleasant thing for any government to find itself in a position in which there is even a single member of their party that does not see eye to eye with them. In the face of even this difficulty, the government have felt compelled, in justice to their own position, and in regard to their duty to the country as imposed by the Imperial Act, the government have felt obliged to take the step they have taken.

What do you think?

1. *"It is not a question of separate schools, it is a question of the constitution of the country." Why did Tupper support remedial legislation?*
2. *(a) In a federal system, what is meant by "centralist"? What is meant by "decentralist"?*
   (b) Would you call Tupper's view of federalism centralist or decentralist? Why?

3. (a) Argue the case that a strong central government is the best protection of minority rights in Canada.

(b) Would the Fathers of Confederation have agreed with you? How can you tell?

32. PROVINCIAL RIGHTS

Wilfrid Laurier, leader of the Liberal party, spoke on the subject of remedial legislation to an English-speaking audience at Massey Hall in Toronto. Laurier's remarks were reported in the Globe, June 13, 1896. *(Reprinted by permission of* The Globe, Toronto.*)*

The principle of provincial rights is the basis of Confederation. (Cheers.) But, strange to say, an old idea, not in accordance with that principle, lingers in the Constitution; and since it is there, it should be met in a statesmanlike manner. The government have adopted a double-faced policy, having a face for each province; a good, pious Roman Catholic face for the province of Quebec, and a stern Protestant face for the province of Ontario. (Cheers and laughter.) Day after day he [Laurier] was proclaimed as a traitor to his race and religion because he had refused to vote for the remedial bill. (Cheers.) He had only this answer to make: that he was true to Canada, because being true to Canada he was at the same time true to his race. In Ontario the Conservatives say that if Laurier comes into power he will bring in a still more drastic measure of coercion. . . . He was there to say not that he would give either a small or large amount of relief to the minority, but that, assisted by his friend, Sir Oliver Mowat, [premier of Ontario and strong supporter of provincial rights] he would settle the question, not by appeal to any class, but by appeal to the sense of justice which was implanted in everyone by the Creator. He was a Roman Catholic and a French Canadian, and therefore might have strong sympathy for the minority. But as he himself would not be coerced by anybody, so he would not consent to force coercion upon anybody. (Prolonged cheering.)

What do you think?

1. "The principle of provincial rights is the basis of Confederation."
(a) What is meant by "provincial rights"?
(b) Why do you think Laurier felt that French minority rights could be best protected by a doctrine of provincial rights? Do you agree with him? Why or why not?
2. How do you think Laurier sold his case to Quebec?

33.   IS THIS COUNTRY TO BE ENGLISH OR FRENCH?

Dalton McCarthy, a Toronto lawyer and prominent Conservative M.P., became the leading spokesman for the Equal Rights Association, the ironically named organization which focussed Protestant bigotry and extremism in Ontario. This reading is an excerpt from a report of a speech given by Mr. McCarthy in Portage La Prairie on August 5, 1889, shortly before Manitoba abolished its denominational school system. The speech was reported in the Manitoba Free Press, *August 7, 1889.*

We have just to remember that the same difficulties occurred in the neighbouring republic. They had French people in the state of Louisiana; but did they allow French to be spoken in the courts, the schools and the legislative halls? They had Spaniards in other parts, and the same attempt was made to keep up the language, race, religion, marching in procession with flags, etc., but the rest of the people, Republicans and Democrats, united and stood on the same platform and the Spanish flag was lowered, and the people became American citizens. The speaker had been in Parliament a dozen years, and had watched this movement growing year by year; and he declared that the people were more French now than ten years ago, and if this thing were not stopped they would be more French ten years hence than now. He had seen it stated in a Winnipeg paper that Mr. Mowat had nothing to do with the Jesuits' estates; but if Mr. Mowat was sanctioning the French language in schools, of which there were over fifty, contrary to the public school law, the people would want to know the reason why. Ontario would give no uncertain sound; and whether Mr. Mowat falls or stands must depend upon his course in regard to this question. Mr. McCarthy had been glad to see it announced that next session the legislature of Manitoba would find a measure introduced to blot out the dual language in the province. (Prolonged applause). He went on to speak of the silence of both sides of the House of Commons when the curse of the dual language was coolly planted upon this province. We were to be brought up with two nationalities in our midst. . . . He had pledged himself to his own constituents to move at Ottawa to expunge the dual language out of the Northwest Territories Act. There was something for the politician to live for; we have the power to save this country from fratricidal strife, the power to make this a British country in fact as it is in name. In order to accomplish this, other issues must for the moment give way. We have got to bend our energies and let it be understood in every constituency that, whether a man call himself Grit or Tory, Conservative or Reformer, his record is clear, his principles are sound and no influence at Ottawa will induce him to betray his great trust. The speaker was glad to inform the meeting that the poor, sleepy Protestant minority of Quebec were at last awake. He trusted before many weeks to address a meeting in Montreal, and to realize that that minority is sound to the core on this question.

What do you think?

1. Describe what you think Mr. McCarthy envisaged as the place of French Canada in Canada.
2. Why did Mr. McCarthy refer to the Protestant minority of Quebec? Do you find this ironic? Why or why not?
3. How would English-speaking Roman Catholics respond to an appeal like Mr. McCarthy's? Why?

34.   FATHER LACOMBE ADDRESSES LAURIER

Father Lacombe, a French-Canadian Oblate missionary, was one of the first and perhaps the most important of the Roman Catholic missionaries working in the Canadian Northwest. Father Lacombe wrote Laurier on January 20, 1896. (O. D. Skelton: The Life and Letters of Sir Wilfrid Laurier *[Toronto, 1921].)*

In this critical time for the question of the Manitoba schools, permit an aged missionary, today representing the bishops of your country in this cause, which concerns us all, permit me to appeal to your faith, to your patriotism and to your spirit of justice, to entreat you to accede to our request. It is in the name of our bishops, of the hierarchy and the Catholics of Canada, that we ask the party of which you are the very worthy chief, to assist us in settling this famous question, and to do so by voting with the government on the Remedial Bill. We do not ask you to vote for the government, but for the bill, which will render us our rights, the bill which will be presented to the House in a few days.

I consider, or rather we all consider, that such an act of courage, good-will, and sincerity on your part and from those who follow your policy will be greatly in the interests of your party, especially in the general elections. I must tell you that we cannot accept your commission of enquiry on any account, and shall do our best to fight it.

If, which may God not grant, you do not believe it to be your duty to accede to our just demands, and if the government, which is anxious to give us the promised law, is beaten and overthrown while keeping firm to the end of the struggle, I inform you, with regret, that the episcopacy, like one man, united with the clergy, will rise to support those who may have fallen in defending us.

Please pardon the frankness which leads me to speak thus, though I am not your intimate friend, still I may say that we have been on good terms. Always I have deemed you a gentleman, a respectable citizen, and a man well fitted to be at the head of a political party. May Divine Providence keep up your courage and your energy for the good of our common country.

What do you think?

1. What was the Roman Catholic church's position on remedial legislation?
2. Would you call this letter of Lacombe's to Laurier a threat? Why or why not?
3. How much influence do you think the Roman Catholic church could bring to bear in Canadian politics at this time? Why? In what way?

Confederation

At the heart of the controversy surrounding French-English relations in Canada is the nature and purpose of Confederation. Some have claimed either that Confederation and the BNA Act in reality gave French Canada very little in the first place, or that the agreement has since proved to be completely unworkable. In the view of these commentators, the Confederation agreement should be scrapped entirely. Others feel that the terms of 1867 have merely become outdated or unwieldy, that the guarantees given French Canada are no longei sufficient, given the modern role of government. Consequently, they feel, the idea of Confederation should be retained, but the BNA Act should be revised. Another section of opinion holds that the terms of 1867 are sufficient and that the French-Canadian leaders of the time were well aware of the consequences of Confederation. Thus, their argument was that the agreement should be retained in its original form, but all Canadians should make a greater effort to live up to the terms set in 1867.

What *was* promised in 1867? What *were* the French-Canadian leaders seeking for their people in Confederation? What opposition did Confederation encounter at the time and why?

To what extent should we be bound today by historical agreements? On what principles of politics or morality could changes in historical treaties be allowed? If the 1867 agreement is changed, are we violating history or adapting to it?

35. SUPPORTERS OF CONFEDERATION

Below are three selections representing the pro-Confederation arguments in Lower Canada. The first two selections are taken from the 1865 Confederation Debates. The third is from a newspaper, Le Journal de Québec.

ETIENNE P. TACHÉ, FEBRUARY 3, 1865

. . . in a Federal Union . . . all questions of a general nature would be reserved for the General Government, and those of a local character to the local governments, who would have the power to manage their domestic affairs as they deemed best. If a Federal Union were obtained it would be tantamount to a separation of the provinces, and Lower Canada would thereby preserve its autonomy together with all the institutions it held so dear, and over which they could exercise the watchfulness and surveillance necessary to preserve them unimpaired. . . .

J. DUFRESNE, MARCH 10, 1865

. . . I accept them (the Seventy-two Resolutions) for many reasons, but chiefly as a means of obtaining the repeal of the present legislative union of Canada, and securing peaceable settlement of our sectional difficulties. I accept them, in the second place, as a means of obtaining for Lower Canada the absolute and exclusive control of her own affairs. I accept them, thirdly, as a means of perpetuating French-Canadian nationality in this country. I accept them, fourthly, as a more effectual means of cementing our connection with the Mother Country, and avoiding annexation to the United States. I accept them, fifthly and lastly, as a means of administering the affairs of the colony with greater economy. Such are my reasons for accepting the Confederation scheme submitted to us by the Government. . . .

LE JOURNAL DE QUÉBEC, DECEMBER 17, 1864

We want to be a nation one day, and as that is our necessary destiny and the goal to which we aspire, we prefer the political condition of which we will be a vital element and in which we will still be in existence, rather than to be thrown into the midst of an immense people, like a drop of water lost in the ocean, where in a few years we would lose our language, our laws, and even the memory of our glorious origins.

What do you think?

1. From the remarks made by Etienne Taché, J. Dufresne, and Le Journal de Québec, outline what you think those French Canadians

who were in favour of Confederation thought that the Confederation agreement meant for
(a) Quebec (Lower Canada)
(b) French Canadians in Canada.
Do you feel that modern-day French-Canadian agitation is an
attempt to see these views realized or do you feel rather that
today's demands for certain rights are for new rights, ones not
thought of in 1867? Defend your answer.

36. OPPONENTS OF CONFEDERATION

The next three selections represent Lower-Canadian opinion opposed
to the Confederation agreement. The first two documents are taken
from the 1865 Confederation Debates. The third comes from a French-
language newspaper, Le Pays.

ANTOINE A. DORION, MARCH 6, 1865
. . . I am opposed to this Confederation in which the militia, the
appointment of the judges, the administration of justice and our most
important civil rights will be under the control of a General Government,
the majority of which will be hostile to Lower Canada, of a General
Government invested with the most ample powers, whilst the powers of
the local governments will be restricted, first, by the limitation of the
powers delegated to it, by the Veto reserved to the central authority and
further, by the concurrent jurisdiction of the general authority or government. . . .

CHRISTOPHER DUNKIN, FEBRUARY 27, 1865
. . . They (the French Canadians) will find themselves a minority
in the General Legislature, and their power in the General Government
will depend upon their power within their own province and over their
provincial delegations in the Federal Parliament. They will thus be compelled to be practically aggressive, to secure and retain that power . . .
there will certainly be in this system (Federal Union) the very strongest
tendencies to make them practically aggressive upon the rights of the
minority in language and faith, and at the same time to make the minority
most suspicious and resentful of aggression. . . .

LE PAYS, DECEMBER 29, 1864
1. Because the new system would be expensive and complicated;
2. Because it would imperil the institutions and the religious faith, as well
as the autonomy, of the French-Canadian nationality, guaranteed by solemn
treaties and Imperial statutes; 3. Because it would impose on this province
pecuniary obligations which were incumbent exclusively and by law on the
other provinces of British North America, and very onerous material
sacrifices, such as direct taxation, without procuring in return in this region

any real or tangible benefit; 4. Because it would very probably instigate, sooner or later, throughout the said provinces, and particularly in this region, civil troubles and perhaps very serious ones.

What do you think?

1. *Compare the views of Taché (in the reading preceding these) and Dorion on the effectiveness of federalism in guaranteeing French-Canadian rights. Whose views have been borne out by history? Support your answer with evidence.*
2. *According to Christopher Dunkin, how would French Canadians ensure that their voice would be heard in the General Government? How would this condition affect politics in Quebec and federal politics? Do you think that Dunkin's prophecies about minority-majority relations have been proved correct?*
3. *Why do you think Le Pays predicted "civil troubles"?*

37. LATER OPINION: TARDIVEL

Jules-Paul Tardivel was a French-Canadian writer of separatist inclination. This selection is taken from Tardivel's newspaper La Vérité, *March 18, 1893. (Cited in K. A. MacKirdy, J. S. Moir, and Y. F. Zoltvany:* Changing Perspectives in Canadian History: Selected Documents and Problems *[Don Mills: J. M. Dent, 1971].)*

Since our newspaper began we have often stated our hope of seeing a French Canada, a New France, emerge on the shores of the St. Lawrence River. Confederation never appeared to us as the final state of our national destinies. It is too vast and contains too many jarring and even hostile elements to become a true fatherland. It is large enough to permit the formation and peaceful co-existence of several independent nations. Our ambitions, as French Canadians, must be to establish solidly in this St. Lawrence Valley, cradle of our race, a new fatherland, French, and let us not fear to add, Catholic.

How and when will the French-Canadian people assume the place to which they are so evidently called among the autonomous nations of the earth? That is God's secret. But sooner or later that hour will certainly strike if we remain true to the Providential mission which He has assigned to us. This mission consists of carrying on in North America the work of Christianization and civilization which Catholic France accomplished through so many centuries and which she might still accomplish today if only she returned to what in the past were her sources of strength and glory.

This providential hour will strike, be certain of it, for it is inconceivable that God could not have willed to make a true nation of the

French-Canadian people whose birth and youth he has so visibly protected. It is folly to believe that the destiny of this prolific and vigorous race, which has acquired such strong roots in the St. Lawrence Valley, is to merge with its surrounding elements or to remain eternally in this violently unnatural state of a race distinct but not independent.

For despite all one might say or do, the French Canadians do form a people apart in Confederation and unless they are renegades to their mission they will never allow themselves to be assimilated. Once this principle is admitted, political union with people with whom they have nothing in common will always appear as an abomination. . . .

Some will perhaps say that the withdrawal of Quebec from Confederation is today impossible. We do admit that it is difficult, but difficult or even very difficult is not the same as impossible.

What appears to be manifestly impossible is the continuation of the present political régime for any length of time, unless the French-Canadian race accepts collective suicide and disappearance as a distinct entity. Change appears inevitable. Some speak of annexation, others of independence. . . .

Annexation to the United States would mean a struggle for national existence against 65,000,000 people. And we already find this struggle difficult against three or four million.

As for independence of Canada, it would in no way ensure the independence of French Canada. We would still be riveted to a people who hate us and who yearn for our disappearance.

Confederation was perhaps necessary twenty-five years ago to avoid a civil war. But it was a transitory form of government and it has now run its course. It has become a threat both to French Canada and to public peace and order. What was supposed to avoid a racial war is today the cause of worsening clashes and must necessarily end in catastrophe.

What do you think?

1. *According to Tardivel, why did French Canada agree to Confederation? Do you feel his analysis was correct? Why?*
2. *Why was Tardivel a separatist? Compare his reasons for Quebec separatism with those of René Lévesque (Pt. 5—The Future, Reading 9). Account for any similarities and differences between the views of Tardivel and Lévesque.*

38.   LATER OPINION: BOURASSA

Henri Bourassa, journalist, Member of Parliament and founder of the Montreal newspaper Le Devoir, was for many years French Canada's nationalist leader. The following selection is taken from remarks made by Bourassa in the House of Commons, March 28, 1905. (Cited in Joseph Levitt: Henri Bourassa on Imperialism and Biculturalism 1900–1918 [Toronto: Copp Clark, 1970].)

Now Sir, the British North America Act, leaving aside all small considerations of detail, had, I think, two great objects in view. The first has been frequently stated, it had for its object to bury all quarrels of the past between Upper and Lower Canada, that was the birth idea of Confederation. The second idea was a larger one, one that had been conceived by imperial statesmen and by Canadian statesmen, it was the loftier idea of creating under the British flag, from the Atlantic to the Pacific, a great confederacy of provinces, the basis of which would be the principle of equality which had been accepted by both races in this country. It was at first to unite the existing colonies and then to make them one nation. It did not enter into the minds of the fathers of confederation to impose the French language upon the province of Ontario, neither upon the provinces of Nova Scotia, New Brunswick, Prince Edward Island and British Columbia, which already had constitutions, which already had parliament institutions. But when they considered—and this was the second object of the Confederation Act—when they considered those virgin lands, when they threw open to civilization those immense territories which had theretofore been only the domain of the Indian and the buffalo, what was the idea which dominated their minds? It was to introduce there an idea that would include both nationalities, to introduce an idea that would bring together the French and the English; it was to create there a British colony, but also an Anglo-French alliance that would endure for all time. That was the mother idea of Confederation which dominated the minds of Sir John A. Macdonald, George Brown and Sir George E. Cartier. Their idea was that in those new territories, provinces should be carved out where the best traditions of England and France would be introduced and maintained for all time to come.

The Solicitor General, I was sorry to hear, made an argument this afternoon that because the French Canadians are less numerous in the Northwest than the Germans, or the Scandinavians or the Doukhobors, there is no reason to grant us the official use of the French language. The Prime Minister argued that it would not be fair to ask for the official use of French because we were only a small percentage of the population in those provinces. Sir, a question like that which was considered by the fathers of confederation and by the framers of the Manitoba Act is not one of those that can be settled by quoting figures. It is true that we are only 4 per cent of the population in those two provinces. At one time there were, besides Indians, no other representatives of civilized nations but the French and the English. But if it is true that in 1901 only 4 per cent of the population was French, it is equally true that only 47 per cent was English speaking, including Scotch, Irish and Welsh; all the rest was composed of foreigners from other lands, men who have no traditions in common with the two original races in this country, who know nothing of our history, who know nothing of our constitution, which is now thirty-three years of age. I say it is the duty of the founders of these provinces, it is their duty to the descendants of those French pioneers who were the first to bring civilization to those western countries as well as the first to plant it on the shores of the St. Lawrence, to join hands with the English-speaking people in the resolve to unite these two races together so as to make that country great, a British country as long as possible; but at the same time to make it, so far as traditions are concerned, an Anglo-French country. . . .

What do you think?

1. *Do you feel that Bourassa's views were reflected in the BNA Act as he claimed? Do you feel that his plans for a bicultural nation were a departure from the views of the Fathers of Confederation including the French-Canadian Fathers? Why?*
2. *Bourassa has been billed by many recent writers as the architect of today's bilingualism and biculturalism policy. Why?*
3. *Construct a debate between Tardivel (in the reading preceding this) and Bourassa. How would their discussions differ from a discussion between René Lévesque and Pierre Trudeau, if at all?*

39.   THE ORIGINAL INTENT DESTROYED

W. L. Morton is one of Canada's most prominent historians. In an article "Confederation 1870–1896" (Journal of Canadian Studies, May 1966), from which this excerpt is taken, Morton argued that the Fathers intended Confederation to create a bicultural nation, but that that intention was lost with the weakening of the strong central government envisioned by the Fathers. (Reprinted by permission of Professor W. L. Morton.)

Macdonald, Galt, Cartier, Brown—all who accepted the Quebec Resolutions and even more, those who, unlike Brown, accepted the Westminster Resolutions, knew how delicate were the compromises, how thin the paper over the cracks, of this constitution, at once traditional and innovating. One delicate subject was education, for example, which in Canada as in the United Kingdom meant religion also. An attempt had been made at Westminster to extend the Canadian compromise of separate schools to the whole Dominion in Section 93 of the BNA Act. But the section did not make the Catholic schools of the other provinces separate; it guaranteed them only if they were established "by law" at the time of union, or established thereafter.

Another such subject was language, and the only language at issue then was French, which was necessarily involved with both religion and education. By the BNA Act it was recognized only in the province of Quebec, and the federal Parliament and courts. But denominational schools carried with them teaching in French as a matter of usage, and were thus a matter of language as well as religion in the Acadian districts of New Brunswick, the French settlements of Ontario, and later in Manitoba.

Confederation had the effect of creating the belief that the French province of Quebec had secured self-government in local and cultural matters, and that elsewhere the Roman Catholic religion and the French language were secured by the guarantee of separate schools in Section 93 of the BNA Act of 1867.

That belief had, after all, been laid down by Cartier, who had declared emphatically: "Under this system of federation which places in the hands of the Central Government all matters of general interest, and to whom questions of race will be indifferent, religious or national rights will not be ignored." The duality of French and English in United Canada was at once politically absorbed and culturally guaranteed in Confederation. It was the shattering of this delusion that by 1896 had made Quebec adhere to provincial rights secured by a federal system of co-ordinate powers and reject a national guarantee of cultural rights secured by the central government.

*   *   *   *   *

The result of the repeal of the education guarantees by Manitoba in 1891 was to make Quebec rely, not on national guarantees but on provincial rights, to safeguard the concern of French Canadians with religion and language. The duality of the Canadian Union, submerged and diffused in Confederation, re-appeared anew, armed with provincial powers, ingrowing and separatist in temper and in Quebec committed to a reliance on one party which has ever since thrust into Canadian politics the possibility of an English "backlash."

*   *   *   *   *

Instead of a national guarantee, imperfect but practical, of the mutual rights of Catholics and Protestants, French and English, the provincial rights of the province of Quebec became the guardian of the French in Canada. This prepared the way for a duality of French and English in Canada reminiscent of that in the United States before 1864. The redefining of the BNA Act into a federal system of co-ordinate central and provincial powers prepared the way for separatism and the demand for special status, or even independence, for Quebec.

What is meant by?

"duality"

What do you think?

1. *Compare Morton's views with those of Christopher Dunkin (Pt. 4 —The Historical Perspective, Reading 36). What do you notice?*
2. *(a) What do you think of Morton's argument that Confederation guaranteed French minority rights across Canada? Do you find evidence in the BNA Act to support him? Do you find evidence in the remarks of Taché, Dufresne or Le Journal du Québec to support him?*

   (b) How strong is Morton's argument that the 1870 Manitoba Act was evidence of the Fathers' bicultural intention?
3. *Do you think that the retention of a strong central government could have satisfied the needs of French-Canadian nationalism? Why?*

40.   A POLITICAL AGREEMENT

Donald Creighton, author of a noted biography of John A. Macdonald, is a Canadian historian of considerable stature. His interpretation of Confederation seen below is taken from his book, Canada's First Century (Toronto: Macmillan, 1970). (Reprinted by permission of the Macmillan Company of Canada Limited.)

The primary aim of Confederation was political—the creation of a great "new nationality"; and the British North America Act was the result of a political agreement among several provinces, not of a cultural compact of two ethnic groups, English and French. Before 1867, British America still remained, and was still regarded, not as a cultural duality but, in the words of George Cartier, as "a diversity of races." "In our own federation," Cartier declared, "we should have Catholic and Protestant, English, French, Irish, and Scotch, and each by his efforts and his success would increase the prosperity and glory of the new confederacy." Language was only one of the many components that made up the curious cultural medley that was British America before Confederation. National origin and national tradition—Irish, Scotch, and English, as well as French—might be equally influential, and religion, so often sharpened by sectarian bitterness, was perhaps the most important of all. The Fathers of Confederation had to take account of these differences; but their great aim was not the perpetuation of cultural diversity but the establishment of a united nation. At the Quebec and London conferences they gave, on the whole, relatively little time to the discussion of ethnic and cultural questions; and the resolutions they adopted on these matters, though important and essential, were few, precise in their wording, and limited in their scope.

The British North America Act contained no general declaration of principle that Canada was to be a bilingual and bicultural nation—or, for that matter, that it would remain "a diversity of races." The Fathers of Confederation were as little inclined to lay down the law about the cultural purpose and future of their new nation as they were to issue a general pronouncement on the nature and probable destiny of mankind. The English and French languages were given equal official status in the Parliament and the courts of Canada, and in the legislature and courts of Quebec. Canada was to establish only two federal courts, the Supreme Court and the Exchequer Court, at Ottawa; and all the other courts in the country were to be provincial courts, constituted and maintained by the provinces. The French language had thus no official standing in the courts of any of the provinces except Quebec; and, perhaps even more important, it was given no protected place in any of the nation's schools. The Fathers of Confederation showed a fair amount of interest in education and its legislative control; but it was very characteristic of these typical British Americans, with their strong denominational affiliations and frequent sectarian biases, that what concerned them was not the role of language, but the place of religion, in the schools. The provinces were given the power to legislate in respect of education; but this authority was limited by some rather complicated provisions designed to protect any rights or privileges concerning separate or denominational schools.

In sum, the distinctive cultural features of French Canada—its language, civil code, and educational system—were confirmed in those parts of the new Dominion in which they had already become established by law or custom. They were not extended in their application to Ontario and the Atlantic provinces. They were given no protected position in the nation as a whole.

What do you think?

1. *What are Creighton's views about the place given to French Canada in the Confederation agreement? How convincing do you find his argument?*

2. *Compare Creighton's views with those of W. L. Morton (in the reading preceding this one). Explain why two prominent historians can disagree so profoundly.*

3. *If, for the sake of argument, one assumes that Creighton's interpretation of Confederation as it pertains to French Canada is correct, do you feel that it is sufficient reason for not supporting a modern government policy of bilingualism and biculturalism? Why?*

4. *How do you think Morton and Creighton would feel about either*

granting Quebec a "special status" or decentralizing federal powers in order to accommodate Quebec's "special character"? Why?

41. A CULTURAL PACT

Mason Wade, author of The French-Canadian Outlook *(1964), a comprehensive two-volume history of French Canada. describes in this passage his view of the French-Canadian interpretation of Confederation. (Reprinted by permission of the Canadian Publishers, McClelland and Stewart Limited, Toronto, and the Editorial Board of the Carleton Library.)*

It is not generally understood among English Canadians that Confederation is not, in the minds of French Canadians, simply a federal union of the British North American provinces, in which the will of the majority should prevail. To the French, it is a pact or treaty between French and English, which guarantees to each group an equal right to its own faith, language, laws, and customs. This interpretation is implied in Cartier's statement that the unity brought about by Confederation would be a unity of diversity:

> If we unite we will form a political nationality independent of the national origin and religion of individuals. Some have regretted that we have a distinction of races, and have expressed the hope that, in time, this diversity will disappear. The idea of a fusion of the races in one is utopian; it is an impossibility. Distinctions of this character will always exist; diversity seems to be the order of the physical, moral, and political worlds.

It is also borne out by Macdonald's view of Confederation as a treaty, and by the safeguards provided for minority rights, both French and English, by the British North America Act of 1867 which constituted the Dominion of Canada. It was first formulated by Quebec spokesmen when these rights were violated soon after Confederation.

The French Canadian's insistence upon provincial autonomy and his opposition to centralization of power in Ottawa are based upon this interpretation, and so is his indignation that the bilingual and bicultural character of Canada is only a partly and grudgingly recognized theory. He feels that he has kept his part of the "treaty" of 1867, and even gone beyond its letter in tolerance to the English minority of Quebec; while the other provinces have flagrantly violated both the letter and the spirit of the pact by their actions in such instances as the New Brunswick, Manitoba, Northwest, and Ontario school questions, and the federal government, by failing to support bilingualism inside and outside Quebec, and by not giving a proportionate share of federal appointments to French Canadians, has likewise broken faith.

What do you think?

1. What is the distinction made by French Canadians, according to Wade, between a "federal union" and a "pact"? Why is this distinction an important one to French Canada?
2. Is Confederation a political agreement or a cultural pact? Support your answer with evidence.

42. A CONTINENTAL FATHERLAND

Michel Brunet is one of French Canada's foremost historians. In an article, "The French Canadians' Search for a Fatherland," from which this excerpt is taken, Brunet describes what he thinks Confederation meant for French Canadians. Brunet's article was published in Peter Russell, ed.: Nationalism in Canada *(Toronto: McGraw-Hill Ryerson, 1966). (Reprinted by permission of Michel Brunet.)*

Confederation could be hailed in 1867 as a great achievement by the British Americans. Had they not succeeded in securing for themselves the northern part of the continent as a fatherland? They could now freely harness their energies and resources to build a continental nation. They sincerely believed that they had solved forever the French-Canadian problem, and the attitude of both French Canada's lay and clerical leaders encouraged them in this way of thinking.

The fact is that Confederation gave satisfaction to most of the French Canadians. The Church had no reason to think that the new political framework was contrary to its vested interests. The Quebec lawyer-politicians were convinced that they had obtained all the guarantees they then deemed essential for the protection of French Canada's cultural values. The new Constitution had many features which greatly impressed the French Canadians of 1867. It created a local administration which would take care of the immediate needs of the population. The French language was official in the province of Quebec and in the federal administration, and the school rights of the religious minorities were recognized in all the provinces. Moreover, the new country was called *Canada,* a name that stirred the imagination of the first white inhabitants of the St. Lawrence Valley.

The Canadiens wanted to convince themselves that this Canada would be the fatherland they had been longing for since the seventeenth century, a continental fatherland which they were ready to build in close collaboration with their English-speaking fellow-countrymen. The Manitoba Act (1870), which gave to the new province a bilingual status, reinforced this belief. The New Brunswick school crisis (1873), the Riel affair (1885) and the Ontario Orangemen's agitation somewhat cooled off their enthusiasm toward Confederation. However, most of their lay and clerical leaders endeavoured to persuade them that they should forget these incidents and keep their faith in the future of a Canada which could be the fatherland of all Canadians.

What do you think?

1. According to Brunet, what did English Canada feel it had won with Confederation? What did French Canada feel it had won? Was there a conflict in the two interpretations? Explain why or why not.
2. "The Canadiens wanted to convince themselves. . . ." Is Brunet implying that the Canadien attitude towards Confederation was based on an illusion? If so, why does he feel the way he does?
3. After assessing the arguments you have read in this section on Confederation explain what you feel was intended for French-English relations in the 1867 agreement. How relevant is this agreement to today's situation? Why?

The 1837 Rebellion

In 1837 two rebellions broke out in British North America: one in Upper Canada and the other in Lower Canada.

Louis-Joseph Papineau, an aristocratic lawyer and politician, led the rebellion in Lower Canada. A severe economic recession combined with racial animosities created a rebellious mood among Lower-Canadian dissidents who wanted to have effective political control not only over the legislative arm of government, but also over the executive arm which was, in 1837, firmly in the grip of the English-speaking minority in Quebec. The 1837 "patriote" has become a rallying symbol for many of today's French-Canadian nationalists. Why?

43. THE "ENGLISH" PARTY AND THE "FRENCH" PARTY

T. F. Elliot wrote the following description of Lower-Canadian politics to his friend Henry Taylor in the Colonial Office. The letter was written October 24, 1835. It should be noted that the "English" party which Elliot refers to was anxious for a union of the two Canadas which, among other things, would effectively diminish the power of French Canadians in the Lower-Canadian Assembly.

... ["The English party"] is composed of almost all the Merchants, with an admixture of considerable Landholders, and of some of the younger and more intelligent Civil Officers. It possess [*sic*] much intelligence, much wealth and still more credit . . . and unity of purpose . . . they know better than any other people how to confer on political association. . . . Yet I do not like the English party. It is fully as ambitious of dominion as the French party, and in my opinion, prepared to seek it by more unscrupulous means . . . but depend upon it that if ever these heats in Lower Canada should go as far as to hazard the connection with the Mother Country, the English will be the foremost to cut the tie. They . . . are by far the best disposed to sympathize with Republican principles; and, I must add, the most capable to wield Republican Institutions. They are the most rancorous, for they remember the power they have lost, and hate their rivals as a sort of usurpers. . . . The "French party" . . . consists mainly of Advocates, Physicians and Farmers, the last very ignorant of politics and indifferent to them and ambitious of their Seats . . . the bulk of the Assembly is inert, and the few Members possessed of activity and intelligence, work in entire subordination to Papineau, of whom they stand in profound awe.

. . . there appears to me to be a deeper motive calculated to bind the French party together, and to give general direction to their policy.

. . . Looking to the circumstances, I cannot think that the French Canadians would be very unreasonable to dread some future extinction of their own tongue and peculiar habits . . . it is not to be doubted that some amongst them fear a lapse into insignificance.

What do you think?

1. *What were the differences in social backgrounds between the "English" and "French" parties? How can you account for these differences? To what extent did this situation remain the same in more recent Quebec politics? Why?*

44. PAPINEAU'S COMPLAINTS

In letters to his friend and collaborator, John Neilson, Papineau expressed his views on the injustice and discrimination that he felt French Canadians lived under in Lower Canada.

The injustice done to my country revolts me, and so perturbs my mind that I am not always in a condition to take counsel of an enlightened patriotism, but rather inclined to give away to anger and hatred of our oppressors.

It is odious to see every office and position closed against our people when the laws do not exclude them; to see them contributing nine-tenths of the revenue and receiving but one-tenth, and to feel that the possession of influence in this country is a passport to persecution.

What do you think?

1. *What were Papineau's grievances?*
2. *"It is odious to see every office and position closed against our people when the laws do not exclude them. . . ." How do you think the French Canadians were excluded from positions of influence? How is this situation paralleled in the Quebec of more recent days, if at all?*

45. A FRIGHTFUL SPECTACLE

An editorial commenting on the rebellion appears below. It was published in the English-language Montreal Herald, *November 14, 1838.*

Sunday night all the country back of Laprairie presented the frightful spectacle of a vast expanse of livid flames, and it is reported that not a single rebel house has been left standing . . . God knows what will become of the Canadians who have not perished, of their wives and families, during the winter which approaches, since they have in prospect only the horrors of hunger and cold. It is sad to reflect on the terrible consequences of the revolt, of the irreparable ruin of so great a number of human beings, whether innocent or guilty. Nevertheless the supremacy of the laws must be maintained inviolate, the integrity of the Empire respected, and peace and prosperity assured to the English, even at the expense of the whole Canadian people.

What do you think?

1. *Who are the "Canadians" referred to in this passage? What do you think the attitude of the* Montreal Herald *was towards the Canadians?*
2. *What was the issue as the* Herald *saw it? How do you feel about this interpretation and why?*

46. THE DURHAM REPORT

After the 1837–38 Rebellions in British North America, Lord Durham, a British reformer, was made governor of the Canadas. His report, an analysis of the causes of the unrest and suggestions for ending it, is one of the political milestones in Canadian history. It is important to remember that in this passage Durham is referring to Lower Canada only.

I expected to find a contest between a government and a people: I found two nations warring in the bosom of a single state; I found a struggle, not of principles, but of races; and I perceived that it would be idle to attempt any amelioration of laws or institutions until we could first succeed in terminating the deadly animosity that now separates the inhabitants of Lower Canada into the hostile divisions of French and English.

There can hardly be conceived a nationality more destitute of all that can invigorate and elevate a people, than that which is exhibited by the descendants of the French in Lower Canada, owing to their retaining their peculiar language and manners. They are a people with no history and no literature. The literature of England is written in a language which is not theirs; and the only literature which their language renders familiar to them is that of a nation from which they have been separated by eighty years of a foreign rule, and still more by those changes which the Revolution and its consequences have wrought in the whole political, moral and social state of France.

*   *   *   *   *

In these circumstances, I should be indeed surprised if the more reflecting part of the French Canadians entertained at present any hope of continuing to preserve their nationality. Much as they struggle against it, it is obvious that the process of assimilation to English habits is already commencing. The English language is gaining ground, as the language of the rich and of the employers of labour naturally will. It appeared by some of the few returns, which had been received by the Commissioner of the Inquiry into the state of Education, that there are about ten times the number of French children in Quebec learning English, as compared with the English children who learn French. A considerable time must, of course, elapse before the change of a language can spread over a whole people; and justice and policy alike require that, while the people continue to use the French language, their Government should take no such means to force the English language upon them as would, in fact, deprive the great mass of the community of the protection of the laws. But, I repeat that the alteration of the character of the province ought to be immediately entered on, and firmly, though cautiously, followed up; that in any plan, which may be adopted for the future management of Lower Canada, the first object ought to be that of making it an English province; and that, with this end in view, the ascendancy should never again be placed in any hands but those of an English population.

What do you think?

1. *How accurate do you think Durham's analysis of the rebellion was? Why?*
2. *What was Durham's attitude towards the French Canadians?*
3. *What was his suggestion for preventing further unrest? How practicable do you think this suggestion was? Why?*

Aftermath of Conquest

After the capture of New France in 1760 the British were faced with the problem of how to govern a population of alien language, religion, law and tradition. The rapid immigration of Americans into the province of Quebec only increased the difficulties, adding as it did another culture to the former French colony. The military governors of Quebec, Murray and Carleton, sympathized with the French Canadians and urged that their traditional way of life be preserved. However, the new English-speaking residents, accustomed to representative government and British laws in the American colonies, clashed with the military governors.

The Quebec Act of 1774 was a major concession to the French Canadians and also a shrewd political move by the British, who hoped that use could be made of the authoritarian traditions of French Canada in maintaining a buttress against the refractory American colonies to the south simply by giving the French Canadians what they thought they wanted. The reaction of English Quebeckers was predictable.

What were the long-term effects of the Quebec Act?

47. THE CAPITULATION

The terms of capitulation agreed to by Britain and France were reasonably generous to the French Canadians. Their property was to be left undisturbed, they were to be able to practice their Roman Catholic religion, and they were to be permitted to return to France should they want to.

Arthur Maheux attempted to give an account of the impact of the capitulation on the French Canadians. (Cited in E. B. O'Callaghan (ed.), Documents Relative to the Colonial History of the State of New York *[Albany: Weed, Parsons and Company, 1855–61].)*

Fear of deportation was very strong. . . . Scarcely four years had passed since the deportation of the Acadians, an event which the people of Quebec could not forget, as they had welcomed them into their homes. . . . But what would be the fate of the Canadians? Born in America, indeed the greater number established for three, four, five or more generations, they had no connections in France, not even relatives able to receive and harbor them. Their country, their only country, was America . . . [they] would not want to leave for France, but would prefer some corner of America. . . .

But would the English accord these privileges? Or would they repeat the cruel stroke of 1755? . . .

When . . . the terms of the surrender had been granted . . . there was unquestionably tremendous relief. . . . The majority were doubtlessly grateful for the enemy's generosity and began to think that it would be possible to get along with these English Protestants.

What do you think?

1. *Why do you think the conquest of New France has been described as a "traumatic" event for the French Canadians? How does this explain the "relief" that Maheux describes?*
2. *Why do you think the British were so "generous"?*

48. TO THE END OF TIME

Guy Carleton, governor of Quebec, discussed the future of Lower Canada in a report dated November 25, 1767.

The King's Forces in this Province . . . would amount to sixteen hundred and twenty seven Men, the King's old subjects in this Province . . . might furnish about five hundred Men. . . .

The new Subjects could send into the Field about eighteen thousand Men, well able to carry Arms; of which Number, above one half have already served, with as much Valor, with more Zeal, and more military Knowledge for America, than the regular Troops of France, that were joined with them.

*   *   *   *   *

Having arrayed the Strength of his Majesty's old and new Subjects, and shewn the great Superiority of the Latter, it may not be amiss to observe, that there is not the least Probability, this present Superiority should ever diminish, on the Contrary 'tis more than probable it will increase and strengthen daily: The Europeans who migrate never will prefer the long unhospitable Winters of Canada, to the more cheerful Climates, and more fruitful Soil of His Majesty's Southern Provinces; The few old Subjects at present in this Province have been mostly left here by Accident, and are either disbanded Officers, Soldiers, or Followers of the Army . . . or else they are Adventurers in Trade . . . barring Catastrophe shocking to think of, this Country must, to the end of Time, be peopled by the Canadian Race. . . .

What do you think?

1. *Why do you think Carleton and Durham (Pt. 4—The Historical Perspective, Reading 46) had different views on the future of the "Canadian Race"?*

49. THE QUEBEC ACT

The Quebec Act formed the foundation of the legal rights of French Canadians and marks the official beginning of a British colony which was French and Catholic. The following selection is from Documents Relating to the Constitutional History of Canada, *Adam Shortt and Arthur G. Doughty, eds. (Ottawa: Queen's Printer, 1918).*

Whatever the motives for the passing of the Act, it is the foundation of the legal rights of French Canadians, and marks the official beginning under Great Britain of a French and Catholic colony.

> And, for the more perfect Security and Ease of the Minds of the Inhabitants of the said Province, it is hereby declared, That His Majesty's Subjects, professing the Religion of the Church of Rome of and in the said Province of Quebec, may have, hold, and enjoy, the free Exercise of the Religion of the Church of Rome, subject to the King's Supremacy . . . and that the Clergy of the said Church may hold, receive, and enjoy, their accustomed Dues and Rights, with respect to such Persons only as shall profess the said Religion.
>
> Provided nevertheless, That it shall be lawful for His Majesty, His Heirs or Successors, to make such Provision out of the rest of the said accustomed Dues and Rights, for the Encouragement of the Protestant Religion, and for the Maintenance and Support of a Protestant Clergy within the said Province. . . .
>
> That all His Majesty's Canadian Subjects, within the Province of *Quebec,* the religious Orders and Communities only excepted, may also hold and enjoy their Property and Possessions,

together with all Customs and Usages relative thereto, and all other their Civil Rights, in as large, ample, and beneficial Manner, as if the said Proclamation, Commissions, Ordinances, and other Acts and Instruments, had not been made, and as may consist with their Allegiance to His Majesty, and Subjection to the Crown and Parliament of *Great Britain;* and that in all Matters of Controversy, relative to Property and Civil Rights, Resort shall be had to the Laws of *Canada,* as the Rule for the Decision of the same. . . .

Provided always, That nothing in this Act contained shall extend, or be constructed to extent, to any Lands that have been granted by His Majesty, or shall hereafter be granted by His Majesty, His Heirs and Successors, to be holden in free and common Soccage. . . .

And whereas the Certainty and Lenity of the Criminal Law of England, and the Benefits and Advantages resulting from the Use of it, have been sensibly felt by the Inhabitants, from an Experience of more than Nine Years, during which it has been uniformly administered; be it therefore further enacted by the Authority aforesaid, That the same shall continue to be administered, and shall be observed as Law in the Province of Quebec, as well in the description and Quality of the Offence as in the Method of Prosecution and Trial; . . .

And whereas it may be necessary to ordain many Regulations for the future Welfare and good Government of the Province of *Quebec,* the Occasions of which cannot now be foreseen, nor, without much Delay and Inconvenience, be provided for, without intrusting that Authority, for a certain Time, and under proper Restrictions, to Persons resident there: And whereas it is at present inexpedient to call an Assembly; be it therefore enacted by the Authority aforesaid, That it shall and may be lawful for His Majesty, His Heirs and Successors, by Warrant under His or Their Signet or Sign Manual, and with the advice of the Privy Council, to constitute and appoint a Council for the Affairs of the Province of *Quebec,* to consist of such Persons resident there, not exceeding Twenty-three, nor less than Seventeen, as His Majesty, His Heirs and Successors, shall be pleased to appoint; . . . which Council, so appointed and nominated, or the major Part thereof, shall have Power and Authority to make Ordinances for the Peace, Welfare, and good Government, of the said Province, with the Consent of His Majesty's Governor. . . .

What do you think?

1. *What assurances did the Quebec Act give the French Canadians about the preservation of their traditional way of life?*

2. How did the Quebec Act reflect the "authoritarianism" or "paternalism" of the Old Regime?
3. Was the Quebec Act a mistake? Should the British have attempted to assimilate the French rather than to actively preserve their way of life? Why or why not?

5

The Future: Policies and Options

The preceding chapters have provided you with the opportunity of examining the contemporary issues and the historical conditions of French-English relations.

But what of the future? Where do we go from here?

This section of readings provides you with the opportunity of examining some of the policies that have been inaugurated to resolve French-English tensions in Canada as well as some of the proposals that have been suggested for future policies. The author has broadly organized these readings into three categories: bilingualism, flexible federalism and separatism. You are cautioned not to see these as mutually distinct divisions; there is a great deal of overlapping and/or interdependence in these categories—they have been created mainly to provide convenience and some clarity.

What proposals in this section seem to you to be the most apt for resolving the contemporary issues? How will your knowledge of the historical conditions help you in making your choice?

Bilingualism

In a previous section in this book, "In the Capital" (Pt. 3—The Contemporary Scene, Readings 31 and 32) you read about the controversy that the federal government's policy on bilingualism has created in the federal civil service. This controversy has created a sizeable body

René d'Arc hears the Heavenly Voice.

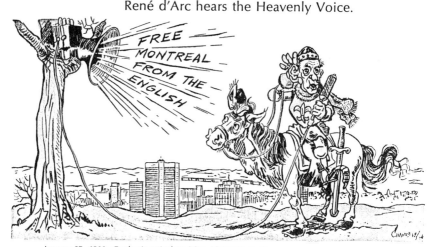

January 27, 1966: Quebec's articulate Réne Lévesque, strong man of the now defunct Lesage government. (Reprinted by permission of the *Halifax Chronicle-Herald.*)

of opinion on both sides of the question across the country.

What does the federal policy entail? Why was it created? What reaction has it received both in Quebec and the rest of Canada? How satisfactory do you think it is for resolving the French-English issue?

1. TRUDEAU EXPLAINS BILINGUALISM

During the 1968 federal campaign Pierre Elliott Trudeau expressed the belief that if minority language rights were guaranteed across Canada, 95 per cent of French-Canadian grievances would be satisfied. This selection, describing the bilingualism policy in general terms, was written by Mr. Trudeau for the Canadian Press, July, 1969 (Reprinted by permission of Press News Limited.)

WHY ARE THEY FORCING FRENCH DOWN OUR THROATS?

That question has been asked by English-speaking Canadians who are concerned about the government's bilingualism policy and about the Official Languages Act, which was recently [1969] enacted by Parliament. The question is based on a widely shared misunderstanding of what our policy on bilingualism means.

In fact, everyone in Canada will not be required to speak French, any more than everyone will be required to speak English. You can grow up in parts of Quebec and never use English a day in your life. You can live in many parts of the country and never hear a single word of French. Most of the people who deal with the government of Canada speak only one language. It is because everyone in the country is not expected to speak both languages, and never will be, that the federal government must be able to speak to Canadians in either French or English wherever there are enough French speakers or English speakers to justify it. Nothing is more important to a person than to understand and to be understood. The most common and most effective tool we can use for this purpose is our language. Any policy which affects such an important aspect of our lives is bound to stir up some controversy.

* * * * *

Some people claim that the Official Languages Act will result in discrimination against those whose mother tongue is neither English nor French. This is one of the most widespread and the most unjustified misconceptions. The Act itself states categorically that the rights and privileges of any language other than English or French, whether acquired by law or by custom, will in no way be diminished as a result of the Act. For instance, the right of people who do not understand English or French to be heard in court through an official interpreter will be maintained.

* * * * *

That is why the Act declares that English and French will be the official languages of the government and Parliament. It imposes no restrictions on the languages or cultural activities of individual Canadians.

A second misconception is that the Act will prevent Canadians who speak only one language from working for the government, the armed forces or the Crown corporations, or from being promoted to important government jobs. There is no clause in the Act which states this, or which will have this result. The object of the Act is to provide government services in both languages where required by the population.

This does not mean that everyone who works for the government must be bilingual. In many areas of the country, including almost all of Western Canada and much of Quebec, government services will be provided in only one language and people working for the government in those areas will need only that language. . . .

* * * * *

Some opponents of the Act have argued that it violates or changes the constitution, the British North America Act, and is, therefore, beyond the powers of Parliament. I am not going to set out a long and technical argument about constitutional law. The fact is that the Act deals only with the departments and agencies of the federal government. It does not deal with matters which, under the constitution, are within the control of the province. It does not alter any of the rights or privileges concerning the English or French languages already guaranteed by the constitution.

*   *   *   *   *

As I travel around the country I find that the advantages of bilingualism are becoming more widely accepted by Canadians, particularly among the young. However urgent it may be to introduce such a policy, and I believe the very survival of our country depends on it, we should not expect to reap its full benefits overnight. That will require fundamental changes in attitudes and institutions which may take years, or even generations. In this historic process the Official Languages Act is an important forward step.

What do you think?

1. Describe in your own words the government's bilingual policy.
2. Why do you think there is a "widely shared misunderstanding" of the government's bilingualism policy?

2.   THE SNARE OF BILINGUALISM

This selection has been taken from the appendix of René Lévesque's Option for Quebec *(1968). (Reprinted by permission of The Canadian Publishers, McClelland and Stewart Limited, Toronto.)*

This latest announcement of the creation of the kind of country we have been denied for the last hundred years is yet another attempt to anaesthetize Quebec public opinion which finally is dangerously awake to its own interests. If the anaesthetic should "take," the emergency would be over for a long, long time. In fact, how many generations would be required (for we must be reasonable, musn't we?) to see transformed into a binational bicultural environment those nine provinces which have never been anything but an English-speaking melting-pot? Another hundred years? That's certainly what they hope. . . . Thus, instead of strengthening Quebec, they talk of a revival of French Canada outside our borders.

Let us say it very, very calmly: what they are proposing to us now is a sucker's game.

First, we must first note the advanced stage of cultural decay of our minorities in the other provinces. . . .

Take a good look at the frightening speed of assimilation. More than a third of the members of our minority groups already declared themselves as English speaking six years ago. In fact, some 34 per cent speak only English.

. . . on checking other censuses since 1931 [it was] also found that the process of assimilation has accelerated constantly. One is forced to believe that since 1961 the situation has continued to deteriorate.

And now, how can they improve their lot? By obtaining (as so many honestly believe and others less naively maintain) advantages comparable to those our English-speaking Quebeckers enjoy?

First on the list would be the urgent need for equally good schools, from primary to university level—for relatively poor minorities which are often highly dispersed and, except in New Brunswick, do not add up to even half the percentage formed by the English-speaking minority in Quebec!

And what would be the result of this most improbable effort? It would throw into a labour market and social climate—completely English in character—a host of people trained and competent to work within a French culture! Or, more likely, it would repatriate them to Quebec as they became prepared (something gained, at least!).

Finally, how is this to happen in a country where at the slightest sign of an economic slowdown the first cuts are made in those services that are the most essential? And at a time when the pressing needs of the present educational system are calculated in hundreds of millions of additional dollars? A wonderful dream—and a sad joke! Trying to sell us such a Utopia would be as fraudulent as the eternal promise made to the Negroes by American segregationists of a school system that would be "separate but equal," a system they will no more see in the future than they have in the past. . . .

To sum up, they would like to substitute for our objective (which is the essential emancipation of Quebec) only a pale shadow, a pious impossibility.

What do you think?

1. *Do you find René Lévesque's reference to assimilation figures effective as an argument against bilingualism and biculturalism? Why or why not?*
2. *"To sum up, they would like to substitute for our objective (which is the essential emancipation of Quebec) only a pale shadow, a pious impossibility."*
   (a) *From this statement, what do you think the attitude of Quebec separatists is towards French minorities and Quebec's relationship to those minorities? Account for this attitude. What do you think of this attitude and why?*
   (b) *Do you think that if Quebec nationalists gave greater support to bilingualism and biculturalism it would be more than the "pious impossibility" they claim it is? Why or why not?*
3. *Read Lévesque's views on bilingualism and biculturalism as he stated them in 1968. Have his views changed since 1963? (See Pt. 4—The Historical Perspective, Reading 11.)*

3. BILINGUALISM—A BLOW TO NATIONAL UNITY

Mark Alchuck was a first year student at Toronto's York University when he wrote "Why I Support a Policy of English Unilingualism" for the February 11, 1971, edition of Excalibur, the York student newspaper. This selection is an excerpt from Mr. Alchuck's article. (Reprinted by permission of Excalibur.)

French Canada exists now as an inward looking linguistic minority in an English speaking sea. Bilingualism will be the final brick in a wall to separate them from the reality of English language numerical superiority. Promoting bilingualism in English speaking provinces and creating French language pockets will increase that isolation. Bilingualism will be the coup de grace to Canadian national unity, the very thing it is supposed to be saving.

Canadian unity will always be threatened, for Quebec is not a province like the others. Quebec is a province of Canada in name only; Quebec is a nation as foreign and as distinct from English Canada as Japan is from Britain. The upsurge in FLQ terrorism is the first labour pain of the birth of a new nation; the separatist Parti Québécois is standing a day and night vigil by the bedside ready to deliver the new state. The French of Quebec are no longer French-Canadians, they are Québécois.

The intellectuals and the students of Quebec have no love for Canada, they are French and a whole generation of French-Canadians have been brought up to decry, if not to hate, the very words Canada and Confederation. This is not an exaggeration, for the Parti Québécois enjoys the support of nearly one-quarter of the Quebec electorate, and their power is increasing.

        *   *   *   *   *

Our only hope of deliverance from the civil anarchy which is rapidly descending upon our nation lies in the reassertion of a single Canadian nationalism. Canada can exist only as one nation with one official language. Our experience over more than one hundred years has shown us that two different peoples can never live successfully as one.

The vain and ludicrous pursuit of cultural dualism which the Liberal government is executing as rapidly as possible will end in the break-up of our country. Bilingualism with all its ramifications, which was never an object of Confederation, must be abandoned. The bilingual experiment has failed, and failed miserably; it is time for a reassessment and a new formula!

What is meant by?

"cultural dualism"

What do you think?

1. *Discuss the following statements made by Mr. Alchuck:*
   (a) *"Bilingualism will be the coup de grace to Canadian national unity, the very thing it is supposed to be saving."*
   (b) *"Quebec is a nation as foreign and as distinct from English Canada as Japan is from Britain."*
   (c) *"Canada can exist only as one nation with one official· language."*
   (d) *"The bilingual experiment has failed, and failed miserably. . . ."*

4. BILINGUALISM AND MULTICULTURALISM

In the House of Commons, October 8, 1971, Prime Minister Trudeau announced that his government was turning to a policy of multiculturalism within a bilingual framework. (Reprinted by permission of Information Canada.)

Mr. Speaker, I am happy this morning to be able to reveal to the House that the government has accepted all those recommendations of the Royal Commission on Bilingualism and Biculturalism which are contained in Volume IV of its reports directed to federal departments and agencies. Hon. members will recall that the subject of this volume is "the contribution by other ethnic groups to the cultural enrichment of Canada and the measures that should be taken to safeguard that contribution."

Volume IV examined the whole question of cultural and ethnic pluralism in this country and the status of our various cultures and languages, an area of study given all too little attention in the past by scholars.

It was the view of the royal commission, shared by the government and, I am sure, by all Canadians, that there cannot be one cultural policy for Canadians of British and French origin, another for the original peoples and yet a third for all others. For although there are two official languages, there is no official culture, nor does any ethnic group take precedence over any other. No citizen or group of citizens is other than Canadian, and all should be treated fairly.

The royal commission was guided by the belief that adherence to one's ethnic group is influenced not so much by one's origin or mother tongue as by one's sense of belonging to the group, and by what the commission calls the group's "collective will to exist." The government shares this belief.

*   *   *   *   *

The individual's freedom would be hampered if he were locked for life within a particular cultural compartment by the accident of birth or language. It is vital, therefore, that every Canadian, whatever his ethnic origin, be given a chance to learn at least one of the two languages in which his country conducts its official business and its politics.

A policy of multiculturalism within a bilingual framework commends itself to the government as the most suitable means of assuring the cultural freedom of Canadians. Such a policy should help to break down discriminatory attitudes and cultural jealousies. National unity, if it is to mean anything in the deeply personal sense, must be founded on confidence in one's own individual identity; out of this can grow respect for that of others and a willingness to share ideas, attitudes and assumptions. A vigorous policy of multiculturalism will help create this initial confidence. It can form the base of a society which is based on fair play for all.

The government will support and encourage the various cultures and ethnic groups that give structure and vitality to our society. They will be encouraged to share their cultural expression and values with other Canadians and so contribute to a richer life for us all.

What is meant by?

"pluralism"

What do you think?

1. *What does Prime Minister Trudeau mean by "multiculturalism within a bilingual framework"? How does he justify this new policy?*
2. *What impact would the new government policy of "multiculturalism within a framework of bilingualism" have on—*
   (a) English-Canadian attitudes towards bilingualism?
   (b) French-Canadian attitudes towards bilingualism?
   (c) Western attitudes towards bilingualism?
   Why?
3. *Is the new government policy an improvement over bilingualism and biculturalism as an attempt to resolve the Quebec issue? Why or why not?*

A Flexible Federalism

The 1867 British North America Act gave Canada a federal structure. The Fathers of Confederation, conscious of the just-concluded American Civil War and anxious to prevent such a calamity in Canada, created a constitution which is different from the American in that residual powers (that is, powers which remain unnamed in the constitution), rest with the central government rather than the provincial governments. The ever-increasing role of government, particularly in the areas of social welfare, has created a strain on this arrangement as the provinces seek more powers, especially taxation powers, to enact social policies appropriate for their populations. Quebec is particularly sensitive in this area, since she feels social welfare policies (and others, such as foreign affairs and communications) are particularly important for defining and influencing the culture of the province. The upshot of these trends in government activity is pressure for revision of Canadian federalism to a looser, more decentralized form. Quebec is certainly not the only province contributing to this pressure—but hers is the strongest and most persistent voice.

There are three major arguments about changing the structure of Canadian federalism. One favours greater decentralization with constitutional amendment. Another also favours greater decentralization but holds that constitutional revision is unnecessary, that there is a natural evolution in Canadian federalism towards decentralization. The third is that Canada needs a centralized federalism in order to enforce strong "national" policies on matters like resources policy, American investment, and social and educational standards which are uniform across the country.

All arguments are strongly presented. Which, if any, do you feel is the most appropriate for Canada's future and for resolving the French-English issue in this country?

5.   DECENTRALIZED FEDERALISM

In the May 1972 issue of the Canadian Forum *two federalist Quebeckers, Pierre de Bané and Martial Asselin, proposed a looser federal structure for Canada so that this country could accommodate Quebec's desire to "control her own destiny" without disintegrating. (Reprinted by permission of the* Canadian Forum.)

In most areas jurisdiction is not clearly defined and is becoming increasingly confused. This is the situation in both Canada and in the other federated countries of the world, and it is an inevitable one. Whereas last century, when government activities were relatively simple and few in number, it was easy to imagine a clear-cut distinction between jurisdictions, such a situation today is purely a product of imagination and cannot correspond to the reality of the political scene. Modern governments are the prime agents in evolved societies, and this is a trend which is continuing to grow. In Canada, at the present time, the public powers are securing one-third of the gross national product; in twenty years it will be half the

GNP. Furthermore, there is close interdependency and correlation not only among the policies of different levels of government but also among those at the same level of government, not to mention continental, international and, soon, world policies.

Finally, even if it were possible to establish a clear distinction among the numerous and complex areas of jurisdiction, this distinction would soon be out of date. It is for these reasons that, rather than attempting to describe in detail the responsibilities of each level of government, we would like to suggest a basic principle which is almost invariably found in federal constitutions: the central government has jurisdiction only over those areas which are expressly assigned to it. This is entirely the reverse of the situation which exists here. The main responsibility of this level of government would be to act as a counterbalance to the whole. There would, of course, be nothing to prevent any province which so wished from delegating some of its powers to the central government.

If this suggestion is turned down, we fear that the strained relations between Quebec and Ottawa will deteriorate still more and will eventually paralyze the country's fiscal system. This is the essence of our thought. It is inspired both by the gravity of the "crisis" which was detected by the Royal Commission on Bilingualism and Biculturalism several years ago now and which has been increasing ever since, and by the keen anxiety which we feel about the destiny of Quebecers.

*   *   *   *   *

Those people who see in this report a defence for secession by Quebec are very much mistaken and have completely misunderstood our purpose. It is our firm conviction that federalism, or the distribution of sovereignty among different levels of government, offers the best solution for the present situation. Examples of federalism across the world show very clearly that this is a system which respects differences to the highest degree, so much so that each federal system is truly unique, a political structure *sui generis*.

What is meant by?

"jurisdiction"
"prime agents"
"public powers"
"gross national product"
"delegate"
"fiscal system"
"sui generis"

What do you think?

1. (a) *Would you say that Canada is more or less decentralized than it was in 1867? Give evidence.*
   (b) *Why do the authors of this selection feel that decentralizing Canadian federalism is the best solution for the Quebec issue? How would they propose to implement this new decentralism? How does their proposal deviate from the BNA Act?*

6. WE NEED STRONG NATIONAL GOVERNMENT

Professor William Neville teaches political science at Trent University in Peterborough, Ontario. In an article written for the November 1971 issue of the Canadian Forum, *"After Victoria: the Choice for English Canada," Professor Neville argues in favour of a strong central government. In addition, it should be noted that Professor Neville in this article argues that Quebec's staying in Canada was no longer possible and that English Canada should prepare for Quebec's secession. (Reprinted by permission of the* Canadian Forum.)

The serious Canadian nationalist, whether he be socialist, liberal or conservative, must recognize the special importance of a strong national government in achieving goals and ensuring national survival. No amount of wishful thinking will alter the fact that the achievement of a strong national government and keeping Quebec in Confederation have become mutually exclusive goals. Moreover, if Quebec has been perceived as the greatest internal threat to our survival, American domination has surely constituted the greatest from outside; and yet our government has been so preoccupied with the one that it has for too long ignored the other.

What do you think?

1. *Why does Professor Neville favour a strong central government, even at the expense of Quebec's seceding from Confederation? Why do you think he feels that a strong national government is of "special importance" in achieving this goal?*
2. *Compare Professor Neville's views with those of Premier Bourassa (Pt. 3—The Contemporary Scene, Reading 4) on the importance of Quebec to Canada's "national survival." What do you agree with and why?*
3. *What do you consider to comprise Canada's national survival:*
   (a) *survival from "American domination"?*
   (b) *Quebec's remaining in Confederation?*
   (c) *both?*

4. *Do you feel that centralism or decentralism is the best means of achieving what you consider to be Canada's national survival? Why?*

7. SPECIAL STATUS

"Special status" refers to a Canadian federalism which is decentralized to the extent that at least Quebec would be given special prerogatives and powers.

Daniel Johnson was the Union Nationale premier in Quebec from 1966 to 1968, the year of his death. This selection is from the text of a brief presenting a proposal for special status submitted by Premier Johnson to the Fiscal Federal-Provincial Conference in September 1966, and published in the November 1966 issue of the Journal of Canadian Studies. *(Reprinted by permission of* Journal of Canadian Studies.*)*

We believe that there exists in Canada a French-language *nation* —in the sociological meaning of the term—with its centre in Quebec. This nation has the firm intention of pursuing its claim by utilizing, in order and justice, all necessary means to its development.

More exactly, what does Quebec want? As a basic function of any nation, it desires to be the master of those decisions concerned with the human development of its citizens (that is, education, social security and health in all their forms), which effect it economically (to be able to set up the economic and financial machinery it believes is required), with its cultural fulfilment (not only in the arts and letters, but also in the French language), and with the glory of the Quebec community (in their relations with certain cour. es and international organizations).

In this respect the new government has set itself a basic task: that of obtaining recognition for the judicial and political affairs of the French-Canadian nation, including the development of a new constitution which recognizes in our country the equal collective rights of English and French Canadians and leaves to Quebec the jurisdiction necessary to safeguard the Quebec identity. Of course, it is not up to the fiscal committee to deal with this matter, but the questions arising from its mandate have such a meaning that we thought we must draw everyone's attention to the universal problem which preoccupies us and that we have the firm intention of resolving. The sharing of resources between governments cannot be resolved without relating such sharing to the special requirements based on the socio-cultural problems of a desire to ensure the existence of a French-Canadian nation.

What do you think?

1. What is the difference between "decentralism," as proposed by de Bané and Asselin (Pt. 5—The Future, Reading 5) and "special status for Quebec," which Johnson's proposal was known as?
2. Would "special status" be more or less acceptable to the rest of Canada than "decentralism"? Why?

8. TRUDEAU REPLIES

In his essay "Quebec and the Constitutional Problem" published in Federalism and the French Canadians (1968), Pierre Elliott Trudeau argued against any change in Canada's constitution. (Reprinted by permission of The Macmillan Company of Canada Limited, Toronto.)

Precisely because they are such a tiny minority in North America, French Canadians must refuse to be enclosed within Quebec. I am opposed to what is called "special status" for these two reasons, among others: first, I would not insult Quebeckers by maintaining that their province needs preferential treatment in order to prosper within Confederation; and second, I believe that in the long run this status can only tend to weaken values protected in this way against competition. Even more than techno-logy, a culture makes progress through the exchange of ideas and through challenge. In our Canadian federal system, French-Canadian cultural values have a good balance of competition and protection from a fairly strong state.

*   *   *   *   *

Canadian federalism is ideal. The federal system obliges Quebec's political culture to stand the test of competition at the federal level, while allowing Quebec to choose the form of government best suited to its needs at the provincial level.

Consequently, there is no need to evoke the notion of a national state to turn Quebec into a province "different from the others." In a great number of vital areas, and notably those that concern the development of particular cultural values, Quebec has full and complete sovereignty under the Canadian constitution.

And so I cannot help condemning as irresponsible those people who wish our nation to invest undetermined amounts of money, time, and energy in a constitutional adventure that they have been unable to define precisely but which would consist in more or less completely destroying Confederation to replace it with some vague form of sovereignty resulting in something like an independent Quebec, or associate states, or a "special status," or a Canadian common market, or a confederation of ten states, or some entirely different scheme that could be dreamt up on the spur of the moment, when chaos at all levels had already become inevitable.

That the Canadian federal system must evolve is obvious. But it is evolving—radically—and has been for a hundred years without requiring any fundamental constitutional reform. In our history, periods of great decentralization have alternated with periods of intense centralization, according to economic and social circumstances, external pressures, and the strength or cunning of various politicians. A recent factor in politics, which is also a verifiable law in most industrial countries, is that the state must nowadays devote an ever increasing proportion of an ever increasing budget to purposes that in Canada are the constitutional responsibility of provincial governments. In other words, Canadian federalism is presently evolving in the direction of much greater decentralization.

> *   *   *   *   *

Our present constitution places all these needs and services without exception under provincial jurisdiction. Already the situation has produced the following statistics (for the years 1953 to 1963): during this decade, provincial expenditure for goods and services rose from 3 per cent of the gross national product to 4 per cent; similar expenditures at the municipal level (which also falls within provincial jurisdiction) increased from 5 per cent to 8 per cent; while federal expenditure fell from 10 per cent to 7 per cent. This realignment of state expenditures has naturally brought about changes in the division of tax revenues between the central and provincial governments. So much so that from 1961 to 1963, for example, provincial income and corporate taxes rose from $655 million to $1,144 million, while federal taxes increased only by $114 million. . . .

The phenomenon becomes even more obvious when one considers the total sum of government expenditure, excluding intergovernmental transfers. "Final" expenditure at the federal level rose from $4.198 billion in 1954 to $6.550 billion in 1964, which represents an increase of 56 per cent. During the same period, provincial and municipal expenditure increased from $2.652 to $8.065 billion, which is an increase of 204 per cent.

Clearly, an enormous amount of power is being transferred to provincial governments by the natural operation of demographic, social, and economic forces, without the necessity of amending a single comma of the constitution. In the circumstances, it seems rather surprising that some Quebeckers should choose this very moment to clamour for a new constitution. Twenty years behind the times as usual, they are at last coming to terms with the reality described in the Rowell-Sirois Report of 1940, and preparing to charge the centralizing dragon just when it has stopped breathing fire.

What is meant by?

"demographic"
"Rowell-Sirois Report"

What do you think?

1. What is Pierre Trudeau's position on special status? On constitutional changes? Compare his views with those of Asselin and de Bané (Pt. 5—The Future, Reading 5) and Daniel Johnson (Pt. 5— The Future, Reading 7). Where do they agree? Where do they differ? In each case, explain why.
2. Trudeau differs sharply from de Bané and Asselin and Daniel Johnson on the necessity of constitutional change. Whose position do you agree with and why?

Separatism

For some Canadians, and among these are French and English Canadians alike, federalism, even with bilingual guarantees included or the division of powers modified, is an inappropriate vehicle for the resolution of the French-English issue in Canada. The alternative they see to federalism is the separation of Quebec from the rest of Canada.

Why are some French Canadians separatists? Why are some English Canadians separatists? What do you think of the separatist proposal and why?

9.   DEMOCRATIC SEPARATISM

René Lévesque, leader of the Parti Québécois, the parliamentary separatist party in Quebec, enunciated his views in a book, Option for Quebec, *published in English by McClelland and Stewart in 1969. This selection summarizing Lévesque's arguments in favour of Quebec separatism, is an excerpt from* Option for Quebec. *(Reprinted by permission of The Canadian Publishers, McClelland and Stewart Limited, Toronto.)*

First, we must secure once and for all, in accordance with the complex and urgent necessities of our time, the safety of our collective "personality." This is the distinctive feature of the nation, of this majority that we constitute in Quebec—the only true fatherland left us by events, by our own possibilities, and by the incomprehension and frequent hostility of others.

The prerequisite to this is, among other things, the power for unfettered action (which does not exclude co-operation) in fields as varied as those of citizenship, immigration, and employment; the great instruments of "mass culture"—films, radio, and television; and the kind of international relations that alone permit a people to breathe the air of a changing and stimulating world, and to learn to see beyond itself. Such relations are especially imperative for a group whose cultural connections in the world are as evident and important as ours.

*   *   *   *   *

That collective personality which constitutes a nation also cannot tolerate that social security and welfare—which affect it daily in the most intimate ways—should be conceived and directed from outside. This relates to the oft-repeated demand for the repatriation of old-age pensions, family allowances, and, when it comes into being, medicare.

*   *   *   *   *

The action demanded of the Quebec government, to be specific, would require at the very least new jurisdictions over industrial and commercial corporations, fiduciary and savings institutions, and all the internal agencies of development and industrialization, as well as the power to exercise a reasonable control over the movement and investment of our own capital.

So as not to belabour the obvious, we shall mention only for the record the massive transfer of fiscal resources that would be needed for all the tasks this state of Quebec should undertake in our name—not counting the tasks it already has, tasks that daily grow more out of proportion to its inadequate means: i.e., the insatiable needs of education, urban problems without number, and the meagreness or tragic non-existence of the tools of scientific and industrial research.

Very sketchily, this would seem to be the basic minimum of change that Quebec should force the present Canadian regime to accept in order to reach both the collective security and the opportunity for progress which its best minds consider indispensable.

We would certainly add to the list. But nothing could be struck from it easily.

For us, this is, in fact, a true minimum.

But we would be dreaming if we believed that for the rest of the country our minimum can be anything but a frightening maximum, completely unacceptable even in the form of bare modifications or, for that matter, under the guise of the constitutional reform which certain people say they are willing to proceed with.

Not only the present attitude of the federal government, but also the painful efforts at understanding made by the opposition parties and reactions in the most influential circles in English Canada all give us reason to expect that our confrontation will grow more and more unpleasant.

From a purely revisionist point of view, our demands would seem to surpass both the best intentions displayed by the "other majority" and the very capacity of the regime to make concessions without an explosion.

If we are talking only of revision, they will tell us, our demands would lead to excessive weakening of that centralized state which English Canada needs for its own security and progress as much as we need our own state of Quebec. And they would be right.

And further, they could ask us—with understandable insistence— what in the world our political representatives would be doing in Ottawa taking part in debates and administrative acts whose authority and effectiveness we intend so largely to eliminate within Quebec.

For the present regime also prevents the English-speaking majority from simplifying, rationalizing, and centralizing as it would like to do certain institutions which it, too, realizes are obsolete. This is an ordeal which English Canada is finding more and more exhausting, and for which it blames the exaggerated anxieties and the incorrigible intransigence of Quebec.

It is clear, we believe, that this frustration may easily become intolerable. And it is precisely among the most progressive and "nationalist" groups in English Canada, among those who are concerned about the economic, cultural, and political invasion from the United States, among those who are seeking the means to prevent the country from surrendering completely, that there is the greatest risk of a growing and explosive resentment toward Quebec for the reasons mentioned above.

*   *   *   *   *

In this parallel search for two national securities, as long as the search is pursued within the present system or anything remotely resembling it, we can end up only with double paralysis. The two majorities, basically desiring the same thing—a chance to live their own lives, in their own way, according to their own needs and aspirations—will inevitably collide with one another repeatedly and with greater and greater force, causing hurts that finally would be irreparable.

*   *   *   *   *

[*Lévesque proposes that Quebec secede from Confederation.*]
For our own good, we must dare to seize for ourselves complete

liberty in Quebec, the right to all the essential components of independence, i.e., the complete mastery of every last area of basic collective decision-making.

This means that Quebec must become sovereign as soon as possible.

Thus we finally would have within our grasp the security of our collective "being" which is so vital to us, a security which otherwise must remain uncertain and incomplete.

*   *   *   *   *

As for the other Canadian majority, it will also find our solution to its advantage, for it will be set free at once from the constraints imposed on it by our presence; it will be at liberty in its own way to rebuild to its heart's desire the political institutions of English Canada and to prove to itself, whether or not it really wants to maintain and develop on this continent, an English-speaking society distinct from the United States.

And if this is the case, there is no reason why we, as future neighbours, should not voluntarily remain associates and partners in a common enterprise; which would conform to the second great trend of our times: the new economic groups, customs unions, common markets, etc.

*   *   *   *   *

We are not sailing off into uncharted seas. Leaving out the gigantic model furnished by the evolution of the Common Market, we can take our inspiration from countries comparable in size to our own—Benelux or Scandinavia—among whom co-operation is highly advanced, and where it has promoted unprecedented progress in the member states without preventing any of them from continuing to live according to their own tradition and preferences.

To sum up, we propose a system that would allow our two majorities to extricate themselves from an archaic federal framework in which our two very distinct "personalities" paralyze each other by dint of pretending to have a third personality common to both.

What do you think?

1. (a) According to René Lévesque, what does Quebec need in order to ensure its "collective personality"?
   (b) Why does he feel that only separatism can fulfill these needs?
   (c) Do you agree with Lévesque when he says that English Canada

would find it "completely unacceptable" to grant Quebec what Lévesque feels it needs within a federal structure? Why?

2. How would Lévesque react to decentralism or special status as solutions to the Quebec issue? Why?

3. Describe the relationship between Quebec and Canada that Lévesque envisages should Quebec separate. Is Lévesque being realistic, given the possible reaction of English Canada to such a move? Explain why or why not.

4. (a) According to Lévesque how would Quebec's secession benefit English Canada? Compare his views with those of Professor Neville (Pt. 5—The Future, Reading 6) and Premier Bourassa (Pt. 3—The Contemporary Scene, Reading 4).

   (b) What type of government do Neville and Lévesque favour in order to ensure national survival—Québécois or Canadian? Do you agree?

(Reprinted by permission of the *Montreal Star*.)

"Just think! You'll be a father of Deconfederation!"

10.   A REACTIONARY PATH

In his collection of political writings, Federalism and the French Canadians *(1968) Pierre Elliott Trudeau outlined his position on the Quebec separatist movement. (Reprinted by permission of The Macmillan Company of Canada Limited, Toronto.)*

Several years ago I tried to show that the devotees of the nationalist school of thought among French Canadians, despite their good intentions and courage, were for all practical purposes trying to swim upstream against the course of progress. Over more than half a century "they have laid down a pattern of social thinking impossible to realize and which, from all practical points of view, has left the people without any effective intellectual direction."

I have discovered that several people who thought as I did at that time are today talking separatism. Because their social thinking is to the left, because they are campaigning for secular schools, because they may be active in trade union movements, because they are open-minded culturally, they think that their nationalism is the path to progress. What they fail to see is that they have become reactionary politically.

Reactionary, in the first place, by reason of circumstances. A count, even a rough one, of institutions, organizations, and individuals dedicated to nationalism, from the village notary to the Ordre de Jacques Cartier, from the small businessman to the Ligues du Sacre-Coeur, would show beyond question that an alliance between nationalists of the right and of the left would work in favour of the former, by sheer weight of numbers. And when the leftists say they will not make such an alliance until it is they who are in the majority, I venture to suggest once again that they will never be so as long as they continue to waste their meagre resources as they do now. Any effort aimed at strengthening the nation must avoid dividing it; otherwise such an effort loses all effectiveness so far as social reform is concerned, and for that matter can only lead to consolidation of the status quo. In this sense the alliance is already working against the left, even before being concluded.

In the second place, the nationalists—even those of the left—are politically reactionary because, in attaching much importance to the idea of nation, they are surely led to a definition of the common good as a function of an ethnic group, rather than of all the people, regardless of characteristics. This is why a nationalistic government is by nature intolerant, discriminatory, and, when all is said and done, totalitarian. A truly democratic government cannot be "nationalist," because it must pursue the good of all its citizens, without prejudice to ethnic origin. The democratic government, then, stands for and encourages good citizenship, never nationalism. Certainly, such a government will make laws by which ethnic groups will benefit, and the majority group will benefit proportionately to its number; but that follows naturally from the principle of equality for all, not from any right due the strongest. In this sense one may well say that educational policy in Quebec has always been democratic rather than nationalistic; I would not say the same for all the other provinces. If, on the other hand, Hydro Quebec were to expropriate the province's hydro-electric industries for nationalistic rather than economic reasons, we would already be on the road to fascism. The right can nationalize; it is the left that socializes and controls for the common good.

In the third place, any thinking that calls for full sovereign powers for the nation is politically reactionary because it would put complete and perfect power in the hands of a community which is incapable of realizing a complete and perfect society. In 1962 it is unlikely that any nation-state —or for that matter any multi-national state either—however strong, could realize a complete and perfect society, economic, military, and cultural interdependence is a *sine qua non* for states of the twentieth century, to the extent that none is really self-sufficient. Treaties, trade alliances, common markets, free trade areas, cultural and scientific agreements, all these are as indispensable for the world's states as is interchange between citizens within them; and just as each citizen must recognize the submission of his own sovereignty to the laws of the state— by which, for example, he must fulfill the contracts he makes—so the states will know no real peace and prosperity until they accept the submission of their relations with each other to a higher order. In truth, the very concept of sovereignty must be surmounted, and those who proclaim it for the nation of French Canada are not only reactionary, they are preposterous. French Canadians could no more constitute a perfect society than could the five million Sikhs of the Punjab. We are not well enough educated, nor rich enough, nor, above all, numerous enough, to man and finance a government possessing all the necessary means for both war and peace. The fixed per-capita gain cost would ruin us. But I shall not try to explain all this to people who feel something other than dismay at seeing la Laurentie already opening embassies in various parts of the world, "for the diffusion of our culture abroad." Particularly when these same people, a year ago, seemed to be arguing that we were too poor to finance a second university—a Jesuit one—in Montreal.

To this third contention, that sovereignty is unworkable and contradictory, the separatists will sometimes argue that, once independent, Quebec could very well afford to give up part of her sovereignty on, for instance, re-entering a Canadian confederation, because then her choice would be her own, a free one. That abstraction covers a multitude of sins! It is a serious thing to ask French Canadians to embark on several decades of privation and sacrifice, just so that they can indulge themselves in the luxury of choosing "freely" a destiny more or less identical to the one they have rejected. But the ultimate tragedy would be in not realizing that

French Canada is too culturally anaemic, too economically destitute, too intellectually retarded, too spiritually paralysed, to be able to survive more than a couple of decades of stagnation, emptying herself of all her vitality into nothing but a cesspit, the mirror of her nationalistic vanity and "dignity."

What is meant by?

"la Laurentie"

What do you think?

1. (a) *What three reasons does Trudeau give for his opinion that French-Canadian nationalists, particularly separatists, are politically reactionary? Would René Lévesque (Pt. 3—The Contemporary Scene, Reading 1) agree with Trudeau? Would George Grant (Pt. 3—The Contemporary Scene, Reading 3)? If not, why not?*
   (b) *What is your opinion of "nationalism" as a social force? Do you think that it is detrimental or beneficial to a society? Why?*

11. CONDEMNED TO LIVE TOGETHER

The following editorial, written by Gilles Boyer, was published in the Quebec newspaper, Le Soleil, *June 19, 1972. (Reprinted by permission of* Le Soleil.)

During his trip through Labrador, the Prime Minister of Canada, who, as such, should certainly be concerned with national unity, has indicated the importance of Quebec to this country by stating that "if ever Quebec should separate from the rest of the country, Canada would cease to exist as a nation." Although this is not a mathematical certainty, there is in fact a grave danger that Quebec's secession, should it occur, would dislocate Canada to an extent such that a truly distinct nation north of the forty-ninth parallel would no longer exist. Which simply means that the rest of Canada is just as necessary to Quebec as Quebec is to the rest of Canada.

Canada is a work of willpower. Once this willpower is lacking, the dissolution of the country could easily occur. If Canada cannot then find the willpower to contend with a radically altered situation, the dissolution will be inevitable.

Canada has been built from east to west, whereas natural geographic and economic trends operate from south to north. Had it been left to these tendencies alone, the Canadian provinces would have become American states. One of the purposes of the 1867 Confederation was to unite the colonies of the north in time to prevent this absorption by the young giant to the south, and to push our borders to the west, to fill a gap which American dynamism was only too ready to fill. Had it not been for this will to remain a distinct nation, accompanied by the desire for co-existence between English and French Canadians, Canada would probably no longer be in existence as an entity separate from its vast American neighbour.

But willpower alone is not enough to maintain a nation unless it is based on solid economic, geographical, and cultural realities. Hence the need to unite the different areas of this vast country and to arrange matters so that, in certain sectors of national life, Canadian diversity may be expressed by one voice, that of the central government. Canada as it was structured in 1867, and as it exists today, is precisely the result of this union of willpower and economic and cultural needs.

In Canada it is unthinkable to break the political union and yet to maintain the existing economic union, because the interplay between the two is too close. A very close economic union can lead only to political union capable of presiding over the economic union. Any separation of a Canadian province, bearing in mind the emotional factors involved in such a serious gesture, would almost certainly prevent the restoration of former economic bonds. Hence the dissolution which would strike Canada as a nation, if Quebec were to leave, due to its pivotal location in the middle of Canada.

Other provinces, especially Ontario, certainly wish to maintain their independence from the United States. There is a danger, however, that this wish, more prevalent in certain intellectual circles than among the masses, would not have sufficient economic support to last for any length of time. Even if it were to unite with the Prairies, Ontario would tend to turn more towards the United States if Quebec were to secede; nor is it certain that the Prairies would prefer to unite with Ontario rather than with the American midwest.

As regards the two extremities of the country, British Columbia and the Maritimes, they would probably be the first to go American, the first because of the barrier formed by the Rockies, and the second because they would be cut off from the rest of Canada by the Quebec border. The attraction of the other provinces to the United States would be that much greater because their standard of living would increase by about 25 per cent and because they speak the same language.

Quebec, which ships 68 per cent of its exports to the other provinces, would be even more isolated than the other provinces, should it secede. Even if secession were to be accomplished peacefully (which in view of past history would be a remarkable exception), it must definitely be assumed that secession would cause resentment which would make it hard to maintain former economic ties, not to mention the difficulties of arranging to liquidate common property, which could only aggravate this resentment. Quebec on its own would be even more unlikely to avoid absorption by the United States, and this would mean the loss of its language.

It is less important to know which needs each other more, Quebec or the rest of Canada, than to realize that they must remain united if they wish to preserve their unique diversities. From the economic point of view, for example, Quebec probably needs the rest of Canada more than the rest of Canada needs Quebec, whereas in the matter of culture the rest of Canada has a greater need of Quebec. If English-Canadians really wish to keep Canada different from the United States, they have in Quebec the greatest factor for cultural diversity in the whole country. The presence of Quebec should therefore not be restricted; it should be extended, especially at the federal level and in the provinces bordering upon Quebec.

Because of its population, which amounts to about 30 per cent of the total population of Canada, Quebec is indispensable to Canada's survival since, with its 21 million inhabitants, Canada is already having very considerable trouble facing up to the American giant. Quebec has also impregnated the Canadian mentality with its culture and values. It has even inspired our national institutions with a zest and diversity which are among the major characteristics of Canada.

If it is not absolutely certain that Canada could not survive without Quebec, it is almost certain that life would be more anaemic than it is at present and that the attraction to America would become still stronger. Quebec would obviously be under twice the amount of pressure. How therefore can it be denied that Canadians of both languages are condemned to live together?

What do you think?

1. *According to M. Boyer, why do Canada and Quebec stay together? How effective do you think his appeal would be to Québécois? Why? How appealing do you find his argument? Why?*
2. *Construct a dialogue involving René Lévesque and Gilles Boyer on the fate of Quebec in relation to the United States should Quebec secede from Canada.*

12. SEPARATION INEVITABLE

This selection is another excerpt from the article by Neville which you read in the section entitled "Flexible Federalism" (Part 5). Here

Neville outlines the costs of keeping Quebec in Canada, suggesting that English Canada should stop trying to satisfy Quebec at the expense of its own needs. Rather, English Canada should prepare itself for Quebec's separating by looking at the advantages and disadvantages of this move for English-Canadian goals. Neville's article, it should be noted, was prompted by the failure of the Victoria Charter. (Printed by permission of the Canadian Forum.)

[*The bulk of Neville's article is devoted to a discussion on how much the effort to appease Quebec nationalism has cost Canada. His points, summarized, include that Canada has—*

1. *failed to solve the problem of division of powers between Ottawa and the provinces because terms acceptable to English Canada are usually unacceptable to Quebec.*
2. *spent unnecessary time and money on such things as the B and B Commission, which is now outdated, the flag debate and the controversy over the monarchy.*
3. *aggravated the problem of regional disparities by alienating the West through its preoccupation with Quebec. Also, since Quebec's priorities are again different from other regions in Canada, the problem of regional disparities is evaded consistently by Ottawa to avoid trouble.*
4. *ignored the cities, because their locations in the province would cause their problems to involve constitutional difficulties with Quebec.*
5. *failed to respond to rising fears about American investment. Canada needs a strong central government policy to deal with this issue; this is impossible, given the Quebec situation.*
6. *experienced the October Crisis of 1970 which created a dangerous precedent and eroded our political traditions as they relate to liberty and dissent.*

Professor Neville then describes the various attempts made to appease Quebec nationalism since the early sixties. Finally he assesses the significance of the failure of the Victoria Charter to win Quebec to approval.]

For ten years we have been increasingly preoccupied with the problem of saving this national marriage. In the wake of Quebec's rejection of the Charter there are now some who are urging upon Ottawa a tough policy. There is much to commend such a policy, but those who pursue it should remember that in fact we abandoned the really "soft" policy five years ago when, after pursuing a policy of co-operative federalism, Mr. Pearson fell under the sway of his justice minister, Pierre Elliott Trudeau. The increasingly tough policy begun in 1966, and the promises for success it held out, helped catapult Mr. Trudeau into the premiership in 1968. His policy, as seen by himself, was to give French Canadians a voice in Ottawa and to guarantee minority linguistic and cultural rights across the country: otherwise there were to be no concessions, no special status, no *deux nations*. English Canada liked the last part of this package enough to accept the first, and it has been the policy consistently pursued, even to the point of bayonets, ever since. The consequence to date, we have already seen: a federalist premier of Quebec with more modest demands than his predecessors cannot, in the crunch, accept the Charter devised by Mr. Trudeau and the other premiers. So far as logic has anything to do with it, this would suggest that a tough policy, rigorously pursued, should in all probability lead to the separation of Quebec from Canada. And while there are more civilized means for achieving this result is it not time we faced the implications of our present situation? It seems clear that while separatists are still a minority in Quebec, they are now sufficiently numerous that the Quebec government—any Quebec government—is obliged to reject plans for constitutional or national development which are acceptable in English Canada. This is to suggest that, while there was a time when national unity could be bought at a price tolerable to both parties, that time is past; and we are now at the point where we must consider the division of our assets as amicably as possible and the seeking of our own national destinies.

The catalogue of the past decade is replete with examples of misunderstanding, bitterness and recriminations. Many of these have been extremely petty but they have played their part and taken their toll. In my view, there is every indication (and few to the contrary) that these tensions will increase and magnify. That will be bad enough in itself, but there is one thing that will make it all a great deal worse: and that is the ostrich-like refusal of English Canada to see what is happening in Quebec. This means that when separation comes we shall be unprepared and unready; that we may well, in pursuit of Quebec, have undermined those institutions which would give us a chance for survival as a new state. English Canada, encouraged by its present prime minister, has been complacent and believed for too long what it wanted to believe about Quebec and the future of Canada. It is time that we began to recognize that English Canadians too have aspirations and preferences, that we have problems to solve, that we have things to accomplish; it is time too that we thought about the problems—and the advantages—that Quebec's departure will confer in reaching our goals.

National unity and unity of purpose are noble objectives but they no longer exist in Canada outside the rhetoric of the politicians. If we do not face that fact squarely then we shall be totally unprepared for the bombshell that almost certainly lies ahead. The spectacle of a Quebec bidding for independence, if we are not ready for it, will be a trauma of gigantic proportions. The vital question then will not be (as it so often is now) "Can Canada survive Quebec's departure?" but, to meet that eventuality, we must now start preparing for it.

What is meant by?

"the Charter"
"co-operative federalism"
"deux nations"

What do you think?

1. (a) *According to Neville, what are the costs of trying to "save the national marriage"?*
   (b) *What advantages do you see in preserving the national marriage?*
   (c) *In your opinion do the benefits outweigh the costs? Why or why not?*
   (d) *What is your feeling about a cost-benefit judgment in the Quebec case? Do you feel that Canadians have a moral obligation to save the national marriage that surpasses "practical" consideration? Defend your answer.*

13.   WHICH FRENCH-SPEAKING NATION?

Eugene Forsey is a widely respected authority on Canadian constitutional history and an outspoken commentator on Canadian affairs. This selection, "Canada: One Country or Two," taken from The Canadian Experiment: Success or Failure? *(Proceedings of the Conference of the First Congress on Canadian Affairs, 1961 [Quebec: Les Presses de l'Université Laval, 1962]), represents Forsey's analysis of "minority problems" which he sees following upon Quebec secession. (Reprinted by permission of Les Presses de l'Université Laval.)*

If the Canadian experiment is deemed to be a failure, an absolute failure, and Confederation is to be broken up into two separate "nations" in the political, legal, juristic sense; if a French-speaking nation is to secede; then the question arises, which French-speaking nation? Quebec? Or French Canada?

If you say, "Quebec," then what becomes of the French-speaking minorities in the rest of Canada? The other "nation" (I wonder what it would be called, by the way) would almost certainly not be pleased by the separation, and might well be reluctant to give its French-speaking citizens all the rights or privileges to which they felt entitled, and to which the people of Quebec felt they were entitled. Even now, many people in Quebec feel that French-speaking Canadians in the other provinces are not getting justice. I can see no reason why separation would lead the majority in the other provinces to be any more considerate of the minority than it is now. This would certainly lead the people of Quebec to demand concessions. The other successor state or its provinces might be very reluctant to grant them; indeed, the central government of the other state might have to tell the foreign minister of Quebec that it was powerless to do anything, since education, for example, was a purely provincial matter.

The result would almost certainly be the creation of a *Laurentia irredenta* in the other successor state, and a furious agitation in Quebec for the expansion of that nation to take in the oppressed brethren.

In short, a separate Quebec nation would be unstable. It would inevitably seek to expand to take in all French-speaking people from coast to coast, or at any rate all of them who wanted to come in (there might be some who wouldn't).

If you say that the new, separate French-speaking nation is to be the whole of French Canada, then you have other problems. Expanding Quebec to take in the French-speaking parts of New Brunswick and of northern and eastern Ontario might be fairly easy. But what about the French-speaking people on the west coast of Newfoundland? Or those in Richmond, Inverness, Yarmouth and Digby counties in Nova Scotia? Or the French-speaking people in Prince County, P.E.I.? Or perhaps in some mixed counties in New Brunswick where it would not be easy to draw a nice, neat line between the two linguistic groups? What about the French-speaking people of Ottawa? What about the scattered French-speaking people of the four western provinces? What about the English-speaking people of Westmount and Montreal West and the Lakeshore? Are you going to set up a series of enclaves, with a Brandenburger Top at the edge of Westmount or on the site of the present Union Station in Ottawa? Will there be provision for airlifts and corridors? If so, you will make Pakistan look like simplicity itself.

The alternative is, of course, a transfer of populations: a new expulsion of the Acadians from Newfoundland, Nova Scotia, Prince Edward Island and the mixed counties of New Brunswick, and of the French-speaking people from the western provinces and some pockets in western Ontario, into a Greater Quebec, enlarged by the addition of large areas from New Brunswick and Ontario.

What is meant by?

"Laurentia irredenta"

What do you think?

1. What "minority" problems does Forsey predict will arise, should Quebec secede, if the French-Canadian nation is defined as
(a) Quebec?
(b) French Canada?
How realistic are Forsey's predictions?
2. What would be René Lévesque's reaction (Pt. 5—The Future, Reading 9) to Forsey's remarks?
3. In this passage Forsey talked about French-Canadian minorities outside Quebec. What do you think might happen to the English minority in Quebec in the event of Quebec separation?

14. THE REVOLUTION THAT QUEBEC NEEDS

Pierre Vallières, before his conversion to the Parti Québécois follow-ing the 1970 October Crisis, was the leading thinker of the FLQ, the separated groups who favour violence as a means of actualizing their goals. In his book White Niggers of America *(Toronto: McClelland and Stewart, 1971), Vallières outlined the nature of the revolution that the FLQ was hoping to foment. (Reprinted by permission of The Canadian Publishers, McClelland and Stewart Limited, Toronto.)*

This revolution that Quebec needs—as do all the countries that are enslaved by capitalism and colonial imperialism—implies nothing more nor less than the disappearance of capitalism itself. That means transforma-tions that are even more profound than those required by the nationalization of foreign capital. It is a question, in fact, of abolishing capital itself, the basis of present society.

We want to replace this economy based on the exploitation of the majority of mankind not only by a new economy but by a new society, in which the category "economy" will not have the same content it does now. We want to replace it with a society in which the producers (the workers) collectively own and administer their means of production and create, organize, and plan their relations of production and the distribution of their products in accordance with ultimate goals that they choose them-selves, for the satisfaction of their true needs, in the framework of an absolute equality of rights, opportunities, and benefits.

Let us acquire the essential political instruments, let us take over control over our economy, let us get a radically reformed social leadership! Wrench off the colonial yoke, get rid of the imperialists who live off the toil of our Quebec workers. Quebec's tremendous natural resources must belong to Quebeckers!

There is only one way to bring this about: a national revolution in a framework of INDEPENDENCE. Otherwise, the Quebec population cannot hope to live in freedom.

But it is no longer enough to want independence, to work within the existing political separatist parties. The colonizers will not so easily yield up their tempting loot. The separatist political parties will never gain sufficient power to overcome the colonizers' political and economic hold. Moreover, independence alone will not resolve anything. It must, at all costs, be accompanied by a social revolution.

Quebec's patriots are not fighting over a name, but over a situation. A revolution is not a parlour game, played for fun.

Only a full-fledged revolution can build up the necessary power to achieve the vital changes that will be needed in an independent Quebec. A national revolution cannot, of its very nature, tolerate any compromise. There is only one way of overcoming colonialism: to be stronger than it is! Only the most far-fetched idealism may mislead one into thinking otherwise. Our period of slavery has ended.

QUEBEC PATRIOTS, TO ARMS! THE HOUR OF NATIONAL REVOLUTION HAS STRUCK! INDEPENDENCE OR DEATH!

What is meant by?

"colonial imperialism"
"nationalization"

What do you think?

1. (a) What were the economic goals of the FLQ based on this passage by Vallières?

   (b) What are the economic goals of the Parti Québécois (Pt. 5— The Future, Reading 9). How do they differ from those of the FLQ? How are they alike? Account for the differences and similarities.

   (c) Evaluate the economic goals of the FLQ and the PQ. Which are the most appealing to you, given the condition of the Quebec economy? (See Pt. 3—Contemporary Scene, Readings 9–15.)

15.   SEPARATISM WITH SOCIALISM

The editorial staff of the radical separatist paper Quebec-Presse commented on Pierre Vallières' conversion to the Parti Québécois in the

December 19, 1971, issue of their paper. (Reprinted by permission of Quebec-Presse.)

And so, Pierre Vallières has decided to leave behind sterile clandestinity and what he calls "armed agitation." He has decided to militate in broad daylight, in democratic structures, towards the political organization and the liberation of the Quebec workers.

If our "justice" allows him the chance, this choice truly corresponds with the task to which all who want to "break the system" in Quebec must subscribe in the present time and circumstances.

The politicizing action of the Front de Libération du Québec (FLQ), however it may be judged elsewhere, will never replace the patient and persuasive work which the political organization of workers demands.

This having been said, Pierre Vallières has chosen to rally around the cause of the Parti Québécois, the principal political force presently organized, on the Quebec scene, which is working toward national sovereignty. As sympathetic as we may be to this choice, it does not allow us to forget suddenly that the Parti Québécois has not yet affirmed, without equivocation, as the party which will ensure not only national liberation, but the economic and social liberation of the Quebec workers.

The PQ is, perhaps, the party which will achieve the national independence of Quebec; it has not been said that it is the party which will lead to the full realization of socialism in Quebec, the only means of struggling effectively against the exploitation of the majority of the people and against U.S. domination of our economy, or American imperialism.

About socialism Pierre Vallières says almost nothing in the texts he has exposed to the public. As for the PQ, it doesn't breathe a word about it, officially, in its programme.

For it must never be forgotten that national independence is only one of the means, one of the indispensable centers of decision that the Québécois must take over to change the system. At least two other means, two other centers of decision, must also be sought:

(1) A real control of the economy by the state (credit, key industrial sectors, natural resources, etc.).

(2) An authentic workers' control of enterprise.

These last two means, equally indispensable, go along with the setting up of a socialist and democratic Quebec.

Now of this, neither Vallières nor the PQ say anything officially. There is in this, however, a fundamental stake: independence will be attained in the interests of the workers if it is given what is commonly called "a class content"; that is, a content conforming to the interests of the majority who constitute the working class.

On this subject, the last [1971] congress of the Quebec Federation of Labour (QFL) has furnished valuable indications. The delegates voted in favour of the right to sovereignty for Quebec, "under the condition that this process must be accomplished by serving the needs and aspirations of the working classes." These needs and aspirations, defined previously during the course of the congress, must go toward "the installation of a socialist and democratic society."

Certainly, as Louis Laberge has declared, "the PQ is the party closest to the interests of the workers, at the present time." But to say that it is the least far away would be more exact.

In order for the PQ to identify itself more with the workers, three conditions would be necessary: first, that certain of its present directors henceforth refrain from certain retrogressive statements and attitudes, the Chamber of Commerce type, regarding the workers' movement and its leaders; second, that the party add to its electoral actions, daily actions of support for the popular struggles; and finally, that the workers themselves, unionized and non-unionized, decide to participate in party activities and in the definition of its orientation and actions on a much wider scale.

Let us be well understood: it would be inadequate, strategically speaking, to create a workers' party to the left of the PQ on the political chessboard in Quebec for the time being, although one might hope that such a party will eventually see the light of day.

Nevertheless, it is equally incorrect to give total support to the PQ as it exists at the present time. Moreover, at the very heart of the party itself, a fair-sized group of militants are unsatisfied with the economic and social programme as it stands and are doggedly working to transform it. They are working toward the democratic adoption by the next congress, in the autumn of 1972, of a program plainly committed to the realization of socialism in Quebec. Until then, unconditional support of the PQ is at least premature for those who believe in a socialist society.

What is meant by?

"clandestinity"
"politicize"
"equivocation"

What do you think?

1. *Compare the positions of Québec-Presse, the Parti-Québécois and the FLQ. What are the similarities? What are the differences?*
2. *Why is the "separatist" element in Quebec split into various factions who often hold conflicting views?*

3. (a) Do you think that Trudeau (Pt. 5—The Future, Reading 10) would apply the label "reactionary" to all these separatist groups? Why or why not?
   (b) Would you apply the label "reactionary" to all or any of these groups? Why or why not?

Suggested Readings

Contemporary

AITKIN, HUGH, G., et al.: *American Impact on Canada*, Durham, N.C.: Duke University Press, 1959.

ALLNUTT, PETER: *Quebec into the Streets*, Toronto: Hogtown Press, 1970.

ARÈS, RICHARD: "L'immigration et l'avenir du français au Québec," *Action Nationale*, 59: 209-27, 1969.

AUF DER MAUR, NICK and ROBERT CHODOS, eds.: *Quebec: A Chronicle 1968-1972*, Toronto: James Lewis and Samuel, 1972.

CHAPUT-ROLLAND, SOLANGE: *My Country: Canada or Quebec?*, Toronto: Macmillan, 1966.

CHARNEY, ANNE: "The Sociology of Violence in Quebec," *Maclean's*, 85:8, 1972.

COGSWELL, FREDERICK, ed.: *One Hundred Poems of Modern Quebec*, Fredericton, New Brunswick: Fiddlehead Press, 1972.

CORBETT, EDWARD: *Quebec Confronts Canada*, Baltimore: John Hopkins Press, 1967.

Conseil de la Vie Francaise en Amérique: *Nothing More, Nothing Less: A French-Canadian View of Bilingualism and Biculturalism*, Toronto: Conseil de la Vie Francaise, 1967.

CRÉPEAU, P. A. and C. B. MACPHERSON, eds.: *The Future of Canadian Federalism*, Toronto: University of Toronto Press, 1965.

DRACHE, DANIEL: *Quebec: Only the Beginning: The Manifestoes of the Common Front*, Toronto: New Press, 1972.

DUMONT, FERNAND: *The Anguish of Quebec*, Toronto: University of Toronto Press, 1973.

ELKIN, FREDERICK: *Rebels and Colleagues: Advertising and Social Change in French Canada*, Montreal: McGill-Queen's University Press, 1973.

Financial Post: "How Quebec Welfare State Evolved" *Financial Post*, 65:11, June 5, 1971.

"French Canadians in English-speaking Provinces," *World Affairs*, 33:13, 1968.

GAGNON, L.: "Growing Poor in Quebec," *Canadian Dimension*, 7:55-6, 1970.

GLASSCO, JOHN, ed.: *The Poetry of French Canada in Translation*, Toronto: Oxford University Press, 1970.

GOLD, GERALD: *Communities and Culture in French Canada*, Toronto: Holt, Rinehart and Winston, 1973.

GOTLIEB, A. E. ed.: *Human Rights, Federalism and Minorities*, Toronto: Canadian Institute of International Affairs, 1969.

GRAHAM, GWETHALYN and SOLANGE CHAPUT-ROLLAND: *Dear Enemies: A Dialogue on French and English Canada*, Toronto: Macmillan, 1964.

GRINDSTAFF, C. F., C. L. BOYDELL, and P. C. WHITEHEAD, eds.: *Population Issues in Canada*, Toronto: Holt, Rinehart and Winston, 1971.

HAGGART, RON and AUBREY GOLDEN: *Rumours of War*, Toronto: New Press, 1971.

HOLDEN, RICHARD B.: *1970 Election: Quebec Crucible*, Montreal: Arès, 1970.

JACKSON, JOHN: "A Study of French-English Relations in an Ontario Community," *Canadian Review of Sociology and Anthropology*, 3:3, 117-131, 1966.

JONES, RICHARD: *Community in Crisis: French-Canadian Nationalism in Perspective*, Toronto: McClelland and Stewart, 1972.

KALBACK, W. E. and W. W. MCVEY: *The Demographic Bases of Canadian Society*, Toronto: McGraw-Hill Ryerson, 1971.

KETTLE, J.: "Quebec Population" *Executive*, May, 1971.

KWAVNICK, DAVID: "Roots of French-Canadian Discontent," *Canadian Journal of Economic and Political Science*, 31:509-523, 1965.

LANGLOIS, CONRAD: "Cultural Reasons Given for the French-Canadian Lag in Economic Progress," *Culture*, 21:152-70, June, 1960.

LASKIN, RICHARD, ed.: *Social Problems: A Canadian Profile*, Toronto: McGraw-Hill Ryerson, 1964.

LEBLANC, PHILLIPE and ARNOLD EDINBOROUGH: *One Church, Two Nations?*, Toronto: Longman, 1968.

LEIBERSON, STANLEY: *Language and Ethnic Relations in Canada*, Toronto: John Wiley and Sons, 1970.

LÉVESQUE, RENÉ: *An Option for Quebec*, Toronto: McClelland and Stewart, 1968.

LORANGER, J. G.: "Separatism and Socialism," *Canadian Dimension*, 6:19-22, April-May 1970.

NEMIROFF, MICHAEL and STANLEY GRAY: "Struggle for Quebec", excerpts from address "Revolutionary Consciousness in Quebec: a New Parochialism", *Canadian Dimension*, 6:23-26, December 1969-January 1970, 2:53, February-March 1970.

MANN, W. E.: *Social and Cultural Change In Canada*, 2 volumes, Toronto: Copp Clark, 1970-71.

MILNER, HENRY: *The Decolonization of Quebec: an Analysis of Left-Wing Nationalism*, Toronto: McClelland and Stewart, 1973.

ORKIN, MARK: *Speaking Canadian French: An Informal Account of the French Language in Canada*, Toronto: General Publishing Co. Ltd., 1967.

Parti Quebecois: *La Souveraineté et l'Economie*, Montreal: Editions du Parti Quebecois, 1970.

—————: *Qui centrâle l'economie du Québec*, Montreal: Editions du Parti Quebecois, 1972.

PELLETIER, GÉRARD: *The October Crisis*, Toronto: McClelland and Stewart, 1971.

PORTER, JOHN: *The Vertical Mosaic*, Toronto: University of Toronto Press, 1965.

Quebec Labour: The Confederation of National Trade Unions Yesterday and Today. Edited by a Black Rose Books editorial collective, Montreal: Black Rose Books, 1972.

Quebec Royal Commission of Inquiry on Constitutional Problems, *The Tremblay Report*, Toronto: McClelland and Stewart, 1973.

Government of Quebec, "What does Quebec Want?" in J. P. Meekison: *Canadian Federalism: Myth or Reality?*, Toronto: Methuen, 1968.

RICHARDSON, BOYCE: *James Bay: The Plot to Drown the North Woods*, Toronto: Clarke, Irwin, 1972.

RIOUX, MARCEL and YVES MARTIN, eds.: *French-Canadian Society*, 2 volumes, Toronto: McClelland and Stewart, 1965, 1969.

RIOUX, MARCEL: *Quebec in Question*, (James Boake, trans.) Toronto: James Lewis & Samuel, 1971.

ROTSTEIN, ABRAHAM, ed.: *Power Corrupted: The October Crisis and the Repression of Quebec*, Toronto: New Press, 1971.

ROUSSOPOULOS, DIMITRIOS, ed.: *The New Left in Canada*, Montreal: Black Rose Books, 1970.

SAYWELL, JOHN: *Quebec 70: A Documentary Narrative*, Toronto: University of Toronto Press, 1971.

SCHWARTZ, R. H.: *Public Opinion and Canadian Identity*, Scarborough: Fitzhenry and Whiteside, 1967.

SÉRAPHIS, MARION, comp.: *The Quebec Tradition: An Anthology of French-Canadian Prose and Verse*, Montreal: Editions Lumeas, 1946.

SMILEY, DONALD V.: *The Canadian Political Nationality*, Toronto: Methuen, 1967.

SMITH, DENIS: *Bleeding Hearts, Bleeding Country: Canada and the Quebec Crisis*, Edmonton: M. J. Hurtig, 1971.

STEIN, MICHAEL: *The Dynamics of Right-Wing Protest: A Political Analysis of Social Credit in Quebec*, Toronto: University of Toronto Press, 1973.

SUTHERLAND, DONALD: *Second Image: Comparative Studies in Quebec/Canadian Literature*, Toronto: New Press, 1971.

THOMSON, DALE C. ed.: *Quebec Society and Politics: Views from the Inside*, Toronto: McClelland and Stewart, 1973.

Toronto Telegram, *Quebec: The Threat of Separation*, Toronto: McClelland and Stewart, 1969.

VALLIÈRES, PIERRE: *White Niggers of America* (Joan Pinkham, trans.) Toronto, McClelland and Stewart, 1971.

—————: "F.L.Q. and the Lessons of the October Crisis", *Canadian Forum*, Jan.-Feb. 1972.

WARWICK, JACK: *The Long Journey: Literary Themes of French Canada,* Toronto: University of Toronto Press, 1968.

Historical

ARSENAULT, BONER: *History of the Acadians,* Quebec: Conseil de la Vie Francaise, 1966.

BERGER, CARL, ed.: *Conscription 1917,* Toronto: University of Toronto Press, 1969.

BERGERON, LÉANDRE: *The History of Quebec: A Patriote's Handbook,* Toronto: N.C. Press, 1971.

BONENFANT, JEAN: *The French Canadians and the Birth of Confederation,* Ottawa: Canadian Historical Association, 1966, CHA Booklet no. 21.

BOWSFIELD, HARTFIELD, ed.: *Louis Riel: Rebel of the Western Frontier or Victim of Politics and Prejudice?,* Toronto: Copp Clark, 1969.

BROWN, R. CRAIG, ed.: *Minorities, Schools and Politics,* Toronto: University of Toronto Press, 1969.

BRUNET, MICHEL: *French Canada and the Early Decades of British Rule 1760-1791,* Ottawa: Canadian Historical Association, 1963, CHA Booklet No. 13.

——————: "The French Canadians' Search for a Fatherland," in P. Russell ed.: *Nationalism in Canada,* Toronto: McGraw-Hill Ryerson, 1966.

BUMSTED, J. M. ed.: *Documentary Problems in Canadian History,* 2 volumes, Toronto: Dorsey 1970.

CHAPUT, MARCEL: *Why I Am a Separatist,* Toronto: McGraw-Hill Ryerson, 1962.

CLARK, LOVELL, ed.: *The Manitoba School Question: Majority Rule or Minority Rights?* Toronto: Copp Clark, 1968.

COOK, RAMSAY: *Canada and the French-Canadian Question,* Toronto: Macmillan, 1966.

——————: "French-Canadian Interpretations of Canadian History," *Revue d'Etudes Canadiennes,* 11:2, May 1967.

——————: *French-Canadian Nationalism: An Anthology,* Toronto: Macmillan, 1969.

COPP, J. T. and MARCEL HAMELIN: *Confederation 1867,* Toronto: Copp Clark, 1966.

DAWSON, R. M.: *The Conscription Crisis of 1944,* Toronto: University of Toronto Press, 1961.

DESBARATS, PETER: *The State of Quebec: A Journalist's View of the Quiet Revolution,* Toronto: McClelland and Stewart, 1965.

DONALDSON, GORDON: *Battle for a Continent: Quebec 1759,* Toronto: Doubleday, 1973.

FARIBAULT, M. and R. M. FOWLER: *Ten to One: The Confederation Wager,* Toronto: McClelland and Stewart, 1965.

GLENDON COLLEGE FORUM: *Quebec Year Eight,* Toronto: CBC Publications, 1968.

GUENDON, HUBERT: "The Social Evolution of Quebec Reconsidered," *CJEPS* 26:40, 533-551, 1960.

——————: Social Unrest, Social Class and Quebec's Bureaucratic Revolution," in Thorburn, Hugh G., ed.: *Party Politics in Canada,* 2nd ed., Scarborough: Prentice-Hall, 1967.

HUGHES, EVERETT: *French Canada in Transition,* Chicago: University of Chicago Press, 1963.

LAPORTE, PIERRE: *The True Face of Duplessis,* (Richard Daignault, trans.,) Montreal: Harvest House, 1960.

LEVITT, JOSEPH: *Henri Bourassa and the Golden Calf,* Ottawa: University of Ottawa, 1969.

—————— ed.: *Bourassa on Imperialism and Biculturalism 1900-1918,* Toronto: Copp Clark, 1970.

MINER, HORACE: *St-Denis: A French-Canadian Parish,* Chicago: University of Chicago Press, 1939, 1963.

MONET, JACQUES: *The Last Cannon Shot: A Study of French-Canadian Nationalism 1837-1850,* Toronto: University of Toronto Press, 1969.

MURROW, CASEY: *Henri Bourassa and French-Canadian Nationalism,* Montreal: Harvest House, 1968.

MYERS, HUGH BINGHAM: *The Quebec Revolution,* Montreal: Harvest House, 1963.

NEATBY, BLAIR: *Laurier and Liberal Quebec: A Study in Political Management,* Toronto: McClelland and Stewart, 1973.

NEATBY, HILDA: *The Quebec Act: Policy and Motive,* Scarborough: Prentice-Hall, 1972.

NISH, CAMERON, ed.: *The French Regime,* Scarborough: Prentice-Hall, 1965.

——————: *The French Canadians 1759-1766: Conquered? Half Conquered? Liberated?,* Vancouver: Copp Clark, 1966.

—————— ed.: *Quebec in the Duplessis Era 1935-1959,* Toronto: Copp Clark, 1970.

NISH, ELIZABETH: *Racism or Responsible Government: The French-Canadian Dilemma of the 1840s,* Toronto: Copp Clark, 1967.

OUELLET, FERNAND et al.: *Constitutionalism and Nationalism in Lower Canada,* Toronto: University of Toronto Press, 1969.

QUINN, HERBERT: *The Union Nationale: A Study in Quebec Nationalism,* Toronto: University of Toronto Press, 1963.

ROBERTS, L.: *The Chief: A Political Biography of Maurice Duplessis,* Toronto: Clarke, Irwin, 1965.

SCHULL, JOSEPH: *Rebellion: The Rising in French Canada, 1837,* Toronto: Macmillan, 1971.

SCOTT, FRANK and MICHAEL OLIVER eds.: *Quebec States Her Case,* Toronto: Macmillan, 1964.

SEIGFRIED, ANDRÉ: *The Race Question in Canada,* Toronto: McClelland and Stewart, 1906, 1966.

SILVER, A. I. and M. F. VALLEUR: *The North-West Rebellion,* Montreal: Copp Clark, 1967.

SKELTON, O. D.: *Life and Letters of Sir Wilfrid Laurier,* 2 vols., Toronto: McClelland and Stewart, 1921, 1965.

SLOAN, THOMAS: *Quebec: The Not-So-Quiet Revolution,* Toronto: McGraw-Hill Ryerson, 1965.

STACEY, C. P.: *Quebec 1759: The Seige and the Battle,* Toronto: Macmillan, 1959.

STANLEY, GEORGE F.: "Lionel-Adolphe Groulx: Historian and Prophet of French Canada," in Laurier Lapierre, ed.: *Four O'Clock Lectures,* Montreal, 1966.

STRATFORD, PHILIP: *André Laurendeau: Witness for Quebec. Selected Essays,* Toronto: Macmillan, 1973.

TAYLOR, NORMAN: "The Effects of Industrialization: Its Opportunities and Consequences upon French-Canadian Society," *Journal of Economic History,* 20:4 638-647, 1960.

TRUDEAU, P. E.: *La Grève de l'Amiante,* Montreal: Editions du Jour, 1970.

——————: *Federalism and The French Canadians,* Toronto: Macmillan, 1968.

UNTEL, FRÈRE: *The Impertinence of Brother Anonymous,* Montreal: Harvest House, 1962.

WADE, MASON: *The French Canadians 1760-1967,* 2 volumes, Toronto: Macmillan, 1968 rev'd.

——————: *The French-Canadian Outlook,* Toronto: McClelland and Stewart, 1946, 1964.

WILLMS, A. M.: "Conscription 1917: A Brief for the Defence," *Canadian Historical Review,* 37:4, December 1956.

Films

New England & New France (1490-1763)
    57 minutes, 55 seconds   b&w   NFB   16mm: 106B 0167 106
Canada and the American Revolution (1763-1783)
    57 minutes, 55 seconds   b&w   NFB   16mm: 106B 0167 107

Ville Marie
    27 minutes, 38 seconds   color   NFB   16mm: 106C 0165 128
The Voyageurs
    19 minutes, 50 seconds   color   NFB   35mm: 105C 0164 032
                                               16mm: 106C 0164 032
Wolfe & Montcalm
    29 minutes, 30 seconds   b&w   NFB   16mm: 106B 0157 070
Adieu Alouette
    NFB   A series of 4 films about contemporary Quebec.
Challenge for the Church
    27 minutes, 14 seconds   color   NFB   16mm: 106C 0172 098
OK . . . Camera
    27 minutes, 37 seconds   color   NFB   16mm: 106C 0172 073
Un Job Steady . . . Un Boss Bon
    27 minutes, 17 seconds   color   NFB   16mm: 106C 0172 087
The Ungrateful Lad
    27 minutes, 10 seconds   color   NFB   16mm: 106C 0172 014
Acadia, Acadia
    75 minutes   b&w   NFB   16mm: 106B 0171 027
Le Quebec as Seen by Cartier Bressin
    10 minutes, 2 seconds   b&w   NFB   35mm: 105B 0369 031
                                             16mm: 106B 0369 031
September Fine at Saint-Henri
    27 minutes, 10 seconds   b&w   NFB   16mm: 106B 0164 023
Visit to a Foreign Country
    27 minutes, 16 seconds   b&w   NFB   16mm: 106B 0162 017
Wake Up, mes bons amis
    117 minutes, 7 seconds   b&w   NFB   16mm: 106B 0170 082
OECA
A Question of Allegiance
    28;10,   008462   color
Durham and the Two Nations
    30 minutes   001887   Mono